Cuba
Open from the Inside

SEA HILL PRESS, SANTA BARBARA

Cuba
Open from the Inside

TRAVELS IN THE FORBIDDEN LAND

CHRIS MESSNER

Sea Hill Press Inc.

www.seahillpress.com

Santa Barbara, California

Book design and layout by Walter Sharp

Photography by Chris Messner

www. cmpictures.com

Cartography by Maps.com

ISBN 978-0-9708050-7-2

Library of Congress Control Number: 2011926750

Printed in the United States of America

To my wife,
Thanks for all your tireless help in this journey.

CONTENTS

Never give up.

INTRODUCTION

NOT LONG AFTER the birth of the Cuban Revolution, my life began as well. Like any young child, I was oblivious to the bigger things that were transpiring around the world. The age-old question for children is, "What do you want to be when you grow up?" Some children seem to already know the answer to that question. While a few can stay the course through life as they grow up and follow through to maturity, constructed by design, most people have twists and turns in their lives. Traumatic situations occur. Unexpected things happen. The course of direction is changed. Different pathways are taken. Some make a conscious action by means of the best-laid plans. Others have no choice at all, the ramifications being what they are, for better or for worse.

As a young child, I didn't really realize that I had any problems. It was when I got held back in the first grade that I first sensed something was wrong. I was dyslexic, but it would be years before I was officially diagnosed.

I was classified differently than the normal kids. The reality for a child in suburban California back in the late sixties was different than it is now. Back then, dyslexia meant you were no longer accepted into regular classes. I was more or less called "retarded," and that was just one of the names people used.

In that "special class," some of the kids were in wheelchairs, and some just looked around, made noises, and occasionally bobbled their heads. It was strange. Supposedly, I was like one of them, but the whole time I felt like something was definitely not right. But nobody was really listening to me. So, I used whatever recess time I had to stay away from all that.

Through it all, my mind seemed to process information in a more visual way. I saw life like snapshots on a storyboard. This visual information was ever flowing, like water. But trying to extrapolate and describe it was challenging. And it was frustrating. I realize now that I had, and still do have, a different way of analyzing things. My challenge is to translate all these different images in my head into words.

I got teased a lot all through school. There was a lot of name-calling. Yes, some fights took place. Why? Who the hell really knows?

As time wore on, I increasingly felt out of place trying to navigate through the school environment. I did what I had to do while trying to figure out where I fit in the cycle of life's food chain. I had aloof moments of being on the outside looking in. I always felt that I was not being understood. The reality, I guess, was that I was really trying to figure it all out.

At times, I felt like a prisoner in my own mind. I began to deflect a lot of this difficulty through athletics. I was big, and athletics was the only endeavor I knew I could handle in a full capacity. With running, it was the longer the distance, the better. I was able to physically and mentally endure. I started to realize that this was the way I could disappear, become invisible in class, and compensate for my shortcomings.

When I saw the pole vault for the first time, I thought, *Hey, I can do that*. I pole vaulted a few times and took a bunch of big falls. But I kept trying, kept trying, and soon enough I started to get it down. Surprisingly, I surpassed many meet records. That is when everything began to take off. Everything started to fit. I gained self-confidence and sensed that I was on a pathway in a new and better direction.

In life, I kept being active outside. I enjoyed surfing. I got into hiking, mountain climbing, and rock climbing. I climbed on El Capitan and scaled other big walls in the Yosemite Valley, including summiting many of the Saw Tooth Ridge peaks, which are above Yosemite by Bridgeport, California.

Around people, I never breathed a word about my inadequacies. Someone who spoke or otherwise interacted with me probably thought I was just fine and as normal as everybody else, I guess. I would try to describe ideas or occurrences, such as the way the light fell on the hills or all the different patterns and shapes caught my eye. I remember hiking in the hills and describing what I saw, and the people I was with would look at me funny like, "What planet are you from?" For lack of better words, I was simply trying to artistically describe how all the elements seemed to be connected with what I saw.

Academically, I just slid by. It was not until late in high school that I was diagnosed as dyslexic. Once I was diagnosed, my reaction was, "Holy Crap! What a load off my mind." I was angry with my parents, teachers, and everyone else who kept treating me like I was stupid. I felt like saying, "See! See! I'm not so stupid like you guys tell me and treat me like I am all the time."

After being diagnosed, I was given this great special education teacher, who worked with me at school. She dressed like an Earth person from the 1960s and had long, blondish, frizzy hair with a few streaks of gray. She happened to be a belly dancer on the side. I always thought that was funny, and yet cool. I was impressed with her. She seemed to really understand what was going on. For the first time, I felt like I had some hope.

My writing and overall academics improved immensely. I could see it. I felt like a real human being. Unfortunately, at the end of that one semester, the class was de-funded. After that, not knowing what else to do, and feeling like I had no other choices, I turned even more into athletics to disappear from life.

I kept running, posting decent times in cross-country 5k and 10k races. In the spring, I competed in track and field, lettering varsity in both sports. I advanced to state competitions and achieved high placements.

Although I really wanted to play football, my parents never let me. I felt that I could have done well. Looking back, well, that's one decision I really resented. Football was and is one of my big passions. They were concerned that I would get injured. The irony is that although I was never injured playing football, it was a freak pole-vaulting accident that changed my life forever.

After high school, I attended the local community college. During that time, some scholarship offers floated in. Recruiters wanted me to transfer to their four-year colleges to pole vault. Some of these recruiters thought I was better suited for the decathlon. At that same time, I enrolled in a landscape horticulture program. I knew that athletics was the one thing I could do well, so I pushed hard in pole vaulting, thinking that would get me somewhere in life. I was training hard and doing really well until one day an incident changed everything. I landed wrong while working out. My right knee snapped to the side and collapsed. I hit the ground. As I turned myself to sit up, a hot surge raced through my body and across my face. I saw bright shooting star-like things floating around in the front of my face. At that moment, things got blurry. Then the reality of the pain hit. It scorched my leg, and I screamed. I thrashed around uncontrollably on the ground and grabbed the back of my right leg, rolling around like I was on a hot frying pan. I couldn't believe the pain. I didn't black out, but it was incredible pain. Just incredible. Finally, after a while, the pain subsided enough that I could just lie there, motionless, panting with tears covering my whole face. My teammates, who were about fifty feet away, doing their warm up drills, said they could hear the leg snap. They said it was so loud it sounded like gunfire, freaking them out: PoP *pop!* PoP *pop!* Each "pop" came like a domino. It was as if each muscle, tendon, and ligament had its different maximum-pressure breaking point before it went off. All the ligaments and muscles either ripped from the bone or tore in half. I couldn't move my leg. I yelled out, "I can't move my leg! ... my toes!" I was paralyzed because the leg had snapped so much. The ACL and lateral collateral ligaments tore, and the bicep hamstring ripped right off the bone. The meniscus cartilage was damaged, and the main nerve was pulled due to the blunt force of the injury.

The prognosis was bad. The doctors believed that I would never walk again. And if I did, I would be dragging the leg. It was a total shock to me. One minute I'm running and in an instant, I'm not. I remember being alone and crying many times, not knowing what I would be able to do in life. Surprisingly, the feeling eventually came back in my leg.

I was twenty years old, living alone in a small studio, and determined that I was going to keep moving forward. I was not going to use the accident as an excuse for failure. I just couldn't. I was determined to walk and make a comeback. I was determined to somehow keep training. What else did I have to fall back on? In reality, I had nothing else. I had nothing, not even the prospect of a good education. I only had a strong back and a will to live. I realized right then the importance of a good education.

All of my scholarship offers were gone, withdrawn. That was it. Everything gone! In the recruiters' eyes, I was now a defective product. It was nothing personal, and I could not blame them for that.

Still, I had to do something. Bills had to be paid. Even when I had the cast on, I took any job that I could find. I remember that big old heavy cast. It stretched from my ankle to just below my hip, and it had a slight bend to it at the knee.

I did whatever I had to do. No one is going to do it for you. A couple of times, I worked with my cast still on, propping myself up and digging trenches with a pick all day. I got sick and threw up afterward. I guess I pushed my body too far after the accident. But I needed the work and the money for rent and food.

My back was strong, and I had a strong will to survive. I got into doing manual labor, working in people's yards, digging trenches, digging out tree stumps. Not able to keep up with school, I dropped out. I continued in the landscaping field. I needed to learn more about the plants, but I continued working on it by trial and error, using what little I had learned in college. I no longer mountain climbed, but I realized that I could get paid for climbing trees. So I learned how to climb trees with ropes and to trim the trees with chain saws. The downside was that I had to endure periodic condescending taunts from people for years about my so-called uneducated, lowly trade.

But then again, it never ceased to amaze me, when people had a tree fall or needed landscape advice, I suddenly became important and needed before being discarded back into the uneducated world once again.

I continued to have lower back pain and my right leg was hurting all the time. Years later, I went to the orthopedist for the first time since my accident. After looking at all the old medical reports, an MRI was performed. It was discovered that the meniscus had partial tearing, and the ACL ligament was barely connected. Many long, loose, and torn fibrous strands were still floating around the knee.

The conclusion was that "medically speaking" I should not even be walking. I really didn't know what to say after that. After all these years of just trying to get by and move on, I never really had time to stop and think about it. Having financial responsibilities, I somehow kept going. Strenuous work was all I knew.

Around this time, by chance, I stumbled upon photography. I went one day to pick up my developed film; oddly, the professionals at the camera store wanted to talk to me. They told me "Look, this is good stuff. You should do something with this." I said, "What do you mean? Doesn't everybody see like this?" And they looked at me, and said, "No, not at all. Your compositions are different. There is definitely a consistency here." That's when I realized, "Wait a minute! Everybody sees things differently." After all those years, I somehow didn't connect all this. I did not realize this before.

A few more years went by. Eventually, I had the time to get more serious, entering pictures that I felt were of interest to me in a few more art venues.

One day I received an invitation to visit a friend who was in Japan on a six-month sabbatical with his family. I thought it was a great idea and a wonderful opportunity for me to immerse myself in something so culturally different, giving me an opportunity to open my world of art as I knew it, and to explore and express my artistic abilities.

The contrasts I found in Japan between centuries-old temples and shrines and the modern and bustling cities were quite interesting. Everywhere in Japan, there is the timelessness of Japanese culture next to the trappings of modernization. I was struck by both the chaos and the serenity. Both aspects of Japan coexisted harmoniously in this geographically small place.

While venturing out on my own, I went to an underground mall in Kyoto. I found it fascinating to watch the people and look around. I happened to walk into a clothing store. I thought maybe I'd buy a shirt. The salesman came up behind me like a tailor with a cloth tape measure. My arms reached longer than his tape measure. All of a sudden, he held the tape measure up in the air. He started talking in a loud voice, so that everyone inside and outside of his store could hear him. I think he was saying something about me being like Godzilla, big.

He turned to me and said, "You! You too big. No have. Japanese big have. So sorry." He bowed up and down and said, "You go."

I had to admire his straightforwardness. I was way too big for the items he had in his store. It was obvious he was just tripping out at my size. By this time, the crowd outside the store was about four deep, with wide, curious eyes all looking at me. I have to admit it was kind of comical. I visually had a funny thought that maybe for good measure I should raise my arms high in the air and breathe fire back at the store and at all the many onlookers like the real Godzilla would do! Ah, but then again, I guess they would not have found that thought funny.

I felt the pictures I came back with were amazing. It was told to me that periodic comments were made by some of the Japanese people who walked by when I was taking pictures at the castles, temples, and shrines. They made comments like, "Who does he think he is? How dare he? That is not a proper way to take a picture of this temple."

But what I saw was something more majestic than the temple itself. It was like, "Here's the bigger picture." And to me, the bigger picture was in the details. I increasingly felt that the veracity of the photographic image was about getting down to what's true, to a truth that's deeper than attitude or "image." It's about isolating part of something, so the whole could be seen.

I'm finding that my eyes really gravitate toward, and are naturally drawn to, abstract and abstract expressionist images. Layering tends to be a theme. All that layering, space, color, light, and shading come together in a way that speaks and stimulates thought, feeling, and imagination. It reflects something larger back at me.

Everything, in fact, reflects something larger than itself. That's the key. For me, the lens is the strongest way to capture my vision of composition and to explain what I view without getting all those funny looks from people who don't understand what I'm trying to say. The words out of my mouth could not move as fast as the images in my head.

This newfound artistic talent has changed me for the better, and in a way, it has vindicated me. What I see now is what I always saw back in the "retard room." I feel photography has made the reality of that legitimate. It gave those early experiences of life a good purpose. I feel free inside now. I have come full circle about it, and nobody can tell me anything different. Nobody can push me around now like they did when I was a kid. Now I can defend myself. Now, instead of being criticized, I am praised for the way in which I see the world. It is a really cool turn of events when I think about it.

My earlier artwork showed a wide range of subject matter. My subjects ranged from detailed architectural studies to pure abstract colorist images. The unifying element was the originality derived from my unique vision.

Life has many unforeseen events that we would never guess would happen. Opportunities rise. Opportunities fall. Some are completely oblivious to the subtleties of life. Seizing an unexpected moment in time, I traveled to Cuba to find art. It was like a part of a puzzle, a piece that I never would have thought in a million years would fit. I did not know what would happen or lie ahead of me in this country that was previously a faceless location that I always remember just seeing on a map. Taking these adventures was an act of discovery, an honest encounter into this unknown world.

I had never before photographed people. Artistically, they never captured my attention. But there was something about the people in Cuba. I found their lack of pretense to be refreshing. There was also an artistic element to everything else on this island. If you look at the pictures I took of the places and people there, my strongest impression of the people is that they're genuine. Here we compete like crazy and hide our intentions. There, they don't compete, and they don't hide much of anything. Life has been refined down to the basics.

In Cuba, you can see the hard lives written on the faces of some of the people. Life there wears on the body. There is a strong sense of pride in themselves and their country, but they are also a very humble people. You can see the way the Cuban people deal with generations of poverty, while maintaining dignity in a peaceful, gentle lifestyle. You can see that.

I returned from Cuba with amazing pictures. With many of these, I have thought, *Wow. I can't even believe I got that.* The pictures are spontaneous and candid. They reflect a rich humanity without pretense or superficiality. I think what happened in my life also gave me an understanding of the difficulties faced by the Cuban people to live, survive, and persevere. I've been there in a way.

Everywhere I looked in this last frontier, there was always something to see. The architecture. The colors. The shadows. The people. It was like when my children watch too much television and get over-stimulated. To me, Cuba was just like that. Everywhere I looked, my eyes couldn't get enough. I could just look all day. I thought I was in heaven, and to think, I went there on a hunch.

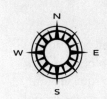

Gulf of

Mexico

UNITED
STATES

Key Largo

Key West

Straits of Florida

La Habana

Yucatan Channel

Isla de la Juventud

Isla de Cozumel

MEXICO

Grand Cayman

Banco
Chinchorro

BELIZE

CARIBBEAN

SEA

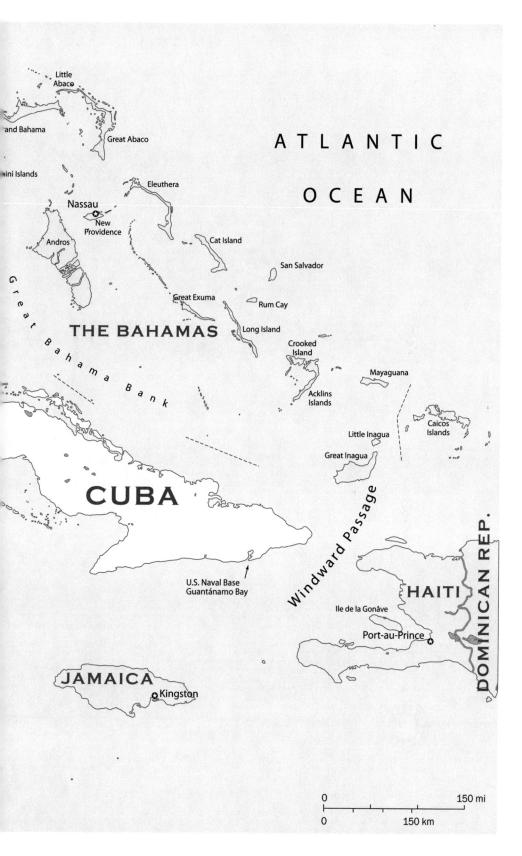

UNITED
STATES

Florida

Gulf of Mexico

Straits of Florida

La Habana
(Havana)

Cuidad de La
Habana

La
Habana

Pinar
del Río

Matanzas

Villa
Clara

Cienfuegos

Isla de la
Juventud

Sancti
Spíritus

Cayman Islands
(U.K.)

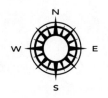

N

W   E

S

CARIBBEAN SEA

0   100 mi

0   100 km

UNITED STATES

Gulf of Mexico

Straits of Florida

La Habana (Havana)
Cojimar
Matanzas
Varadero
San Francisco de Paula
Regla
San José de las Lajas
San Diego de los Baños
Las Terrazas
Cárdenas
Santa Ana
Güines
Viñales
Pinar del Rio
Sagua la Grande
Santa Clara
Remedi
Playa Larga
Yaguaramas
Cienfuegos
Isla de la Juventud
Península de Zapata
Playa Girón
Bahía de Cochinos
Manicaragua
Sanc Spírt
Embalse Hanabanilla
Trinida
Topes de Collantes

Cayman Islands (U.K.)

CARIBBEAN SEA

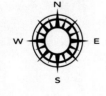

N
W · E
S

0   100 mi

0   100 km

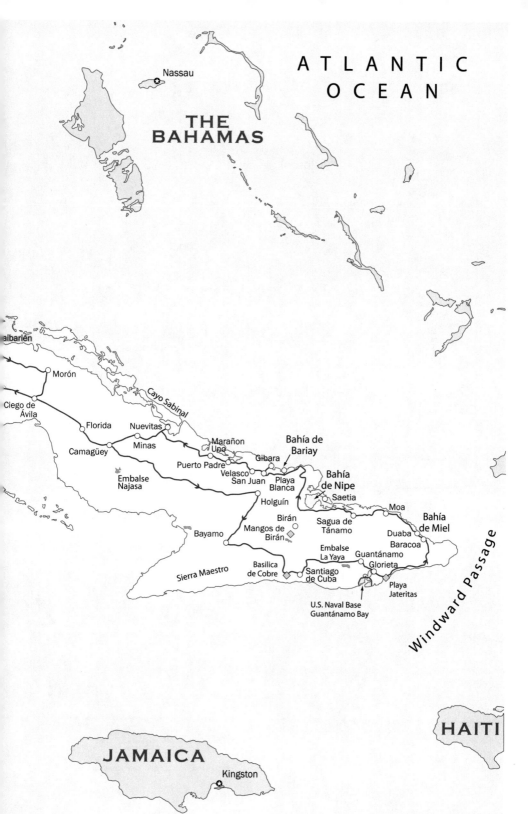

ATLANTIC
OCEAN

Nassau

THE
BAHAMAS

aibarién

Morón

Ciego de
Ávila

Florida

Camagüey

Minas

Nuevitas

Cayo Sabinal

Marañon
Uno

Puerto Padre

Velasco

San Juan

Playa
Blanca

Gibara

Bahía de
Bariay

Bahía
de Nipe

Embalse
Najasa

Holguín

Saetia

Moa

Bahía
de Miel

Bayamo

Birán

Mangos de
Birán

Sagua de
Tánamo

Duaba

Baracoa

Embalse
La Yaya

Guantánamo

Glorieta

Basilica
de Cobre

Santiago
de Cuba

Sierra Maestro

U.S. Naval Base
Guantánamo Bay

Playa
Jateritas

Windward Passage

HAITI

JAMAICA

Kingston

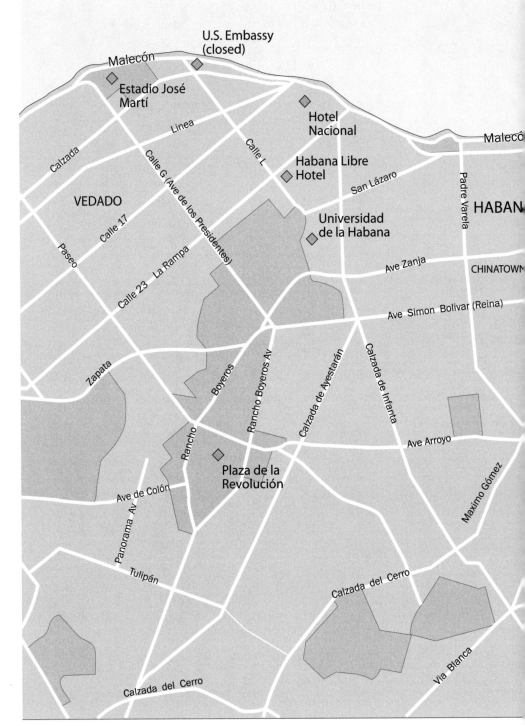

Straits of Florida

Malecón

U.S. Embassy
(closed)

Estadio José
Martí

Linea

Calle L

Hotel
Nacional

Malecó

Calzada

Calle G (Ave de los Presidentes)

Habana Libre
Hotel

San Lázaro

Padre Varela

VEDADO

Calle 17

Universidad
de la Habana

HABAN

Paseo

La Rampa

Calle 23

Ave Zanja

CHINATOWN

Ave Simon Bolivar (Reina)

Zapata

Boyeros

Rancho Boyeros Av

Calzada de Ayestarán

Calzada de Infanta

Ave Arroyo

Rancho

Plaza de la
Revolución

Maximo Gómez

Ave de Colón

Panorama Av

Tulipán

Calzada del Cerro

Calzada del Cerro

Via Blanca

Castillo de los
Tres Santos Reyes
de Morro

Via Monumental

Cojimar →

Castillo de San
Salvador
de la Punta

Fortaleza de San
Carlos de la Cabaña

CASABLANCA

Trans-Bahía
Tunnel

Museo de
la Revolución

Castillo de la
Real Fuerza

Ave de Italia

Hotel
Ambos
Mundos

LA HABANA VIEJA
HAVANA OLD TOWN

Dragon
Gate

Ave de la Bélgica

Desamparados

Bahía

de la

Habana

Ave del Puerto

REGLA

San Francisco de Paula
"Finca La Vigia" →

Via Blanca

Primer Anillo del Puerto

0		0.5 mi
0		900 m

1

CONNECTIONS

THIS IS A story of an unlikely destination—a true tale of confronting a land full of color, beauty, and spirit—a land whose people inhabit a cultural time capsule, weathering hardships with generosity, resourcefulness, and dignity. Full of historical significance, theirs is a place largely shut off from the world, in a different time, held back, isolated, and forgotten. It is the enigmatic island: Cuba.

After a flight that went smoothly, I was very happy to finally arrive and land in Havana. I slowly disembarked the plane and walked the passenger ramp. As I passed by guards, they scanned me with their eyes, and they scanned the other passengers who went by them, one by one. I passed their security dogs, about three or four, which looked like a type of spaniel to me. The dogs did not appear too threatening. However, I could not help but notice that all the eyes of the Cuban authorities focused intently on us passengers and our every move.

The path through the terminal was narrow and direct. There were big glass walls acting as barriers. Guards were standing at designated points to direct us through, as we continued to follow the determined pathway. After finally getting through the terminal and reaching customs, I arrived to an area where the movement of all the disembarking people began to slow down. I then found myself starting to stand stagnant in a bottleneck area with many other people. There I found myself waiting in front of an array of many faceless individual white doors.

Eventually, I was allowed to pass through one of these doors. It closed behind me after I went through, and I found myself in a very small, enclosed area with a counter about chest high and a closed door on the other end. I stood in front of the counter, and before I realized what was going on, a picture had been taken of me.

Cuban security did a lot of looking—looking at my passport, looking at the pictures they just took of me with my face staring from their computer screen. They spent a lot of time slowly focusing on the picture of my face on their computer, then at my passport, and then slowly looking back at me. I stood there, unsure of what they might be looking for. Without warning, I heard a low-pitch buzzing sound that was coming from the knob of the other door, the exit door. This became the first intersecting point by the Cuban officials, as I was allowed to continue through this unlocked door. On the other side, I was told to put my luggage through the scanners. I had to put everything through, even my film—no exceptions. The divergent foreign travelers around me looked slightly confused. But I knew what to do because I had visited Cuba before.

In the United States, the authorities will hand inspect film rolls, but

definitely not here in Cuba. It is said that X-rays do not damage film, and on my two previous trips to the island nation, my film came through just fine. But I always took film as a carry-on item. If the film had went through in checked baggage, where the X-rays screen at a higher intensity, it would have come out so overexposed that it would have rendered the film useless, like being exposed to full sunlight. All of my film would have been destroyed. As an artist, I always get a little concerned about going through any X-rays.

In a foreign country, something can always be just a little off, a little bit different from what we are used to in the United States. The electrical outlets in Cuba are a prime example. Some are 110 volts, some are 220 volts, and sometimes you just don't know. In the hotels, they are not always marked, and the electrical outlets often look alike. I have experienced electrical shocks, that numbing sensation, by just brushing my hand on a hotel bedside lamp.

It was because of these unknown elements that I was feeling a little uneasy about any of my film going through the X-rays. But at the same time, you can't argue with the iron wall of Cuban security—that's just the way it is. So I sent through my one carry-on bag, and next, I sent my large camera pack through. I went through too, and that's when it all started to go wrong. The X-ray technician looked agitated.

"Is something wrong?" I asked, not quite sure of what was going on.

She slapped a small sticker on my carry-on bag, "You have to come with me," she said in broken English.

As I followed, she escorted me down the corridor. I could see her gesturing out to her other comrades as we passed. I could pick up from the energy mirrored off their faces that something was not right. All the while, she called out for assistance.

"What's wrong? What's wrong?" I asked, as she guided me through the terminal.

"It's OK," she said. "It's OK. Don't worry," she said again in her broken English.

We walked further and moved from the terminal. I was told to stand off to one side, behind a stand of barrier blinds at portable tables that were set up. The technician put a guard on me, and she kept calling out for somebody. Perhaps it was a person of even higher authority. The other security people did too. It seemed that it had to be this one person.

I got a little worried. Minutes passed. He arrived from around the corner. He wore military dress. I could not help but notice his shoulders displayed epaulets made of thick cloth. At about six-and-a-half-feet tall, he reached roughly to my height. I am probably a bit taller. His hair—trimmed in a short, military style—did not move. His eyes pierced the air right at me. When he charged out orders in Castilian Spanish, the others jumped. His voice was deep, and when he spoke it was like he said, *I'm taking over now!* He was a man of discipline, definitely in charge, a definite imposing figure. And there we were, standing across this table, this military boss on one side, and me on the other. I took a deep breath—not sure of what was about to happen. I sensed that something was not right. All I could think was, *Oh, God, help me!*

He stared at me longer, with a glaze of contempt in his eyes. My camera pack was below. My carry-on bag lay on the table between us. There was a very long pause. I could see him slowly sizing me up, as he continued staring, not taking his fixed eyes off me, while not saying anything. . . .

With an authoritarian demeanor, he then spoke the words, "Open it up!"

I did not know what to think, but I complied. I had no choice. I opened the bag, and he yanked out all my stuff. It spilled out onto the table. He immediately saw the first of two laptops I brought—both of them gifts for Jesús, my best friend and most trusted confidant in Cuba. I met Jesús when he worked as the tour guide for my first two trips to the country.

I arranged those trips through a reality tour provider. The first trip was in 2007 and focused on agriculture and sustainability. The second trip, in 2008, focused on architecture and urban planning. Each was made possible in part by my position as one of four land-use professionals on a seven-member city architectural review board.

But this, this was my third trip, in March of 2009—this was going to be different. I was no longer associated with the umbrella of the past reality-tour organization, and I had planned to be gone for many days on a potential three thousand mile journey across large swaths of the island and its perimeter. I wanted to venture to and through some of Cuba's most out-of-the-way places. Since I thought that I would have some extra space in the car, and thinking it might be fun, I invited Jesús to ride along. Prior to flying to Havana to meet Jesús, I planned to spend one night at the Courtyard Marriott in Cancun, Mexico. My time in Mexico was short by design. After bidding my wife and three children farewell, I arrived from California and stayed fewer than twenty-four hours. I did not want to spend any more time in Mexico than necessary. And I really did not want to experience again what I went through previously in Cancun, immediately before my second trip to Cuba.

On my second trip, I got caught up in the American Airlines debacle of 2008, when thousands of travelers were stranded, as the airline grounded more than one thousand flights to inspect electrical systems. All of the airline's flights out of Santa Barbara airport to Dallas, where I needed to go, were grounded. I was rerouted to Los Angeles and flew from Los Angeles to Dallas. This put me a few hours behind. Because of these delays, it looked like I was not going to make my scheduled meeting in the Cancun terminal with the rest of my tour group—a meeting at which we were supposed to receive our Cuban visas and my airline tickets to Havana.

I was heavily weighed down because I had brought two extra-oversized suitcases filled with nothing but humanitarian gifts for Jesús, Pilo, and Chiqui (pronounced "Cheek-e"). The latter two people were friends I made on my first trip to Cuba. The items included clothes, hats, soap, toothbrushes, shoes, pencils, over-the-counter medicines, blank CDs, three very special pairs of new Oakley sunglasses in cases, and beef jerky certified by the US Food and Drug Administration. I also brought Disney short story picture books for their children and boxes of Cracker Jacks. (Every kid should be able to try Cracker Jacks!)

Upon arriving in Cancun, I entered the international terminal and retrieved all my checked luggage. I had to go through Mexican customs. A line of travelers stretched out in front of me, and I noticed something odd occurring. Everyone going through was asked to push a button on a glass display. After they pushed the button, the display turned either red or green. Green meant a traveler was allowed to pass through. Red meant no passage, and the person in question was stopped and inspected. The lights were on a rotation, it seemed, so approximately every fifteenth person who went through would be stopped by the red light. I began to notice that one of the inspectors asked a lot of questions and kept looking toward the back of the room, like he was eyeing somebody behind the scenes.

Three people in line in front of me each landed on red. Then I came up. The inspector asked where I came from. I told him Texas.

"Push the button," he said.

I pushed the button, and it turned green. I kept moving, but the inspector yelled out at me, "Stop! Come back here." He told me that the display turned red.

"No, it didn't," I said. "It was green."

He argued, "Red."

"No!" I said. "It turned green."

There was a short pause, then he said it turned red and green at the same time. *Right*, I thought. He told me to push the button again, and then he looked back across the room, like he did for the other people. When I pushed the button, the display, not surprisingly, turned red. Did someone override the rotation?

"We have to look through your suitcases," the inspector said in his smug voice. He opened the suitcases and started pulling out all my stuff. He had this satisfied look on his face, like it was Merry Christmas!

"You can't have this," he said. "You can't have that."

He wanted all the beef jerky. I had big bags of beef jerky. "I had no problem coming through here the last time with it," I told him. "I brought jerky on my first trip in my carry-on bag."

He gave me a run-around rambling reason as to why I was not allowed to have these things.

I said, "It has the FDA approval on it, and besides, I'm not even staying here in Mexico. I'm catching a flight to Cuba that I'm already late for, and I need to get moving."

"No!" he said. "You can't have these things." By now, it had become very clear that this was a shake down. I started to get really angry! I spent so much time and effort getting all those gifts together. I had such heartfelt compassion for my friends, and I wanted to try and help ease some of the burdens of their daily lives.

Suddenly, before I realized what I was about to say, something came over me and burst out of me. I yelled, "How dare you! These are gifts from the church to the people of Cuba!"

I was just loud enough for everybody to hear, and everyone around started watching us. I decided in that instant not to push too hard, because a Mexican *federale* (federal policeman) with a machine gun happened to be walking by. I thought that I could be dragged off to a back room, as I was not sure of who could be on the take around here. This corrupt inspector slowly started putting everything back in my suitcases, all the while awkwardly looking around and trying to justify his actions, as though he wasn't doing anything wrong. He slid my bag aside. A woman inspector came over and did a little extra looking. She had a condescending air about her, and she asked how much all the stuff in my suitcase was worth. I thought for a moment that they might try to hit me up for a tax, or maybe hit me up with a pay-off scheme.

I played dumb and said, "I don't know, between fifty and one hundred dollars."

She tried to put me down, like I was cheap, but that was it. She zipped it up, and I zipped out of there, hoping that maybe, just maybe, I had time to catch my flight to Havana. I jumped on a shuttle that took about five minutes to carry me to yet another terminal.

When I got to the other terminal, I was thrilled to learn my flight to Havana was delayed. I went to the counter to obtain my ticket and visa. But as it turned out, the liaison for my reality tour in Cancun did not give my Cuban visa to the counter staff. This meant I could not get my ticket. Plus I had not logged the necessary advance check-in time, thanks to American Airlines.

I was not sure what to do. It was late at night, humid, and I had sweat dripping off my head. I stepped out of the terminal in Cancun, and I got pounced on. Everyone was trying to help me to move over here, to do this, to get me there. A few of these folks saw I was frustrated and also quite tired. I was awkwardly carrying the oversized suitcases along with my carry-on bag, which was hanging over my shoulder, and a large, heavy camera pack. A couple of guys said they could take me to an inexpensive hotel, one with discounts for people who miss a flight, supposedly. They showed me a picture of the hotel. I wanted to sit in the terminal all night, but there was really nowhere to do that. So I thought, *OK, OK, I'll get in this taxi.*

We left, and as we were driving, I started to realize we were oddly moving away from the city. The night sky was getting even darker. I then began to realize that I was not in a taxi. We drove on, and it kept getting darker. I got even more agitated.

The one guy kept patting me on the back, picking up on my uneasiness, saying, "It's OK. It's OK," as if to calm me down.

That in itself made me even madder, and I began to believe that something was wrong. I thought they might kidnap me, rob me, or even kill me. It just did not look right. We drove on. About twenty minutes into this, I was ready to unleash and start going postal, because I thought I was being kidnapped. But a hotel appeared, seemingly out of nowhere. We drove around the back and through a special employee entrance with a security gate. We got out. I was escorted to the head maid. She had a small makeshift office. The guys and the woman negotiated for a room.

The maid said, "One hundred dollars."

"No way," I responded. That got it down to eighty dollars. "Fine, whatever," I said.

It was about midnight. I was escorted through a maze of walkways. Some of the elevators did not work, but we made our way up into the back area of this hotel. I saw people who looked like they might live there permanently. It seemed really odd. I got into a room. I locked the door. The "taxi" guys told me they would come back in the morning to get me. *Really?*

I grew concerned they would not come back, and that I would miss my flight. I paid them fifty dollars for the round trip.

In the morning, they sent another guy back, so I had to pay thirty-five dollars more to get taken back to the airport. By this time, I was just glad to get back to the terminal safely, and I tried to look at this game as the cost of doing business. I made my flight.

As I planned for this current adventure, my third trip to Cuba, I worried about having to travel through Mexico again. Every day in the major news media, I saw stories of kidnappings, beheadings, and gun battles related to drug-turf wars. The United States was repeatedly issuing travel warnings for Americans to avoid going to all of Mexico.

I did not want a repeat of the stress of what happened to me on my last trip in Cancun—and I certainly did not want something worse. So this time, I prearranged for a legitimate taxi shuttle to pick me up and take me to the Cancun Courtyard Marriott, where I had an assured reservation. After landing, I went through customs. When I left the airport security area, I immediately was approached inside the terminal, but not by anyone I was expecting. Some were airport loiterers and some were workers at the airport. It was odd that it came out that I was going to Cuba and how they knew. They asked, was I "looking for a great time?" They made off-hand remarks like, "live it up." Their tone and body movements were very suspicious. It made me believe that they were connected to the drug trade in some way, but they did not come right out and say it.

Instinctively, I responded with, "No trouble. No trouble," in a somewhat joking manner, so as to distance myself and keep from being pulled deeper into their probing conversations. I could discern that they were trying to feel me out, to see where I fit in the parameters of the drug underworld—whether I was a courier, or had a contact in Cuba, or was a potential rival.

I worried about going through Mexico again, but unbeknownst to me, the problems were waiting for me at the airport in Havana this time. After breakfast, I checked out of the Marriott and took its free shuttle to my terminal.

While in Mexico, I had two main objectives—to obtain a Cuban tourist visa and to not miss my flight across the Gulf. I purchased the visa from the Click Mexicana airlines. It had to be filled out precisely. They wanted to know my passport number, name, and my reason for visiting Cuba. I had to check in at least three hours before takeoff. I also had to present that same visa when I left Cuba, along with twenty-five Cuban CUCs for the Cuban departure tax. If you do not do this, you will have trouble. On my second trip to Cuba, when I flew across the Caribbean to Havana, I happened to sit next to some Americans who were defying the travel embargo. They were going to Cuba for a few days to check it out. But I have always wanted to travel legally.

In order to travel legally to Cuba from the United States, I had to jump through hoops every time. The paperwork was tedious. I had to obtain several letters of recommendation and document my purpose for travel. The mayor of my city, a staff city administrator and a fellow colleague on the architectural review board, wrote the letters of recommendation for me. Basically, the whole process was geared toward proving that I was who I was, explaining what I was doing, and documenting how I qualified. Once approved, my sworn affidavit was only good for a set period of time. If I stayed in Cuba longer, I would have trouble.

Returning to America was always a concern of mine. I had heard of people having problems and experiencing hassles despite traveling legally. I was told how important it was to be truthful with the US Customs officials. In answer to the question, "Where have you been?" I suppose I could answer, "Mexico," without mentioning Cuba. But I never did that, and it is not advised.

Heck, even if you do play by the rules, things can go awry. I was barely back in Cuba, and here I was, already detained in a back room.

Dating back to 1930, the international airport in Havana was named in memory of Cuban patriot José Martí, a poet, professor, journalist, and philosopher who championed independence from Spain. The airport looks a bit older than those in America. Inside, the Cubans have tried to make it a little more modern. But on the runway coming in, new arrivals can see old passenger or cargo airplanes off to the side of the tarmac in a line on a grassy area. Some appear broken in half—their electrical wires dangling from the fuselage—as though mechanics cannibalized them for parts. I could discern their age, as they looked like something from the old black and white days, having faded paint, perfectly round passenger windows, and the ends of their wings and tails curved and exaggerated. They most probably dated back to the 1950s if not earlier.

Now on my third trip to Cuba, I was experiencing new problems. After the interrogator saw my laptop, he pulled out my camera and the forty rolls of slide film I had packed. He also saw the disposable camera that my wife, Anne, had sent along. She knew that when I traveled I did not typically take pictures of myself or of my companions, since I am usually concentrating on my own photographic artwork. So my wife wanted me to take a cheap camera, so I could get shots of what she wanted to see—namely me, friends, and places I stayed. The disposable was still packaged in its colorful cardboard box, unopened. The interrogator told me to open it up and pull it out. It was vacuum-sealed in foil.

As he broke the seal, I said, "It's just a disposable camera." He wanted to open the camera itself, which would have exposed the film. I told him no. It was the only time I stood up to him. He relented, and moved to other questions.

I thought to myself, *Why is this happening?* I felt progressively worse, increasingly worried that my trip was about to end. But I was not trying to do anything wrong.

The interrogator moved to my forty rolls of film. "How many pictures per roll?" he asked.

"Thirty six," I replied. I couldn't really figure that one out, unless he just wanted to test me, thinking maybe I was carrying this stuff in without really knowing anything about it.

From my camera pack, he moved to my only other piece of luggage, my regular carry-on bag, and pulled out my other laptop. This inspired an explosion of new questions, and his voice grew even louder.

I now realized that there was no way I could tell him these laptops were gifts to my friend Jesús. Yet I had to explain fast.

"This is my laptop, and my other laptop is a backup," I said. "That other laptop is old, old, old. It's over ten years old." It was indeed about that old, but remained in good shape. "It's just a backup for my pictures. If one computer goes bad, at least I've got something," I said. "I will be in Cuba for three weeks. I have no resources. I could plug it into the wrong electrical outlet, hit a 220-volt line, fry it, and I'm screwed."

He didn't like my answers, but then again, what else could I say? There was a short pause. He looked at the back of my camera. It was not digital, there was no digital screen, and I had forty rolls of slide film. Here I was with these computers and no way to transfer my film from the camera to the computer. He was so aggressive, and yet he failed to notice that I didn't really need my computers for my photography. I did not know computers very well, and I was trying to convince this guy that I did. I guess theoretically I could have gone to a photo place and made files. I think he was basically blinded to this because he was like a pit bull.

He turned to my clothes—every pocket, every seam, everything! He stuck his hand inside every sock. He pulled out my shorts. One pair, two, three, four, and then he went on a verbal barrage and belittled me for not packing any long pants. Well, the truth is, I hardly ever wear long pants.

Anyone who knows me knows I never wear long pants. If I do, it's like, "What's wrong with Chris?" But I did not explain this to him. One, I did not think he would understand, and two, I did not think that this, this *El Comandante* (the Commander) wanted to hear about it.

He turned to my stash of underwear. He went through every pair, and at this point I got an idea that I thought maybe I'd just try to loosen things up. So I leaned over and said, "Hey! At least they are all clean."

He had his head down, but he looked up and right at me quite slowly, and it was a steely look with his eyes, and his jaws were clenched tightly. It was as if he were saying, *Don't even fuck with me!* And I just thought to myself, *OK . . . that was definitely not a good idea!*"

It was obvious that this guy was on a mission. He was intense. He was methodical, and at times he would just go into a rage.

"You're a liar!" he yelled at me. "I don't believe you!"

"How many times have you been to Cuba?" he demanded.

I told him this was my third visit, and his voice grew louder. "What?" he shouted.

"What were the dates?" he demanded. I told him.

He questioned me about how I make money. I told him I was visiting for a research study. I explained that I was a landscape contractor, and that I work with plants and trees. Then he mocked me. How could I afford to come on these trips if I was just a gardener? And all the while, he took notes.

"How much Spanish do you speak?" he demanded.

"A little bit." I said it in English.

"What state do you live in? What town are you from?"

I told him, and again, he mocked me. "You're from Santa Barbara, and you don't even speak Spanish?" he said loudly.

I felt he was definitely trying to intimidate me, to get me to try to speak Spanish. I sensed that if I did, I could slip. My Spanish was limited.

"You come here and you don't speak Spanish?" He shouted!

It was as though he was daring me to try, to try to get me to say something wrong. I'm sure if I did, he would go on and on, and this could open up a new line of questioning.

I had to say something. I told him, in English, that the Spaniards came all the way up the coast of California and built missions.

The questions went on and on. "How much money do you have?" he shouted.

"Forty-eight hundred Euros," I replied.

But I realized, *Holy Crap! I'm off by an extra thousand. If he checks my pockets, I'm screwed.*

Right before I left home, I last minute stuck that extra cash in my pocket, as I was beginning to feel the gravity and uncertainty of this trip. US and international credit cards do not work in Cuba. There is no US Embassy. There is nothing of the sort, and I would be all on my own. Because of the embargo, there are many restrictions. You cannot even use American traveler's checks. I had to plan for all possible contingencies, and hoped that I would not run out of money. Had he found the extra money I had in my pocket, I don't know what would have happened.

This guy acted possessed—like he smelled blood from five different directions. He appeared to grow angrier. And yet, I didn't have anything he could really stick me on. That was the key. I figured that he might have harbored a preconceived suspicion about who I was. Maybe it's because I'm tall, broad shouldered, and weigh 240 pounds. Maybe it's because I have blue eyes and short-cropped hair. At age forty-eight, heck, I suppose I look like I could be ex-military. Plus, on this trip, I only had two carry-on bags for my entire stay, whereas the usual traveler to Cuba probably brought at least one or two larger suitcases, if not more.

Like I said, I didn't have anything, and so he started to question me— again and again—about how much money I made and how I could afford to get here.

"I make my money as a landscape contractor," I said. "I trim trees. I landscape."

It was all true. Or at least it had been true. I worked in landscaping and trees for about twenty-five years. It was how I made my way, stretching way back to my early twenties, when I severely injured myself in a pole-vaulting accident. I had to forgo college because of that accident, and pulled myself back from paralysis. It was bad.

I told him, "I'm a landscape contractor." He tried to put me down for it. I was going to pull out my wallet and show him my official state contractor's license card. Even though I'm retired, I still retain my license. I realized this move might give him an opportunity to go through my wallet. *Who knows what might get trumped up out of that?*

So I said, "OK, look. I don't know how to explain this."

And he looked at me like he thought he finally had something.

"Oh, please do," he said in a condescending tone, as he gestured theatrically with his hands like, *Let's hear this one!*

So I tried to explain that I'm a member of a board.

He made a face like he did not understand. His expression said, *What?*

"A board of seven people," I said. "A committee."

"Oh, OK. Proceed," he said.

"It's called the DRB," I said. "An architectural design review board."

I told him that I qualified to come to Cuba because I serve on an architectural design review board for my city, and that we have similar architecture to that of Cuba. I came to research, take pictures, and document Cuban architecture and landscaping. "We oversee our city on design, on architecture, on land use," I said. "I am one of the land-use professionals on issues such as landscaping, trees, and drainage. I even know some architecture, and that's what I bring to this board. Your city and my city have a lot of similarities. Spanish history, architecture, and things like that. We have small farms and organic farms that bring food into the city." I brought out the affidavit that permitted my travel.

He yelled out, "It says here 'professional'!" I did not know, or understand, what brought that comment on. He changed the subject, going on and on about my maps. He looked at my maps and demanded to know, "Where did you get these?"

"My wife," I said. "She works for a map company." That was true. It was just a map. It even had the price tag on the back. But he went through that whole map, every crease in that map. He opened it, but he also ran his fingers in the creases.

Again, he said, "Where did you get this map? This is the best map I have ever seen."

It was almost like a compliment. I think it was meant to get me to open up. He had moments of that good-guy, bad-guy thing. He berated me at first, but then he backed off and changed the subject—again—I think because he didn't find anything of substance in the map or get me to open up about it.

Right after that, he opened my flipbook calendar, my daily planner. It was about three inches by six inches. On the front page of the notepad, I had written down the places I'd really like to go to—Remedios and the Bay of Pigs—and man, he just lit up on the Bay of Pigs. I tried to calm him down.

I said, "Well, there's a museum I'd like to see there." I mean, yeah, I wanted to see the museum, but I wanted to see other things too. I tried to play up on the museum to calm him down.

I had also written "Bayamo," and I had jotted "cane" underneath, meaning cane fields, sugarcane fields. Cane was real big in that area.

He just went off on that. "Cane fields? What?" he yelled.

Right then, I wondered, *Is there something over there that is sensitive that I don't know about? Military maybe?* I had no idea. "I want to get pictures of sugarcane," I said. I told him that sugarcane is seven times more energy efficient than the corn-based fuels we use in America, and we could learn a lot from that.

He looked at me with a pause and said calmly, "I did not know that."

Then he went on. I was concerned because he also saw that I had written "Gitmo" on there. Surprisingly, he didn't bring that up. Perhaps because below "Gitmo" I had written "Columbus." Columbus landed at Guantanamo on his second voyage in 1494. And in Baracoa, over by Gibara, is where he actually set foot in 1492 on Cuban soil for the first time.

El Comandante taunted me. "So, you're going to go to all these places?" he said.

"Well, I'd like to," I responded slowly. "But I don't know if I can."

There was a pause. Then he snapped back at me. "But if you could, you would really want to go there, wouldn't you? With forty-eight hundred Euros, you should be able to do more than just that!"

He began to very slowly and meticulously flip through all the empty note pages of the day planner. All of a sudden, I experienced a heavy pressure, a swelling in my chest, as my heart started pounding. Feeling that deep warmth from my beating chest made my forehead begin to perspire. He flipped almost through to the end of the notepad; I had just remembered what I had written on the back of the last page. I thought, *Oh, my God. Here it comes*, because all the way to the back of the notepad, I had Jesús's name, address, and phone number—pretty much all sorts of written information that I'm sure this El Comandante would have loved.

Any information about my Cuban contacts would have given him something to go on, and the last thing I wanted to do was bring any trouble to my friends, especially with the way El Comandante was acting. I really didn't know what he might level at them. Sure, I put all that info on the back page, but I did it for easy reference, so I could just flip to it. I honestly wasn't trying to hide anything. But I'm sure he would have seen it differently.

As he was approaching the last few pages, I felt sure that this was it. I was sweating and holding my breath, trying to do everything I could to not look obviously concerned. I was fully aware of the all-consuming movement of my heart and the tingling of adrenaline rapidly pumping through my whole body. At that moment, without any rhyme or reason, he paused near the last few pages of the notepad and then . . . and then he just mysteriously stopped! It was like he was in a deep thought about something. All of a sudden, he just closed the notebook, just like that. He never even saw the back page. And I thought to myself, *Oh, my God. Thank God.*

El Comandante yelled out for a guard to stand at attention and watch me while he went away for a while. He left me standing there. I looked at the guard, who stared back at me. We said nothing.

Later in my trip, I found out that back in 2008, Jesús's house had been raided. He had an illegal satellite dish inside an air conditioning unit mounted to a window. Jesús told me that Cuba has different levels of police, and that one type looked around for that sort of violation. It's not that they did not want Cuban citizens to have outside television. My understanding was they did not want access to all the propaganda broadcasting from Florida—messages like, "Leave. Come to America. You can do this." News, education channels, the history channels, Disney, Cartoon Network, they did not seem to care about those. At the hotels, I was able to watch European CNN world news, even in the lobbies in full view of the Cubans working there.

So they raided the house. Normally, Cubans put the satellite up and then charge neighbors to plug into it. That incurred a fine of several thousand pesos. But Jesús didn't do that. He just had it up for himself and his family. He did say that the police were surprised that he was not running cable and renting out access to other people. They issued a fine of fifteen hundred pesos. They took his computer along with the satellite dish because the computer was hooked up to the dish. If Jesús had been there, he could have unplugged it from the computer drive, but he wasn't home. At that time, he was off for a month working on another part of the island. His wife was left to deal with the situation on her own. That was intense for her, from what I understand. She didn't want all the police coming in because she is the principal of a school. The police had come to her school, which was embarrassing enough for her.

She asked, "Am I under arrest?"

They said, "No." Yet, all eyes of the school were on her, watching. She refused to get into their police car. She deliberately walked home and met them there to make her point. The police wanted to come into the house but were refused, saying, "No, only you can come in," referring to the head guy, and actually, he turned out to be pretty nice, I was told.

Once I learned from Jesús that the authorities took his computer, then I understood why I had experienced such difficulty reaching him via e-mail. In the lead up to my trip, I was stressed out trying to line things up. Yet, I was not always able to communicate with Jesús to make plans. I had a heck of a time—so much so, that I was almost to the point of canceling my whole trip. Planning to travel about three thousand miles around the island and at the same time being unable to nail down my itinerary with

Jesús was daunting. It did not help that much that all of the country was on dial-up, and that mail takes about four to eight weeks to deliver via a third party nation, if it even made it through at all.

After some time, El Comandante returned. He dismissed the guard. My ordeal in detention lasted nearly all afternoon. All my luggage had been pulled open and laid on the table. And as I said, El Comandante did not seem to like my laptops. He lorded over both of them—all the time, questioning and questioning me. He put another guard on me again, and he left again.

He commanded; he yelled out; and then, *boom!*, somebody would hop to it.

He said something in Castilian Spanish that sounded like, "Stand here. Guard him!" Then he walked away, and I had a guard standing with me, watching me the whole time.

I spoke to the guard in English. "Sure is taking a while," I said, but I got no response. I added, "Is everything OK?"

I got that same answer in broken English, "It's OK. Don't worry."

I started to clue in to the situation. I surmised that this guard did not know English. I was pretty sure he did not understand me. I realized that "It's OK" is probably just a pat answer they use to keep things calm, even if there was an issue—a policy to get people to relax. Instead of engaging in conversation, they repeat, "It's OK. Don't worry." What can you say to that?

I just stood there not knowing what to do. I was not sure if they were watching me on camera or not. This time, it seemed that El Comandante had been gone a long time. On the other side of the partition, I could hear people coming and going. Occasionally, another traveler would be pulled aside for a short while, and then let go. And, yet, here I was, caught in this confusion.

When El Comandante returned, he again asked what I did for a living. What was interesting was that when I had filled out the immigration papers on the flight to Cancun—and I'm telling you, it was a godsend—the form had a line for occupation, and I put "artist" to begin with; afterward I thought something wasn't right about that. I tore up the form and filled out another one. I sat on that to think for a while, and I ended up writing "research study," because that's really how I got my paperwork from America. When he left, I think El Comandante called Mexico and asked, "What did he put on that paperwork?" to see if there were any discrepancies.

When he returned from his long absence, he said loudly, "All right! I'm going to take a computer. You can't have two. Which one?"

I pulled out the old one. Nothing was on the hard drive. "You can take this one. It's old. It's insignificant."

He agreed, repeating my claims that it was cheap and practically worthless. He kept pounding this home, to the point that I almost told him to just keep it; I didn't need that one. I thought that might get me on my way quicker. I began to sense that if I said that, the guy would hit me up for bribery. And yet, I felt so compelled to say, take it, you can have it. It was as if that was what he *wanted* me to say. But, no! I bit my tongue, and I didn't say anything.

After a very long pause, in which El Comandante just stared at me, waiting, like he expected to hear something from me, he suddenly pulled out a form and wrote on it.

"You can't have two computers in Cuba," he said. "What I am going to do is, I am going to give you five days free, and then I'm going to charge you per day, plus a fine." He paused, then asked, "So how much is this computer worth?"

I said, "It's nothing, it's not worth anything. I keep telling you that."

He gave me that slow, stony, steely look again, the look that said, *Don't fuck with me.*

Without thinking, I immediately came up with a value. "Twenty five dollars," I blurted. I just threw that out there. Whatever. He recorded the serial numbers and made me sign the form. He threatened me, "Don't you dare lose that piece of paper. And when you come back to leave, you present that form, pay the fine and fees, and you will get your computer back."

"Sign here." He commanded, and I did. Then, he abruptly roared, "Now get out!" He turned and walked away.

All my stuff laid scattered about across their table. There was absolutely no way that anyone was going to help me to collect up all my belongings. I was left to find my own way out. Feeling as one might feel after walking through fire, I packed it all up while trying to hold myself up and keep my composure the best I could. As I turned to leave, there happened to be another military official who was sternly staring at me. This caught me by surprise. Now, how long had he been standing there behind me? I did not know. He stood there. Flanking his side were two other, probably lower level, military men. He snapped out at me too, and I thought, *Great! He's got his own line of questions.*

"How much money did you bring?" he said angrily as he gritted his teeth, seething in a deep, low-tone voice.

My first thought was to say that I had already told his other *companero* (colleague). At that moment, I could not figure out why this new comrade needed to know.

"Forty-eight hundred Euros," I said. But it was as if he didn't believe me. He appeared really, really angry, like he literally wanted to take me and haul me away along with my heart and spleen on a platter. He had positioned himself in such a way that I had to walk right past him, brushing against him. I began to walk out slowly, not wanting to stop because I think he was fishing, hoping in some way I would trip up, falter, or break down and say something that would give him an inroad to another line of questioning. I was certain he would detain me further. Dreading any more questioning, and not knowing what was in store for me next, I just thought, *You know, I'm not going to elaborate any further.*

I just walked steadily and slowly, and I purposely did not look back. I found my way out to the last doorway, where guards purposely stood on each side. As I approached closer, the doors automatically opened. Not knowing what would happen next, I just tried to stay composed the best I could. I continued walking cautiously between them, as if I were threading a needle. They both stared at me the entire time, as I slowly and apprehensively passed on through.

I got outside and the sky was darkening. I changed some of my Euros to Cuban CUCs. My fingers were a little shaky as I searched for the exact amount through my pockets.

El Comandante had wasted all his time with me and he got absolutely nothing for it. Well, nothing but an old laptop. I felt violated, and for much of the next two days, I felt dejected and emotionally drained. If that guy were a trial lawyer, he'd make good money in the United States, I thought.

I hailed a taxi and headed toward my hotel, the Hotel Vedado. I think the driver could tell I was feeling down. He did not ask, but I could tell that he could tell that something traumatic had just happened. He tried to cheer me up. He told me about certain sites along the side of the road—a university, Pan Am Arena, and other places.

I wasn't rude, but I did not feel like talking. "*Gracias,*" I said. "*Gracias.*"

I could tell this taxi driver was trying to be humane and compassionate. He tried to speak English to break up the silence, but I was not really into conversation. I felt withdrawn and beat down. I was trying to maintain my composure, but I felt isolated and dejected—not knowing what to think any more. It was a twenty- to thirty-minute ride to Havana proper.

Leaving the international airport and heading into Havana, the contrasts between the United States and Cuba become stark. Everything in Havana has an aura about it. The best way to describe it is that it is like a time capsule. Architectural influences could be traced to different centuries or even decades, including the Soviet era. Reflecting the latter, I saw buildings, walls, and cement square posts with a forty-five-degree tilt at the top and barbed wire. It's no secret that old American and Soviet Lada cars still roam the streets. In parts of Cuba, life can be very hard, and some neighborhoods very poor. On my second trip, I had visited a place where two-by-fours joined one-inch by six-inch planks. I peered through the cracks and saw that somebody called this home. I saw an old lady in a wheelchair in one such structure. In the small creek outside, I saw raw sewage floating by.

Built in the 1950s, the Hotel Vedado is centrally located and close to the ocean in the Vedado district of Havana. In order to keep the wide peripheral view of the ocean unobstructed, development was strictly forbidden in the Vedado district during the Colonial era.

The ability to earnestly see off into the crest of the distant horizon provided an early warning to the residents of Havana of any potential attackers fast approaching the city. Though I could have stayed elsewhere, I had stayed at the hotel on my first trip, and decided to start out at a place I already knew. However, the Hotel Vedado looked different from then. As I checked in and looked around this time, I sensed a new vibe. More tourists were around during my first trip. I wondered if hurricanes Gustav and Ike had anything to do with this. I had heard those two back-to-back hurricanes caused much damage and big food shortages. They apparently hit the crops hard.

I grabbed dinner inside the hotel, and I noticed that I had to pay, whereas before the hotel provided a meal along with the room price. At twelve CUCs, dinner seemed a bit pricey here at the hotel. But considering what I had just been through, I didn't want to go out where I might get hassled or hustled. I decided to stay in and eat. I watched European CNN world news. I took a shower and laid down. My room was on the fourth floor. I was very tired and mentally exhausted from the day's troubles, so I went to bed early. I did not feel motivated to go out and take any pictures.

The next day, I knew I needed breakfast and some coffee. As I was looking at my maps, I thought, *All right! I've got to get out of this funk I'm in. I've just got to pull myself out of this.* I decided to make my way along the waters edge on the Av de Malecón. The Av de Malecón, famously known as the Malecón, was constructed in 1901 by the United States during its occupation of Cuba after the Spanish American War in 1898. The Malecón, acting as a type of cement breakwater and boardwalk, has an interesting heritage over the years for a place of social gatherings.

As I walked along the Malecón, I saw off in the distance, across the mouth of the Bahia de la Habana, outcropped at the furthest most point on the eastern side of the bay, the Castillo de los tres Santos Reyes de Morro. This grand fortress made of rock and stone, which was built during the time period of the Age of Sail, has been majestically standing guard there for over four hundred years. It was always beautifully in my view as I walked along the Malecón.

I eventually came upon the Castillo de San Salvador de la Punta, which was built between 1589 and 1600. Large cannons, set up long ago on both sides of the bay to thwart invaders and pirate attacks, are still in position and manning their posts today. During its heyday, this fortified block fortress had a massive floating chain connected to it. This bronze chain was stretched 270 yards across the bay every night from here to the El Morro fortress. A loud canon firing from the mother ship, which was anchored inside the bay, alerted city residents that the chain was closing the entrance to the bay. At dawn, another canon firing would signal the pulling back of this massive floating chain and the reopening of the Bahia de la Habana.

The Malecón ends at Castillo de la Real Fuerza, another stone fortress built between 1558 and 1577 to protect the city from pirate attacks. This fortress was built after Havana was raided in 1555 by Jacques de Sores, a French buccaneer. When I reached the end of the Malecón, I continued walking into Habana Vieja, or Old Havana. In the seventeenth century, the Spanish Crown built a large wall around the city. Although most of these walls were torn down over time as the city grew, some of the foundations still remain. This historic heart of Cuba sits on the western edge of the harbor. Walking through the narrow streets, open plazas, and arcades of Old Havana was like walking in an open-air museum. I saw many beautiful *mediopuntos*, which are half-moon, stained-glass windows. These large, arched features appear over balconies, doors, and windows. Old Havana architecture is a mixture of lavish Baroque and colonial styles.

I had a really good walk. I was able to air and clear out my head. I was never once bothered by *jineteros*, who are Cuban hustlers, which was good. I did not want anyone to talk to me. I wanted to be left alone. I wanted to just look, and relax, and be in my own world and breathe. I took pictures and watched the huge container ships that were coming and going. While looking down some alleys, I took numerous pictures of old cars, the art deco buildings, the eclectic architecture, and just plain daily life. I was gone for about six or seven hours. Later, Jesús told me that if the government put a tail on me after I left the airport, and if they saw me walking around all the next day, they probably thought, *Hell, this guy is nothing. Why are we following him around?*

I went back to the hotel, took a shower, and got ready to meet with
Jesús and his family. I went to comb my wet hair and found that I did
not have my comb. I knew that I had packed a comb in my travel bag. I
distinctly remember putting soap, toothbrush, shampoo, and a comb in my
bag. Then I realized that my four-year-old son, Garrett, had been hanging
close to me while I was packing. He had taken my comb out of my travel
bag and didn't put it back. *That little stinker!* I thought, *Where am I going to
find a comb in Cuba?* I can't just go down the street to the local supermarket
and get a new one, as there are no supermarkets just down the street. These
necessities are hard to find in Cuba. It's one of those things that I could
spend too much time looking around for. It would be easier for me to just
go without a comb than try to hassle with finding a new one in Cuba.
Throughout my entire trip, I had to "comb" my hair with my fingers, and I
was reminded of my son each and every time.

The plan was for me to meet up with Jesús that night and have dinner
at his mother's house.

He met me at the hotel lobby, but he was prohibited from coming to
my room; that sort of rule was common here in Cuba. But it felt great
to finally see my good friend once again. We gave each other a big hug
and chatted and conversed in the lobby for a while. After some time of
catching up about our lives and families, I asked for his bag, and I rode up
the elevator to grab the remaining laptop and a few other gifts for his kids
and wife. I wasn't going to bag up the computer in the hotel lobby, where
anyone might be watching. Jesús was happy and excited that this was going
to be a much needed and wonderful resource for his family. Once finished
at the hotel, we looked for a taxi to take us over to his mother's house.

"Let's take a potato chip," I said, pointing toward one of these small
yellow cars that fit two or three people. They look like a three-wheel golf
cart with a half-moon yellow shell that passengers fit tightly inside. The
Cubans call it a *cocotaxi*.

Jesús looked at me funny, like, *What the hell?*

I said, "Yeah, dude. That looks like a potato chip to me. Let's go!" And
so, off we went.

Jesús wears his long hair in a neat ponytail. He is college educated and
an effective communicator. He is confident, insightful, street smart, and
funny. He's a kind-hearted family man. When he says he will take care of
something or will be somewhere at a specific time, he follows through. He
enjoys food, particularly pork, pineapples, and bananas. He likes to drink
beer and rum. He hopes to someday eat a big T-bone steak because he's

never had one. He likes old TV shows, especially *Abbot and Costello* and their famous "Who's on First" sketch. He has worked in restaurants, and at the time of my visit had only left Cuba one time on a trip to Greece. He planned to return there with his wife. I asked him how his wife would feel about leaving the island for the first time. His response? "Joyful." All of these attributes made Jesús a great friend, and he and I really hit it off.

Jesús's mother's neighborhood is pretty amazing. I remember him saying while passing through the neighborhood on my last trip that "this is the heart of Cuba." I could stand there and look down some of those streets, and it created the illusion of stretching for miles, just miles. It was almost like being in a corn maze. You could just go and go and go. Wires crisscrossed above the narrow, potholed roadways, connecting the concrete homes and buildings. At some of the homes, people sat on their porches. They had the front doors open and their black and white TVs on, with coat hangers doubling as antennas. And that was it. What do you do? Other folks were coming and going, working perhaps, but not many had cars. Some had bikes or scooters. I saw horse-drawn carts with wooden wheels. The owners cut old bike tires and nailed them all the way around the wooden wheel to keep it from wearing down. It probably took about three bike tires, tacked on by small nails, to go all the way around one wheel.

I considered it an honor to visit Jesús's family. His mother's place was on the fourth floor of a multifamily structure. We made our way up the central stairway. At the top, the strangest thing happened. The door opened, but nobody was there. It turned out that this was the first of two entryway doors. There were many pulleys crudely placed in strategic corners up, around, and against the stairway walls. Many different lengths of twine were tied successively together. I could see each of the countless individual frayed and knotted connections as they ran through the many different pulleys, and together with the pulleys, they made their way down the corridor. Occupants could pull a string in the living room to spring the locked door that was down below. I thought that was wild.

Jesús did a great job providing for his family. His parents were sweet, as were the many other relatives who came by to meet me. Actually, Jesús's mother and stepfather, not his biological father, lived there. His dad died many years prior. His stepfather, Omar, told me, "*Mi casa es su casa*," meaning my house is your house. This phrase can be an overused, hollow cliché. But he said it as he shook my hand, and I could tell he meant the words from his heart.

They all got along so beautifully. Jesús's family welcomed me with open arms. They spoke very little English, and with my limited Spanish, this made for interesting times. Jesús told me his two daughters understand English, but are lazy about speaking it. He said he purposefully talks to them in English because he knew that if they were to have higher paying jobs and a better future, they would need to know English.

One thing that took a while for me to get used to was the custom Cuban women had when greeting or bidding farewell to either men or woman. They did one kiss toward the side of a cheek, but did not actually kiss the cheek. They made loud and long over-exaggerated sounds of kissing two or three times, but only touching cheek-to-cheek once. In other countries, you know, they do three, four, or five peck kisses on either side of the cheek. It just seemed odd to me. For men who were greeting or bidding farewell to other men, handshakes or a pat on the shoulder were the norm.

Jesús's mother had two indoor cats. They appeared very well cared for, unlike the near feral cats or dogs I saw roaming Havana. From the rooftop of their home, Jesús's family had a pretty nice view. It was like a refuge up there, a place the family could sit and talk and not be fearful or distracted by the bustling of the street. On the next-door roof below, I could see a bunch of cats hanging around, sitting, resting like they were waiting around for something.

I asked Jesús, "Hey, what is that?"

He said, "Oh, they know that my mom likes to throw food from the balcony as a little treat for them."

I thought that was interesting. The cats were all there just waiting patiently to see if they could get a handout, like, *Meow. Where are you? We're all waiting here.* I could also see the roofs of other nearby homes. At all of these, water was fed in by gravity from individual tanks on the roofs.

Inside the house, I saw various household items piled high in the corners of the rooms. In Cuba, they do not throw anything away. Jesús's mother knitted and sewed, so she had fabric and yarn in large bags. On the balcony were car parts and small cut pieces of pipe. I saw some piled up bricks. I could see about the same type of things on everybody else's balconies too.

We all ate dinner in one room, so they moved extra tables around. It was like Thanksgiving. They prepared this huge red snapper for me that they got fresh this morning, and they cooked the whole fish right there. It covered an entire turkey platter—head, tail, skin, and all. We could peel the meat right off the bones, then flip the fish over to the other side. They also served fried plantains, Cuban bananas, a staple food. They cut the fruit into three-inch lengths, fried the sliced plantains, squished them into patties, and sometimes dropped garlic or shrimp in there. Then they fried it again. These are called *tostones*, and they tasted so good.

Oh, this meal was good! We also had black beans and rice, and Cuban Bucanero beer. (I have since noticed that the Jamaican Red Stripe beer available in the United States tastes a lot like the Cuban Bucanero.) We had Bucanero Max, which has an extra kick to it. On a large plate, they also served sliced red and green tomatoes along with thinly sliced cucumbers and cut onions, which is known as a Cuban salad. It was a wonderful feast. As we ate, we spoke about family and about embarking on our anticipated trip.

After dinner, I finally was able to talk with Jesús. It felt so good to talk with somebody I knew, and in English, about the interrogator, El Comandante.

Jesús said, "Chris, you have to realize that with this military guy, that's his job. You've just got to really think that, that's his job."

Jesús said that when he helps tours back to the airport, he sometimes gets questioned. He has been ordered, "Show me your ID." He could tell I was still a little beat down from the ordeal, and still not sure what to make of all of it. I knew that getting out of town and onto the road to start this adventure would be good for me.

I told Jesús my high points—what I would most like to see—with the caveat that it was all subject to change, and that we would just try and flow with things on a day-to-day basis. It's best to try and be as flexible as possible and roll with unexpected changes. Who knows what will happen. We might have flat tires or breakdowns. We agreed to meet at nine in the morning and make it to the car rental office, which was back at the airport, by ten o'clock.

At the end of the meal, as is customary, they served hot Cuban coffee, espresso-style with a light, airy, sweet sugar. After dinner, Jesús and his family walked me through the maze of the dark and low-lit narrow streets and alleys of Old Havana to find a taxi. I could hear people all around me, and music in the dark distance. I thought to myself, *These are the exact same alleys that Ernest Hemingway walked. The same sounds he heard and the same sights he saw, which have barely changed with time.*

We arrived at the lineup of cabs, and Jesús tried to find me a good one. "Some of the Soviet Russian Lada cars you don't want," he said, noting they were cheap and unreliable. He flagged me a better taxi and negotiated the price—five CUCs. We went our separate ways for the night.

VENTA DE
FLORES
MONEDA NACIONAL
ROSAS ROJAS → 1.00 C/U
ROSAS AMARILLAS → 2.00 C/U
AZUCENAS →
GLADIOLOS CORAL → 3.00 C/U
GLADIOLOS ROSADOS
GLADIOLOS DE COLORES → 5.00 C/U
GIRASOLES
LIRIOS → 5.00 C/U
MARIPOSAS → 5.00 rmao

2

REFLECTING

I AWOKE THE next day feeling rested and relaxed from my sleep in the hotel bed. I thought, *It's really going to happen.* I was excited about finally getting past the intense pressures of the barriers between our two countries. I felt eagerness, excitement, and anticipation about exploring this uncharted Cuban frontier.

I rode down the old elevator toward the large dining room that had several food stations. At one station, I found cut tropical fruits—mangos, papayas, pineapples, and guava. At another station, I found breads of a European style, which were accompanied by thin layers of white cheese. An old Cuban woman stood behind a small square grill, ready to scramble eggs. She used two eggs for each serving, plus a choice of already diced up ingredients—onion, ham, and something green I could not identify. I tried the eggs, ham, and onion. I decided to try the green item, still not sure of what it was. But I'm always game to try something new, well, at least once.

It was a good breakfast. To finish it off, I drank four or five hot Cuban espressos. OK, maybe six. I absolutely could not stop at one.

The other diners in the room appeared to be South Americans from Bolivia or Venezuela. I could tell by their accents and their mannerisms. As I finished my breakfast, in came a wave of French, Russian, and German tourists who looked as if they had just gotten up from bed.

I finished eating and went back up to my room to get my things and prepare to meet Jesús in the hotel lobby, at our prearranged time of nine o'clock. Jesús and I walked out to find a taxi. Just outside the hotel, Jesús struck up a conversation with one of the taxi drivers. Jesús decided we would go with him, even though his taxi was an old Russian Lada. The driver seemed to be a pleasant fellow. Upon learning I was an American, he wanted to speak to me in the little bit of English that he knew. I reciprocated by trying to speak to him in my little bit of Spanish. In the back seat, Jesús had a hilarious time laughing at our attempts. Since he could speak both languages, Jesús knew that our varying topics of conversations were not making much sense. As for my excuse, well, it was probably all of those great espressos I had earlier that were now kicking in.

The driver took us to the airport, where we would pick up our rental car. It cost twenty-five CUCs from the hotel and took us about twenty-five to thirty minutes max to get there. The driver unloaded our stuff and left the airport. He was a nice fellow, but unfortunately, we had told him to drop us off at the wrong terminal. We got out at terminal three, but we should have chosen terminal two. It was too far to walk with our luggage; plus it was starting to get hot. We decided we needed another taxi. I counted twenty taxis all in line in front of this one terminal, but none of the drivers we asked wanted to help us. It was too short a drive, and it was obvious they could make more money driving people from the airport into Havana. I came up with an idea.

I said to Jesús, "Hey! Ask the last guy in line. What does he care? He's last in line. He can take us over to the other terminal and then come back and be pretty much in the same spot in line as he is in now. He shouldn't care."

Now, Jesús is a sharp guy and pretty street smart from living in Havana, but I definitely caught him by surprise when I blurted that out. Jesús agreed it was a good idea.

The driver said, "*Si*," without any hesitation. It was about three CUCs for us to take that short hop.

We got to terminal two, unloaded our luggage, and found the car rental kiosk office. We filled out the paperwork, discussed return procedures, and inspected the car for any damage or possible mechanical problems. We were then given the keys to the car by the attendant as he reached out to shake my hand, and then he said the words, "Good luck!" We were now free to go.

The car, a silver Kia Picanto, was quite small. I did not realize how small this car was going to be until I actually saw it. It was so small I thought, *Dang! It almost looks like one of my kids' match box cars.*

Even the tires were no higher than about twenty inches. I thought, *Wow! I'm not sure how I'll fit in it.* But, then again there was nothing I could do about it; I had already prepaid and made all my calculations for gas. I knew I had reserved a small car, but not that small. One of the many preparations I had to make for this trip was to decide how much money I would need to bring. This was stressful for me because I knew there could be no room for error. I could not allow myself to run out of money in Cuba. Because of the strict US embargo, American credit cards and traveler's checks were neither allowed nor accepted. There was nothing to fall back on, and no American Embassy to help me out if I ran into any troubles, as one did not exist anymore. Since the United States broke off diplomatic ties with Cuba, the American Embassy has been closed since 1961. I would virtually have to be on my own.

I had to calculate the costs for my transportation, food, and lodging. In addition, I would be having Jesús along for this intimidating undertaking of mine, I could not expect him to pay his own way. Regarding the calculations for gas for the rental car, I didn't know how many times I would have to fill the tank because I was unsure of exactly where this arduous adventure would take us. Before I left, I was not sure of the price per liter for gas in

Cuba. I also had concerns about actually being able to find filling stations when I needed them, especially way out across the countryside, so I wanted a car with good gas mileage. I determined that the Kia got about fifty-eight miles per gallon, and that its tank held about nine gallons (thirty-five liters). I reviewed my maps to determine how many kilometers I might travel. I converted the kilometers to miles and the liters into gallons. This gave me a gauge for estimating how much fuel I would use. Since I did not know the price of petrol in Cuba, I used the price of gas in America. Just in case I made any errors, I added in a little extra and hoped for the best.

We picked up the car, and I was happy to see it had air conditioning and was an automatic. In Havana, people filled the streets—walking, riding bikes or rolling along on *bici-taxis* (bicycle taxis). As we were about to pass by, the people got really close to our cars and held out their hands to signal for rides. Driving an automatic made it a lot easier for me to react quickly when necessary. I would be doing all the driving on this trip because Jesús did not have a driver's license. Not many Cubans own cars. Even with all the tension between our two countries, ironically, my US driver's license was valid in Cuba.

On my first two trips to this island, my lack of luggage was a curiosity to both Jesús and Chiqui, who was the tour bus driver. His nickname, Chiqui, means small (actually Chiqui is as big as I am, and as gentle as a teddy bear). He and Jesús kept commenting on how they never saw anybody come to Cuba with as little luggage as I brought.

For this trip, I figured that wearing what I could repeatedly for a couple days or so would be fine. I was there for my art—not for show or to be a tourist. I looked at it this way: I would take a shower every day and wash the clothes in the tub when I needed. I could hang them up, and they would be dry within a few hours. By doing that, I was able to travel light and could move more freely. As it turned out, Jesús had a much bigger bag than I did, but we managed to fit them both in the back seat of this small car along with my heavy camera pack.

Being scrunched into the little Kia was a hassle, but in hindsight, I did feel we were generally off to a good start. Jesús and I were getting on the same page. I was happy to be out and about and feeling like I was finally going somewhere. At this point, I wanted to get away from the crowded city. I really wanted to get a feel for driving, just hitting that road.

I tossed all the luggage in the back seat, got in the front, reached down for the lever, and pushed the seat all the way back until there was no leg room behind me. My size being what it is, this was still a tight fit. I felt like a sardine in a tin can!

I turned the key and off we headed toward the Bay of Pigs. To Cubans, the Bay of Pigs, or Bahia de Cochinos, is a pleasant, touristy recreational area frequented by Cubans and foreign tourists. I wanted to go there and see what the famous battle was about, to see the beachhead landings of Playa Larga and Playa Girón. I heard the museum at the bay displayed tanks, airplanes, and other historical items left from the battle. The whole place represented a history that I wanted to explore for myself, to experience in a noncommercialized form before Cuba opens to the outside world. Who knows what the folklore will say after it does.

We had to drive very slowly, inching along as we tried making our way out and away from the car rental kiosk. Masses of people milled around terminal two—a few hundred people outside and even more inside. This terminal had the only direct flights to and from Miami. As I understand it, those flights were mainly for Cubans with families in the United States.

I could see that there were many happy people, and at the same time, there were faces of many sad ones, depending upon whether the plane was arriving or departing. I had to drive very slowly through the crowds that were pressing close to our car. I then noticed Cuban airport security and military personnel mixed in with citizens and travelers who were milling about. They glanced at us as we drove through the crowds of people, our car creeping ever so slowly away from the airport. I carefully made my way out, so as not to hit anyone.

Leaving the airport, we traveled on a rural asphalt beltway that wrapped around Havana. What lay ahead was a world of uncertainty. I felt a little nervous about the driving to come. I soon realized that driving in a foreign country is a vastly different feeling than walking around in one. The beltway in Havana is different from a beltway in a big American city. Although wider than most streets in Cuba, the Havana beltway is more like a rural road with one or two lanes.

As we drove through the outskirts of Havana, I noticed high-rise buildings that looked like apartments. Some buildings in groupings of three or more strongly resembled government-built architecture found in the former Soviet Union. The materials used to construct these buildings looked out of place compared to much of the Spanish architecture material used for other structures I found in Cuba. Jesús told me that these apartments needed to be constructed quickly to provide much needed housing for the Cuban people. The Russians provided the materials, the design, and the professional supervision. However, Cubans created micro-brigades of workers from all sectors and constructed their own housing using their own labor. Although the Russian design was easier to reproduce on a large scale, I felt this "revolutionary architecture," as it is called, resulted in buildings that were of boxy, flat, dull, square, and unattractive. The unattractiveness of these structures made them stand out from the other buildings.

While driving through Cuba, we commonly saw laundry hanging out to dry. The dominating clothing in Cuba tends to be very bright. The residents have been very creative in how they hung their laundry to dry from these Soviet style high rises. High-rise residents attached a stick to both sides of their windows in order to suspend a clothesline. The sticks protruded at a ninety-degree angle from the buildings. To maximize the space available to dry their laundry, rows of wire or string were tied from one stick to the other.

There was so much laundry hanging from all these makeshift clotheslines that, unintentionally, the clothes created a beautiful abstract scene. Having a natural pattern of bright colors, textiles, and shapes, they wrapped around and covered the building on a grand scale. In contrast to the unattractiveness of the structures, the laundry hanging out to dry looked like a beautiful work of art, the effect of this hanging laundry reminding me of the artwork of the artist Christo and Jeanne-Claude. Unlike the temporary materials used by Christo and Jeanne-Claude, the laundry hanging out to dry was constantly reoccurring, placed there out of necessity. The clothes and materials changed, and each change brought new wrappings of colors, textiles, and patterns. I wanted to soak it all in, but I was driving and had to keep my eyes on the road.

It became really obvious really fast that I had to get my bearings driving in a foreign country. I was also starting to have some major concerns with understanding the traffic signs; some of them were not where I expected them to be. Driving was tricky in Cuba because of all the people along the roads. I had to anticipate their body movements. Some of these people had horses or oxen with carts. Fortunately, Cubans drive on the right side of the road. It would have been even more confusing for me if I had to drive on the left.

From the beltway, we took a right turn toward the southeast and entered onto the wide-open three-lane Autopista Nacional motorway. Once on the motorway, past the exchange and picking up freeway speed, I now became unclear of my bearings. I had never seen anything like this; the lanes were not marked or painted, so there was no true separation from one lane to the other. While driving, I had to feel my way around past the other cars in a complete free-form manner. It felt like I was driving on a never-ending airline landing strip.

I don't remember any landmarks of this area. I had to be concentrating and keeping my eyes on the road. After a while, I did settle down a bit, and I started feeling a little better about my driving. From the Autopista, going east past San Jose de las Lajas, I saw brown grassy fields and big one-hundred-foot Cuban Royal Palm trees, the national tree of Cuba, scattered across the landscape. The Cuban Royal Palm has dense crowns and huge arching fronds that each stretch about twenty feet in length. They reminded me of the giant valley oaks that dot the Santa Ynez Valley wine country near my home in California. At times, I spotted rows of papaya trees.

Jesús kept an eye out for checkpoints because some of them are very difficult to recognize. Jesús said that one clue is a sudden drop in the speed limit before a checkpoint. The speed might quickly fall from 100 hundred kilometers per hour (62 mph), down to 80 kilometers per hour (50 mph), then to 40 kilometers per hour (25 mph). However, this was tricky because sometimes the speed limit did not fall at all—a checkpoint might appear without a warning.

We hit our first checkpoint when leaving Habana Province and entering Matanzas Province. It would be the first of many. Jesús got excited and yelled out, "Slow Down!" Sure enough, about five police officers stood around right on the road. Jesús yelled again, "Slow Down More!" They stared at us as we drove very slowly past them, giving us stone-faced looks. Of course, I could not be sure what was going on in their minds, but as for me—Hell! I kept both my hands on the steering wheel, looked straight ahead, and tried to act like this was just a normal, everyday occurrence for me.

Past the checkpoint, the road conditions were uneven. At times, I saw gravelly sand on the asphalt highway. A few times, I drove more toward the middle of the roadway than necessary because of the rough, unlevel roads. Drivers passing by honked at us. "Chris!" Jesús said. "You need to move over!" Geez! And here I thought I had been driving OK.

The weather was comfortable—I felt a bit cooler driving through here than I had in Havana. In the beginning, I didn't stop to take any pictures. But I remembered seeing many buzzards. I looked around a little and kept driving. If something amazing came along, I intended to stop to take a picture, but I wasn't completely comfortable with the idea of pulling over when I saw something to photograph. (At home, some of my friends get uptight if I pull over too many times while driving.)

I would sometimes mention to Jesús that I saw something that looked like a good picture. Jesús asked me, "Why didn't you take the picture?" I couldn't give a good answer. A few times, I would need to turn around and to go back for the photograph after we were a half-mile down the road. Subconsciously, I guess I was trying to be polite. Jesús got angry with me.

"Chris," he said, "If you see something, pull over and take the picture." It took a few times of backtracking before I settled down to the idea of stopping randomly. But, after all, that is why I came to Cuba.

I continued driving down the Autopista Nacional, passing more fields with giant Cuban Royal Palms scattered about. Some of the trees appeared to be indiscriminately dead, their massive, tall trunks stood empty, with no palm fronds. Who knows how long they had been standing there. Acting as lightning rods, apparently the dead palm trees were struck by lightning during the many thunderous tropical storms that rip through Cuba. These dead trees were a sporadic sight that I periodically noticed while traveling all across the island.

The Autopista started a long, gradual decline. I sped along at about 100 kilometers per hour, and just when I had started feeling that I had gotten the hang of driving on the motorway, out of nowhere, at the bottom of this downhill run—WHAM!—I nailed some slightly buried railroad tracks. And I'm telling you, Jesús about crapped in his pants and out his shirtsleeves. He was screaming, and I was doing everything I could do to keep from letting the car fishtail. We were swinging left, right, and left, and right again! Afterward, I kept repeating, "God, I can't believe it." I'm so glad my reflexes were fast. We could have flipped and rolled multiple times in that little sardine tin can of a car. That would have been quite a way to start the trip. I hit those tracks so hard that I'm surprised all four tires didn't blow. It was a definite wake up call. Who would have expected railroad tracks to be in the middle of the freeway?

I looked at Jesús and exclaimed, "Where in the heck did they come from?"

"This is a Cuban freeway, not an American one!" Jesús excitedly shot back.

Now, for a moment there, you would think that we were arguing like an old married couple. Eventually, we calmed down and finally reached the turnoff to the Bay of Pigs. Like many places in Cuba, this turn had no sign postings announcing the turnoff. We almost flew right past, but Jesús had a sense about where to turn; though he did not know exactly where. If we had missed the turnoff, it would have been many miles before we could loop back to this spot.

The turnoff came right up on us, and as we made the turn, the road started to drop down. We drove down the road a distance, and Jesús pointed

CUBA OPEN FROM THE INSIDE

out an old, large sugar mill that was built in 1904. During the battle of the Bay of Pigs conflict, Fidel Castro made this sugar mill his headquarters. Today it is a museum, the Museo de la Comandancia. I saw colorful and interesting looking propaganda signs placed here and there; though most were broken apart when Hurricane Ike ripped through. Mainly these signs touted the victory over the *Yanqui imperialistas* (Yankee imperialists).

As we made our way down this lush turnoff road, I started to notice small monuments appearing randomly to the left and right of the road. These monuments marked the exact spots where Cuban defenders died in the three-day battle, which lasted from April 17 to 19, 1961. In the battle, Castro used an SU-100 tank destroyer, which is now displayed in Havana in front of the Museum of the Revolution (formerly known as the Batista Palace).

Further down the turnoff road is the Peninsula de Zapata, named for a bygone landowner named Francisco Zapata. In 1636, he was granted this area by the Spanish Crown. It later became a preserve. It looked interesting on a map and sounded so from the way Jesús described it. But from the road, it's just a thick, grassy swamp. Jesús told me this area is home to a species of crocodiles that are only found here. At one time, they were almost extinct. They were protected starting in the early 1960s and re-established with help from breeding programs. Tour agencies periodically would hire Jesús to bring groups of bird watchers to this area because of the rich diversity of native fowl. Many endemic birds found here include the blue-headed quail-dove, the Zapata rail, the bee hummingbird (the world's smallest bird at two inches in length), the Cuban black-hawk, and the Cuban pygmy owl. Many migratory birds can be found in the reserve as well. I understand the swamps also have Caribbean manatees. These can grow to thirteen feet long and weigh about 1300 pounds. In the spring, the beaches and the roads are invaded by thousands of large crabs wandering around with outstretched claws looking to mate. I did happen to see such a display on my second trip, in a different area near Cienfuegos. It was quite an amazing sight to see.

This whole stretch of road in this area reminded me of parts of Louisiana. There were a few patches of open land, but from what I could see, the rest was swampy bogs. There was little to no traffic on the road. There was, however, a traffic checkpoint we had to go through located past Palpite. This checkpoint featured a long red and white wooden bar across the road, with a weight on one end of the bar that rose up so we could pass. I had to drive through very slowly, so they could look at the car and us. Jesús gave a little hand wave, and I think that helped.

So there I was, ready to really see the infamous Bay of Pigs, to see what this battle was about. We were able to drive right up on the sand to see the beachhead and the museum in Girón. I admit, I had preconceived ideas of what it would all be like; it was not quite what I envisioned. The only pictures I had seen of the beach were in documentaries related to the battle. It's a beautiful beach. I thought, *This beachhead is one of the actual places where they landed. Wow! It's hard to imagine that a big battle took place right here in this tranquil pristine place. You could be lying on this beautiful white sand, lying here under some of these coconut palm trees with a light breeze fluttering through the palm fronds, and hearing the light sound of the waves.*

Playa Girón was named for a French pirate, Gilbert Girón, who frequented this area at the turn of the sixteenth century. Who could have known that this area would become so famous over three centuries. I stood there in silence and looked around quietly. Occasionally a local jinetero wanting to be my friend hit me up. I would reply, "*Yo bien,*" and wave him away. Move on. Not interested.

I took pictures. There were no cliffs—only a pure, flat white-sand beach. A couple of areas had huge coral-like stones that jutted toward the bay. The white-sand area is where the landings took place. A battle force would not want to drop its boats, tanks, and men on the hard coral because the coral would wreck the boats and make the men easier targets for gunfire. On display was a military airplane with a star on its side, tanks, and other weapons that were either used or captured in the battle. Jesús stayed off in the distance by the car. He could tell I was having a deep moment within myself, looking around. He struck up a conversation with locals who happen to be walking by.

Standing here thinking about the history of Cuba, I saw the rhythm of the tides. The tides come in and out and wash the beach clean. Over centuries, many people have explored and colonized Cuba as far back as the Guanajatabey, Sibony, and Taino Indians. Each wave of people brought new changes. When the US embargo ends and the tide goes out, what vacuum will occur? And what exactly will fill it? I thought, *What will happen after Castro?* Many Cubans have known no one other than Fidel Castro, and after all many have come to revere him like a father. When the US embargo ends and Cuba opens, yet another new wave of people will arrive. Major changes will occur, and with them more commercialization. Standing here, it was difficult to believe that I was really in Cuba, again seeing it for what it truly is, the real Cuba, not some portrayal. And I thought, *This thing is bigger than I realized.* At one time this place was the edge of the known world and a major hub for shipping—the United States was not even born

yet. During this time, America was undeveloped and unexplored. Ironically, now America is well developed, and Cuba is the unexplored frontier.

I was glad and feeling lucky to be here before the floodgates open. I feel I'm seeing the natural beauty of this land before it becomes developed and commercialized. Once the floodgates are indeed opened, Americans will rush in with gold fever. Collectors will come in, and all the old cars will disappear. In an indirect way, its isolation has given Cuba its unique culture. I saw that culture in the movement of the people—the horses, the carts, the bikes, and the old cars. And I saw it in their music. Cuba's isolation has created unique microcosms at all levels. Even endemic plants and animals are preserved, and in a way, have been protected. Ending the embargo would improve Cuba economically. Sure, I want the people to have a better life. I sensed, though, that the Cuba I was standing in at that moment would become a folkloric memory. I sensed that the Cuban microcosm I was witnessing would not be the same.

Turning away, I walked over to a small baseball field and took pictures. It just so happened that the world baseball championship was being played during my time in Cuba, so I decided to make a point of taking pictures of any random baseball fields or stadiums I saw. Baseball is king in Cuba. Large or small fields, it didn't matter. I stopped just about everywhere to take pictures of baseball fields, some had horses, cows, or goats walking across them; others appeared manicured for the pros.

Walking back to the car, I saw an old abandoned gas station. The walls were faded shades of blue, worn with the passage of time. Painted on one side were the words, "*Seguros de la Victoria,*" which means "Certain of the Victory." The blue sky and Caribbean clouds in the background made for an interesting composition. I thought it would be cool to document the architecture of gas stations across Cuba as well, and so I made a point to photograph as many as I could.

On my first two trips to this island, I made it a point to photograph the old theaters and cinemas. The last cinema built in Havana was constructed in 1959. Cuba has a rich history in the arts, with diverse theaters and cinemas. Most of the time, I stood out when I shot the pictures, because of my size and the size of my camera. People watched me, probably curious why I was taking a picture of a baseball field, a gas station, or a cinema. To them, it was just an everyday place. To me, it was a whole new world.

As we left Playa Girón, we stopped at the roadside stand to pick up snacks and drinks for the road. We drove northeast along a back road, away from the Caribbean coast and inland toward the town of Santa Clara. The surroundings began to change. As we drove inland, the topography became like a large prairie. I saw brown grassy pastures, bean fields, and other agricultural crops. Occasionally, I saw people working in the fields and a man on bare horseback directing them. In a remote area, not far from the village of Yaguaramas, we happened to come upon a monument located at the side of the road. Next to the monument was a Cuban flag flying from a flagpole. Both the monument and the flagpole seemed oddly placed in the middle of nowhere. I stopped to check it out. Interestingly, what really caught my attention was that the primary name on the monument was not a Spanish name. It was an American name—Henry Earl Reeve, a brigadier general nicknamed *"El Inglesito."* I learned that Reeve fought for Cuban independence from Spain during the Ten Year War. Apparently, he was killed in battle here where we were standing, this exact location, on August 4, 1876. This monument honoring him was built in September 1968. Reeve was born in Brooklyn in 1850, had read about the Cuban uprisings, and volunteered to fight for Cuba's independence in 1868. With an expeditionary force, he arrived in Cuba in 1869 aboard the ship *Perrit*, which was ambushed by the Spanish as it landed. All those aboard were put before a firing squad, shot, and presumed dead. But Reeve somehow survived. He had just enough strength to pull and drag himself out from underneath all the dead bodies that were piled about, and he sneaked away. A Cuban army unit picked him up. For the following seven years, Reeve fought over four hundred battles. Until his last battle, of course, right here.

As we continued to drive northeast, the weather began to get cloudy. It looked like it could storm; fortunately, it didn't. As we got closer to Santa Clara, the highway and roads got a little busier. After driving over a few small, rolling mountains, I started to see Santa Clara on the far horizon and could make out the top of a very large structure, something resembling industrial stadium lights. My first thought was that maybe it was a baseball stadium. As we neared Santa Clara, I had to keep my eyes on the road because of the increased traffic and the people moving alongside the road. As we crested over a hill, something in the center of the road caught my attention. We drove up on a dead dog in the middle of this asphalt beltway.

That's one of the memorable things about Cuba: there are stray dogs everywhere. I could not tell how long it had been lying there, but what really caught my attention was the frenzied buzzards fighting and tearing away at its carcass. Man! They were going for it. It looked like a picture out of *National Geographic*. Buzzards all over that carcass, hitting each other's wings, fighting. I thought, *Dang. That's raw life's reality.*

Santa Clara had little roundabouts. As we came to one, I had to quickly maneuver the car, "Stay right. Stay left. Go straight!" Jesús would say.

But soon enough, Jesús said, "See up in the distance? Those lights? That's Ché's huge monument and memorial."

He of course was referring to Ché Guevara, the Marxist revolutionary. The monument was elevated on higher ground, above the city. We were now headed right toward it. The road went uphill a bit, and then, all of a sudden, we happened to appear right in the middle of this grand, dedicated memorial area.

As I looked for a place to park, Jesús gave me last minute instructions regarding the memorial. "Be careful," he said. "You are free to walk around, but you cannot take pictures from the back of the monument." I asked why, and he continued to say, "Because the entrance to the mausoleum is behind there and underneath this monument. A strict show of reverence is enforced there, and because of that you are not allowed to take pictures."

At the top and to the left of the monument steps, there was a huge bas relief of Ché on a stone wall sixty feet long by twenty feet high. The bas relief showed Ché with various commanders and comrades and depicted events from his revolutionary career. In the center of this, towered an impressive statue of Ché with his arm in a cast, a nod to one of his battleground injuries. The statue is made from twenty tons of bronze and stands 22.3 feet high atop a tall rectangular pillar. Inscribed at the top of the pillar in large lettering is, "*Hasta La Victoria Siempre,*" or "Onward Victory Forever."

I began to notice that this place was full of symbolic elements. Positioned high on this pillar, Ché is purposely facing South America, a symbolic reference for South America to be inspired by Ché and his role in the Cuban revolution.

The statue has oxidized over time, its patina coming from the green stains of weathered bronze that were naturally bleeding down from the top of the pillar. The sculptor, Jose Delara, planned this in his design and used this to visually stress and metaphorically show that Ché is forever rooted in Cuba, even though he was not born in Cuba, but in Argentina.

To the right of the statue of Ché was a smaller square column. Chiseled on one side of this column is the last text of the last letter Ché wrote to Fidel Castro before Ché left for Bolivia, where he was killed. Overall, the use of geometrical elements in this memorial represent Ché's steady and strong persona.

After completion of construction, the monument was dedicated on December 28, 1988—that day marked the thirtieth anniversary of Ché's capture of Santa Clara from the Batista army. During this decisive battle, Ché used a bulldozer made by the American company Caterpillar to remove the railroad tracks of the railway line used by the Batista army. The train with Batista reinforcements derailed, which effectively helped to end the Batista dictatorship. Interestingly, the bulldozer is still there on display.

Ché's remains and the remains of thirty-eight other men who fought with him were dug up from the jungles of Bolivia. They were brought to this site in Cuba on October 17, 1997, and placed in the mausoleum. Fidel Castro lit the eternal flame at the entrance to the mausoleum, which happens to be behind and underneath this monument from where we were standing.

As I stood on the upper level of this monument and looked out across over the road we had just traveled, I saw a very large, very wide, square-shaped plaza. To the right and left sides of the square, each had a row of fourteen Cuban Royal Palm trees, twenty-eight total, to represent Ché's birthdate of June 14, 1928. The end of the square farthest from me presented large billboards, one which read, *"Fue una estrella quien te puso aqui y te hizo de este pueblo,"* meaning "It was a star who brought you here and made you part of this people." The wide hardscape walkways of this plaza contained patterns and colors, which when viewed from the top of the monument, looked like an army of people holding hands. It was my understanding that this was the artist's way of showing that Ché wanted the people of the world united as one.

We finished our tour of the memorial and drove through Santa Clara, which was founded on July 15, 1689, by a group of settlers from the village of Remedios. Tired of dealing with the marauding pirates who were constantly raiding Remedios, the settlers decided to move further inland to Santa Clara in order to distance themselves from these troubles. Ironically, we were on our way to Remedios.

We drove across beautiful rolling hills on our way to Remedios. We traveled many hours since leaving Havana, and by the time we reached Remedios, it had been a full day.

We planned to spend one night and most of the next day in Remedios before leaving for Holguin. In Holguin, we would be meeting up with Chiqui, who would be working there as a bus driver for a tour group. This would be the only time that our paths would cross Chiqui's path and allow for a short visit.

Founded on April 13, 1514, Remedios is an old colonial town with about thirty thousand residents. It is located two hundred miles from Havana along the northern Cuban coast toward the Gulf of Mexico.

Except for those perpetual marauding pirates, Remedios has been more or less unnoticed and undeveloped for centuries because of its out-of-the-way location. This peaceful, quiet town contains many very well preserved examples of sixteenth and seventeenth century colonial Spanish architecture. Many of these buildings remain intact. The Iglesia San Juan Bautista de Remedios, one of the town's churches, was built in 1545. It has a neoclassical bell tower, a Baroque interior, a mahogany decorative *alfarje* (carved wooden ceiling), and gold-covered ornate altars. Because of the constant pirate attacks, locals intentionally painted over the gold altars with white paint to hide their precious gold from these invading pirates. Over time, more coats of paint were added, and the hidden gold was somehow forgotten. It was not until centuries later, during a restoration project from 1944 to 1954, that workers rediscovered the gold altars. There is a sense in Remedios that life remains unchanged.

We found a casa in the area near the town square, but it was full. The owner, a kind fellow, recommended another casa and even led us there.

This casa, La Buganvilia, turned out to be better than the first one. The house was situated in an area with a dense concentration of other colonial homes, which were painted in a variety of different colors. Parallel to the street, the façade had a large wooden front door and a window to the side. The window had wooden shutters and nineteenth-century iron grilles with a wrought-iron ornamental motif on top.

Inside, there was no vestibule. The entry opened into a large living room with high wooden-beamed ceilings. Continuing on, we entered into a lush, green open courtyard. The owners offered us a room situated toward the front of the house with two beds.

"We'll take it," we said.

We arranged for dinner to be ready for us when we returned and decided to take a walk as there was still some daylight left. We made our way to the town square. One of the first sights we encountered was a fair taking place. I soon learned that this was the Cuba International Book Fair, an annual event that moves from province to province, promoting reading and literacy. *Leer es crecer,* meaning "reading is growing," was their motto, and its overall purpose and goal is to provide literary opportunity and access to all Cubans. There were booths that displayed books and others that displayed artistic and literary activities. Along with food and music, this fair had a old, primitive-looking amusement-park rides. One ride was constructed of materials that looked like old metal trash barrels that were cut and resized to resemble airplanes. They were hung horizontally and suspended by chains. The airplanes were about a foot off the ground and went around slowly in circles. At first, I only noticed the happy children on the ride, but after taking a closer look, I noticed that each plane had a red star on the back tail wing and was made to look like a Russian MiG fighter jet. I got a chuckle out of this because it reminded me of taking my own children to fairs in America, where the planes are made to look like American fighter jets. The whole area had this carnival atmosphere, and the festivities continued until late at night.

As we continued walking, I saw a group of young boys standing on a colonial arcading walkway with pastel colors supported by many fluted Corinthian columns. The excited boys stood single file in a line, and at the front of the line stood an old man holding the reins of a very spirited pony. The boys handed the old man a small coin, probably a one peso coin. The old man helped each boy mount the horse before he let go of the reins. Each boy paid and was given a turn to ride the pony by himself down the long side street and back to where the old man stood.

After our walk around the town square, we headed back to the casa for dinner. We entered the house and saw that the owners had set up a beautiful table next to the open courtyard.

For dinner I had three lobster tails. Jesús had pork. We shared *potaje*, a thick black and red bean soup with garlic, onions, and added spices. We had rice, which we ate with potaje on top, and a plate of salad consisting only of thinly sliced cucumbers, onions, and tomatoes. There was beer, a lot of beer, to celebrate our first night.

During dinner, Jesús got a surprise call on his cell phone from my friend, Pilo, a professor whom I had met on my first trip to Cuba in 2007 while visiting the village of San Diego de los Banos in the Pinar del Rio province. This village sits between two mountain ranges and is known for its natural mineral springs. It dates back to the early seventeenth century, when a slave stumbled upon the mineral springs. This slave was infirm, but after bathing in the mineral springs, he was cured. Word spread quickly about the healing properties of the mineral baths, and the people started arriving.

While in San Diego de los Banos, I stayed at the El Mirador, which was built in 1954. Pilo had gotten word that there were Americans staying there, and he eagerly rode his bike some fifty miles to get acquainted and converse. On that trip, he brought with him a very large book entitled *Adventures in American Literature.* Pilo was so proud of that book and carefully pulled it out of its protective wrapping to show it to me. He told me that it was a university book, which probably cost a lot of money, and that he had read it many, many times over.

Our conversation turned to education, and Pilo alluded that he did not make much money as a professor. Due to difficult times, many teachers had left the universities to make more money elsewhere. But Pilo, having deep convictions about the importance of teaching and education, recognizes the sacrifices and knew what money can't buy. He knowingly chooses his path. Realizing the hardships ahead and enduring them, he continues teaching. I found Pilo to be a humble, soft-spoken man—eager to talk, eager to listen. A genuine kindness radiated from him. I continued our friendship by corresponding with Pilo by mail.

Pilo wrote English pretty well, though somewhat broken. Because of the embargo, no direct mail service exists between the United States and Cuba. All mail must go through a third country. Our letters typically take a few months to reach the other person. Sometimes a letter may never be delivered, as I found out. Before I left on my second trip, I received a letter from Pilo. In his letter, Pilo graciously asked if I could bring some much-needed items to Cuba for him. Fortunately, his letter did reach me in time, and I was able to gather the items Pilo requested, and then some:

> Dear friend Chris,
> It is good news again about your arrival at Havana and know that you and your lovely family are well. You are already invited to visit my apartment, meet my small family and have dinner with us. It will be great thing if we can meet and have dinner at home. I'll be very proud if you accept my invitation. I'm teaching English History and literature at the University. I do a lot of cycling, the weather is very nice here; but we always have a burning sun. I wonder if you could do me the favor of buying me there in America a baseball hat (a cap) and cargo short. I need it for the bike. I always wear a baseball cap where ever I go. Once we meet I give you the equivalent of the items' price in C.U.C. If unfortunately it is impossible for you to visit my town my brother in law visits me every weekend and he has got a motor cycle, so he is a trustable person, he can bring me the package to my place here. Thank you so very much for your help, your kindness, your precious time, your solidarity, charity and everlasting friendship. We are all very grateful and hopeful. In the meantime my best wishes to you and your marvelous family. See you soon! Yours friendly, with warm hug and shake hands.
> Pilo

Unfortunately, on my second trip, I was not able to connect with Pilo. I assumed that my group would be staying at the Hotel Vedado, as that is where my group stayed during my first trip. I wrote Pilo before the trip and informed him of this. At the last minute, I found out the group for my second trip would be staying at the Presidente Hotel instead.

There was not enough time for a letter to be delivered back to Pilo to let him know about the change. I felt bad because I had no way to contact him to let him know about the hotel change. I left the extra items I brought for Pilo and his family with Jesús. Jesús knew about the troubles and the hassles I had in Mexico when the Mexican custom agents tried to steal my suitcases. He promised that somehow he would get these things over to Pilo. Some of the items I took to Cuba for Jesús, Chiqui, Pilo, and their families were essential everyday items. Although very commonplace and easy to obtain in America, these items are very difficult to obtain in Cuba. Jesús and Chiqui were very grateful to have these little necessities of life and promised that my efforts would not be in vain, as they would get Pilo's things delivered.

Months went by, and I wondered whether or not Pilo ever received these items that I knew he and his family really needed. I realized the delivery would be difficult for Jesús, as Pilo lives far from Havana in the province of Pinar del Rio. Eventually, I received a letter from Pilo informing me that he had received the package. He apologized for his delay in writing, but he explained that life had become very difficult for him since Hurricanes Gustav and Ike ripped through his province:

Big hello from Pilo my dearest friend Chris and your whole family,

I let you know once more that your package arrived in good order. My brother in law visit Jesús and pick the package. He did and everything worked well. Then in a couple days he brought it home to me. Jesús and the bus driver Chiqui were very nice, kind and reliable people. All these stuff are very useful and enjoying a brand mark quality. We had a special lunch with the Jerky beef. Our daughter tried jerked beef for the first time and I can't remember the last time I had it either. The cap and T-shirt all fit. It is a big surprise, the Oakley cycling sunglasses. They are no doubt the best I've ever seen and the first I wear. It is very refreshing when I wear them under the burning sun which cause a blinding glitter on the road. These sunglasses are just the great thing! You can take for it for granted no one will be able to take them from me. I like them very much and I keep them a souvenir. Thank you very much for your help, your charity and your commitment. It is pretty much appreciated and we never forget your kindness trying to ease our lives a little bit. It was a pity we were not able to meet each other once more. Maybe you will be able to revisit Cuba once again and it could be possible. I'm sorry it took me such a long time to respond, but communications were interrupted for more than 20 days. Now we have electricity from 6 PM to 8 in the morning. The two hurricanes hit our hometown. The eye of the hurricane was here. We felt the calm, after it the stormy winds once again blowing at 340 kilometers per hour. It swept and devastated the entire area. The landscape is bleak like after the dropping of a nuclear bomb. More than 200 thousand houses were damaged in Pinar del rio Province. We only had 8 casualties, but it will take many years for our lives to return normal. There are a lot of economic problems, we are facing shortage of food and high food prices, high prices of fuel. All this brings about inflation, Cubans are undaunted, we are enduring. We are living rough times, so the cost of living is getting higher; anyhow, there is one thing you can be sure of. I won't never get rid of my bicycle or the Oakley sunglasses. Each day they are more useful! I pen off now. In the meantime stay healthy and have success in your lives and future plans. Thank you very much for your time, your kindness and especially your friendship. We very much appreciate it for always. Hoping to hear from you soon. We are endlessly grateful! Love and warm hug.

My small family, daughter Elisana. my wife Yazmin,

And your Cuban friend.

Pilo

Because of the political wall that's between America and Cuba, communications are very hard and very slow. Before this current trip, I made sure to send Pilo a letter a few months in advance to let him know that I would be coming out once again. I was hoping that this time things would work out, and that we would be able to connect. I did not receive a letter back from Pilo, and I began to wonder if something was wrong.

Out of the blue, Jesús's cell phone rang, and it was Pilo! Unfortunately, when Pilo called me in Remedios, Jesús only had a few minutes left on his phone card. We could not use up those remaining minutes in case we needed the phone in an emergency, and we had no idea when or where we would find a place to buy more phone cards. As I found out, it was very difficult to find places in Cuba to purchase phone cards.

Before handing his phone to me, Jesús explained the problem about the minutes. I was delighted to finally make contact with Pilo again. Pilo was very happy to talk to me, so happy that he kept talking and talking. I wanted to talk to him, but I could tell by the look on Jesús's face that our last minutes were running out. Because of the time and language issues, I was not able to explain to Pilo in a short amount of time what was going on.

I said, "I'm sorry. I am about to have problems with this phone." I told him that I had to get off the phone because the battery was dying. I let him know when I would be back in Havana, so we could try to connect again. I felt badly about this, and I hoped that Pilo did not think I was being rude to him. I didn't know what else to say.

After dinner, there was one more item of business we had to take care of: we had to find a safe place to park the car for the night. This turned out to be a nightly ritual. We could not just park the car on the street overnight because, more likely than not, someone would steal something from the car. We paid a gentleman down the road to watch the car, and I drove through the narrow streets to this man's house. He opened up two small doors on the side of his house, and I drove the car inside. The doors opened up to a large courtyard where five other cars were parked. Viewing the house from the street, I would never have guessed that it had such a large space inside for parking cars. We walked back to our casa and settled down for the night.

For the trip, Jesús brought a surprise bottle of Havana Club 7 *años* rum. He cracked opened the new bottle and poured the first of its drops on the floor. He explained to me that this is a Cuban custom, done as an offering to the African deities known as *orishas*, meaning the gods. The first drink is given to the orishas as a way of asking for permission to drink from the newly opened bottle. Whether at a park, a party, or a bar, I noticed this custom practiced throughout Cuba.

We drank some of the rum straight up in our room. It wasn't too high octane, carrying a little hint of a smoky flavor, but it was definitely pleasing to the senses—and relaxing. Jesús also brought out another surprise, a miniature hand-held DVD player for the trip! He was able to plug it in with a couple of wires into the back of the TV in our room. But the real surprise was what he had on it. I was a little taken back and bewildered at how in the heck, of all things, he had two recordings on that DVD player: a 2005 and a 2007 show featuring Jeff Dunham, an American ventriloquist and stand-up comedian, along with his array of an animated cast of puppet characters.

Jesús obtained a copy of these recordings from one of his friends, and they all think it is one of the funniest things they have ever seen. I do not know how his friend obtained these recordings, apparently from the black market. Jesús was quite proud of his recordings, and brought this as a treat because he wanted to share it with me. I was in a state of astonishment as to how the black market could reach out to some of the least likely and remotest areas. I never would have guessed that something like this would turn up. This became the first of many nights that we would watch these recordings. Jesús imitated the characters at relevant moments. I could not hold back from laughing at the sounds of Jesús's comedic Cuban accent when quoted lines of its characters. That first night in Remedios, we were too tired to watch the whole thing through. As we called it a night, we could hear the music and dancing from the fair in the distance.

About four o'clock in the stillness of the morning, I woke up and could hear a couple across the street having an intimate moment. At first, I was a little surprised at how well I could hear everything. But then I remembered that in these old colonial towns, the streets are very narrow, and none of the windows have glass panes. Since it never gets cold there, there has never been a need for windowpanes. Wooden shutters or slats protect the windows. That's it.

I told Jesús about it in the morning. His reaction was, "Ah Dang! I missed it!" he said. He told me a story about when he was a little kid in his village. Many times they would hear, "Armando! Armando!" coming from next door. The next day, when he and other children played outside around the village square, the kids would run up behind this woman as she was walking. The kids would laugh and skip behind her saying loudly, "Armando! Armando!"

Around seven thirty, we got up and had breakfast—scrambled eggs and Cuban espresso. Jesús couldn't believe how much I was drinking, but to me it didn't seem like much. I was really enjoying it. "Besides," I told him "If you get sick with the runs, this stuff will definitely firm everything right up." Jesús seemed to understand, so with a smile, he poured himself more espresso just for good measure.

After breakfast, we went for a walk that lasted most of the morning. We checked out the whole town. It was beautiful, just beautiful. I could not believe the authenticity of this place. If I go back to Cuba, I will definitely visit Remedios again. In all my travels across Cuba, Remedios is one place where I felt comfortable walking and taking pictures of various people and things.

I did not see many propaganda signs in Remedios. Like every other town or village in Cuba, Remdios has a CDR, *Comites de Defensa de la Revolúcion*, meaning "Committees for the Defense of the Revolution." But that was it. No huge billboards.

In the distance, I kept hearing loud noises. This went on for about an hour. And then without any warning, out of nowhere, a Mikoyan MiG-29UB Russian jet fighter came streaking past. The MiG banked hard, and a few white streaks came off the body of the aircraft. It flew so close that I could see the pilot. A few more planes streaked by, banking here and there. I wanted to take pictures, but I stopped at the last second. After El Comandante's interrogation at the airport, the last thing I wanted was any more trouble.

Kids ran around. Sometimes they came up to me and said, "Do you have something for me?" I didn't give them anything. I felt that if I did, I might start a frenzy.

I saw guys riding bikes with fresh-baked rolls piled three feet high on the back of their bikes. As they made their way through the streets, they yelled loudly from the top of their lungs, "Pan! Pan! Pan!" meaning "bread for sale." I saw one gal walk past with a milk crate with string tied to it. She walked down the street dragging the crate. It had no wheels, and to me she looked like she was walking a dog. Kids played street ball. Horses trotted by.

At one point, we were walking down the street when this guy began to motion to me. "Come. Come here," he said as he motioned with his hands and arms.

He wanted me to go into his house. So I did. He took me to the back where they were cutting up a pig for the market. The homeowner was so happy. He kept smiling. He said a few words but I didn't understand them. Then he picked up the pig's head and held it aloft with two hands, so that I could take a picture of him with it. I smiled and did so. He was a nice fellow.

We continued down a side street. On the corner of José Martí and J. Crespo Moreno streets stood a very old colonial wooden house. The house had wood planks of varying widths ranging from four to twelve inches. The planks were flat and lay horizontally in no particular order. After so many years in the hot Caribbean sun, the unpainted wood was now bleached and weathered to light gray tones. The house barely held together. I stood across the street, out of the way of the passing bicyclists and horse carts. I wanted to take pictures of this house. I wanted to capture the old door and the weathered wood-grain patterns, which had an appeal to my eyes that I wanted to capture.

For fifteen minutes, I stood observing my surroundings and taking pictures. Jesús, who had been standing a small distance off to the side, started laughing. I turned to him and gave him a look, "What?" He proceeded to tell me that an old man had been watching me the whole time. This old man was rambling on and on that he had never before seen anyone take a picture of Francisco's house. He wondered what in the world could be so interesting about Francisco's house. It made no sense to him; to him it was just a house. The old man didn't see the historical significance of these homes that have been standing here for hundreds of years. This town is all he knew, and these houses were part of the passing scenery. Here, the cycle of life has continued over the years, unaware of the march of progress occurring around the rest of the world.

Continuing on our walk, I saw many small places, old colonial buildings, dedicated to fixing flat tires; these people who run these shops are called *poncheros* (flat tire repairmen). After seeing the conditions of the roads in Cuba, I understood that people were constantly getting flat tires. I saw the importance of having a constant supply of patching materials and compressed air for cars and bike tires. I was impressed and amazed at the resourcefulness of these little repair shops. Lacking proper tools, they were very ingenious with creating makeshift tools that got the job done.

It was nearly time to hit the road again, though I didn't want to leave. We walked back to the house where the car was parked and paid the owner three CUCs for storing our car overnight. We drove to the casa to pick up our things, pay our bill, and say our respectful good-byes. Then we continued along the coast to the fishing village of Caibarien. I didn't know anything about Caibarien, but from the map, I decided it was a good direction to head.

3

HISTORY IN THE ROUGH

LEAVING REMEDIOS, CAIBARIEN was just a small hop east, about six miles. Since Caibarien is right on the coast of the Gulf of Mexico, I assumed we would find a big, bustling harbor. I thought it might be interesting to check out, but instead we found a small bay with a docking area for fishing boats.

We drove through town toward the boats, where we tried to find a safe place to park. I had to park off this part-asphalt, part-dirt road and was especially careful to find an area where it looked like we would not easily get a flat tire. Throughout this trip, I had to constantly be on guard against flat tires. It's not like in the United States, where we can park our cars about anywhere and not worry about these things. In Cuba, there is always fine debris such as nails and concrete chunks on the roadways—as well as rough and sporadic potholes. Things fall off of people's carts; trash invariably spills onto the street. Moreover, I did not see any street-sweeping trucks in Cuba. Occasionally, I saw someone sweeping off the street curbs with a palm frond, and pulling a trash can on a cart.

We found a clean, open spot of dirt that looked good enough for us to pull over to park the car. Jesús and I walked to the small harbor docking area, which was not far away. I saw a dead cat that was camouflaged in the wild, thick, uncut grass. The cat was hollowed out and appeared to have been there for a few weeks. I don't know why it caught my attention.

As we walked closer, we could see that part of this small bay was blocked off with a large chain-link fence. Jesús noticed a small sign on the fence. He immediately froze, stunned and apprehensive.

"What's wrong?" I asked.

"The sign," Jesús said. "It says that this area is a military naval base." Even though the base was small, Jesús felt that it would not be a good idea to take pictures here. Well, I wasn't there to take pictures of their base. The small fishing boats looked interesting out in the water. They were moored to rows of bamboo or small poles that had been lashed together. It reminded me of scaffolding. Instead of a vertical scaffold, this one was lying horizontally across parts of this small bay. How the boat owners got out to their small boats I don't know.

We stood there for what seemed for quite a while, unsure what to do. I could see Cuban military personnel starting to observe us from the other side of the fence. Although we weren't trying to bring attention to ourselves, it was hard not to with the large camera pack on my back and the big telephoto lens carried in my hand. I thought it would look even stranger if we just turned around and quietly walked away.

I said to Jesús, "*Mira!* Why don't we just ask them for their permission to take pictures?" I didn't want any trouble; I only wanted pictures of the bay.

Jesús walked over to the guards and said, "Look, I am a tour guide, and my friend here is an artist. He would like to take pictures of the harbor and the boats. But we wanted to respectfully talk to you first." We were granted permission on the condition that I only shoot in a certain direction—toward the water and away from the naval base.

After cautiously taking my pictures, we turned to head back to the car. About fifteen feet away from me, a buzzard came out of nowhere. It flew gracefully in a tight, downward corkscrew motion and floated with a precise drop right down on that dead cat lying in the thick grass. *My God, they can find anything! They are everywhere!* I thought to myself.

Across the street, I spotted an old train station, a blue building with white trim. Over many years, the paint had faded from its past days of glory. The roof was made of red tiles. On one side of this building, in a straight row, were several tall, narrow, open rectangular entrances. On the building I read the name of the town, Caibarien, and the year the structure was built, 1929.

Old, rusted passenger cars sat on the tracks behind the train station. They looked like something from the 1930s or 1940s. I don't know whether the train station was still in use or not. As I took pictures of this station, I heard noises in the distance, the sounds of a few children nearby playing baseball in a field of dead grass and dirt. They appeared to be having a good time just being kids.

We left Caibarien and traveled a wonderful road that ran parallel to the Gulf of Mexico on the northern side of the island. The road cut through cane fields, farmlands, and small towns. As we drove, I spent my time looking around. The tranquil scenery resembled the California wine country. Even the road was in great shape. On the more open parts of the road, we did not see any other cars for miles. According to Jesús, not many people travel this area. Sugar mill refineries were scattered here and there. Several times, I stopped to take pictures of the mills and the cane brought in for processing. These mills had big smoke stacks with thick plumes of smoke billowing out. Many of the smoke stacks had dates on them from the 1800s. The smaller sugar mills had old, long flat-bed trucks with tall side boards on them that could drive right into the mill. The larger sugar mills had railroad tracks for the connected line of boxcars to be pulled directly inside. Both trucks and trains were filled to the brim with sugarcane that had been harvested and broken up by the combines out in the fields. They were so full that the sugarcane nearly spilled over onto the ground.

Our next stop was the town of Moron. This farm town was more modern than the other villages and towns that we had passed through. We were running low on fuel, and this looked like a good place to stop and fill the tank.

It was the first time we stopped for gas. We pulled into a gas station and an attendant came out to the car. "*Todo arriba?*" he asked. This surprised me and caught me off guard, being used to American gas stations, where it is rare to have an attendant come out and greet customers and ask to fill up their gas tanks. While the attendant filled up the tank, Jesús went down the street to pick up food that we could eat in the car. We wanted to continue driving while we ate.

While standing there next to my car, I heard sounds, "Psst. Psst." Someone behind me was trying to get my attention. I ignored this, assuming it was another jinetero. This continued for a while. *Dang! This guy's not backing off.* I turned around to see who it was. It turned out to be an older man who was pointing at one of the tires on the rental car. He was trying to tell me that the tire needed air. I thought, *Wow, this guy is right. The air is really low.* Without asking if I wanted help, this old man put air in the tire and checked out the other tires.

"*Gracias, Gracias,*" I said, and I gave him a tip.

Apparently, this guy was not employed by the gas station. At a number of gas stations, we encountered men who were not employed by the stations but worked there nonetheless. They sat there all day long, making money from tips. Sometimes they held the key to the bathroom. Usually the toilets in the gas station bathrooms would not flush on their own, let alone have toilet seats or paper. One of these men at the gas station would pour a full bucket of water in the tank to clean out the toilet after anyone used it and see that the bathroom stayed clean. Well, as clean as it could be. I'm sure that my wife would have a list of excitable "rights of refusal!" comments. But, for a guy, what can I say?

Jesús returned with the food, and we were ready to hit the road again. As we were leaving the gas station and about to drive onto the road, someone came up quickly and started pounding on the driver side window. Normally, I would have ignored it, figuring that someone was trying to hustle me, but since the last guy turned out to be helpful with my tires, I rolled down the window while idling there, thinking that something else might be wrong with the car.

"*Si?*" I asked. But before I could realize what was happening, the man immediately dumped a bunch of handmade trinkets into my hands and on my lap. Included in the batch were coconut carvings that looked like "see no evil, hear no evil" monkeys.

"What?" I said. I could not believe it, "No! No! No!"

But he persisted saying, "*Si. Si. Si.*"

I tried to give it all back to him, but I wound up with even more, different, crap in my lap! I was trying to get back on the road, and I didn't want to be rude. I kept moving the car slowly, and he kept right on walking in sync with the car—his head still inside the car window. Out of the chaos, I did notice that this man's face had a genuine innocence about it. But it was hell trying to get those trinkets back to him and close my window. As fast as I gave the stuff back to him, he put more stuff back in my lap. I kept thinking, *Where the hell are Penn & Teller when you need 'em? Just make this guy and his stuff disappear!*

Finally, I was able to get that window closed and get the heck out of there. This guy must have been in his fifties or sixties. But who really knew? Not me. Life is hard in Cuba, so some Cubans look older than they actually are. Truth be told, he was probably younger than fifty.

After leaving Moron, we dropped down toward Ciego de Avila, which got us back on the Autopista Nacional, the main highway that threads through the center length of Cuba.

Although we should have stopped in Camaguey for the night, I wanted to continue on and push to Holguin, where Chiqui was working as a driver for a tour group. I didn't want to miss seeing Chiqui, as it may be the only time I would get to visit with him.

It began to get dark and a light, sporadic sprinkling of rain began. As we kept pushing on, the drive started to get scary. The wide lanes of the main Autopista Nacional highway had turned into a narrow, two-lane road. Apparently, the construction project in the 1980s to widen the Autopista Nacional highway in this area was never completed. Jesús told me that the Cubans started working on this highway at the two furthermost ends of the island. The plan was to work their way in toward the middle, so that both ends would be connected with more lanes. But after the Soviet bloc's financial meltdown and pullout from Cuba, the road-widening project was abandoned. The further we drove inland on this highway, the more we could see the conditions of the original road deteriorating and becoming even more dangerous. Jesús started mumbling something about this middle highway section, *central de la carretera*, approximately 350 to 400 miles, not being finished properly. This particular part of the road was built during the late 1920s, and seemed to be even more narrow than usual. The person in charge of the construction apparently embezzled money from the project, purposely taking a foot and a half off each side of the road.

From what Jesús told me, it sounded like when the guy got caught, he didn't have a very happy ending.

I knew that some construction projects were halted in Cuba when the Soviet Union suddenly pulled out of Cuba in the early 1990s. The Soviet Union's economic crisis meant the end of Soviet aid to Cuba. I did not realize that the pullout by the Soviets stopped just about everything. It began what Castro called the "special period." Because of the intense driving, I had trouble listening and did not think to ask Jesús follow up questions about this.

This narrow road was very dangerous, with everybody driving fast in both directions. It was also getting very dark, as there were no streetlights or, for that matter, any other lights anywhere.

People trotted slowly on horses at the edge of the road. Horse-drawn buggies in the middle of the road came and went in both directions, most without any type of modern reflectors on the back. A few buggies had red oil lanterns dangling from the rear by a rope. Although having the lanterns did improve their visibility, the lanterns were not very bright, and it was still very difficult to see. Without street lighting, everything seemed even darker, and I found my eyes had a hard time adjusting. Once in a while, we suddenly came upon big trucks without any rear lights. Other trucks would honk their horns, as they flew past us spewing out black smoke as they went. There was so much black smoke, we could not even see the trucks when they passed.

Occasionally, from out of nowhere, people would stagger onto the road, then suddenly jolt back off the road into the complete darkness. I could not figure out why, but Jesús realized it was a Friday night, and these people had most likely been drinking. As they had no means of transportation, they were walking, or rather staggering, to their destinations somewhere.

People would also rush to the edge of the highway when they heard a car coming, hoping to get a ride to wherever they were heading. Other people would rush to the edge of the highway to sell whatever it was they had on hand, holding it out in the air in front of them. They ran out in groups of two, five, or even ten people at a time holding their stuff up. One guy even had a huge, white, very much alive turkey! He was holding the bird up high in front of him, upside down by its feet. Oh my God! I became so stressed out from trying not to hit anyone. My natural human instinct was to jerk the car in the opposite direction away from where these people rapidly jumped out onto the edge of the road. But I could not do that because the lane for the oncoming traffic was too close to us. I never knew when an old army truck, sugarcane truck, or horse carriage might be in the other lane coming toward us. Some of these trucks and horse carriages did not have lights; I could not see them until the last minute. Having to be on guard for these things made the driving intense.

I was amazed that we didn't see more accidents. I don't think there was any way to get immediate help to the scene of an accident. It was definitely survival of the fittest. It was so dangerous I don't know how we got through it. I told Jesús, "I never ever want to drive at night again."

He agreed and said, "Chris, I don't care. We will drive until just about dark, and that's as far we'll go."

We could finally see the lights of the city in the distance and knew we were almost to Holguin.

It was late when we got to Holguin, and I was exhausted from driving on that dangerous road. We wanted to stay at the same hotel Chiqui was staying at, but it was full. We called around and finally found a casa run by two old widows who must have been in their early seventies. Because of the one-way streets, it took us a while to find the casa. The façade in front had nineteenth century iron grilles over the windows. The windows themselves had stained glass work at the top of the panes, popular in the 1800s. In this neighborhood, a very narrow sidewalk ran alongside the homes. We entered the casa by going up one small, square half step from the sidewalk to the front doors. A very small, white, clean, fluffy, happy dog greeted us as we stepped inside this beautiful, authentic casa. The black, white, and brown marble flooring had tight, small, intricate geometric patterns and a small glass chandelier hung from the high wood-beamed ceiling. *Wonderful old ladies*, I thought, *just like grandma's house.*

We put our things in our room and left to meet Chiqui before it got to be too late. We told the nice grandmas that we would be back after dinner. We met up with Chiqui around nine o'clock.

We had a wonderful meeting with Chiqui. We gave each other a big hug and sat down in an open-air café at the hotel. We had pizza and a round of drinks. I downed two beers to mellow out my nerves from the crazy and stressful drive. Jesús and Chiqui conversed in Spanish. At first, I didn't know what he was talking about because Jesús was speaking so fast. When Chiqui's eyes grew big and his mouth dropped open, I figured out that Jesús was telling him the story of us hitting those hidden railroad tracks on the Autopista Nacional at over sixty miles per hour. Chiqui stared at me with big wide eyes and looked at me like I was some kind of Evel Knievel. I could tell that he knew we were lucky to have survived that. Jesús continued talking even faster in Spanish, and then Chiqui started to laugh so hard that he almost fell out of his chair. I knew that Jesús was telling him how he and I were arguing so excitedly back and forth like an old married couple after the railroad tracks incident.

After that, it was time for another round of drinks. Then Chiqui made an off-the-wall comment that if I were a Cuban, I would have been drafted into the military because of my size, just as he was. It turns out that Chiqui had served in some capacity in the special forces of the Cuban military; a sharpshooter, as I understand. I thought, *Wow! I would never have guessed this about him.* Then he said he got out of it when he could.

This particular night, Chiqui was in Holguin with a tour group. He was driving a tour bus that was about half the size of one of those normal big buses. Chiqui is as big as me, maybe bigger. *But at least he can fit easily into the bus that he drives*, I thought. Apparently, he crisscrosses Cuba all the time, so he seems to know a lot of the roads well.

During our trip, Jesús and Chiqui sent each other text messages. For them it was an inexpensive way to keep in touch. Jesús would let Chiqui know where we were going. If Chiqui was aware of any problems on the road or troubles in the area where we were headed, he would text Jesús with this information. For instance, later on in the trip when we left Guantanamo and made our way through the steep mountains on the La Farola pass to Baracoa, Chiqui warned us about the blind, hard steep curves in this area. These curves are especially dangerous because the large tour busses can whip around the blind corners. With their size, weight, and the force of gravity in play as they come down a hill, these tour busses can wipe a small car right out.

After our visit with Chiqui, we had to get back to park the car before it got too late at night. The elderly ladies at the casa told us that they knew someone across the street who could help us. The friend of the neighbors turned out to be an old lady who was taking care of her mother, and who happened to have a garage. We knew that this old lady could not stay up late waiting for us, so we had to cut short our visit with Chiqui.

The old lady had a garage all right, but it was built for a Model-A car, if that! I was barely able to get our sardine tin can of a car in there. I even had to pull both the car door mirrors in. Once I got the car in, the other problem was how the heck to get out of the car! I opened the door as far as I could, breathed in, and squeezed my body out. I think I popped a button off my shorts while I was trying to get out between the tight wedge of the door and the car. After I got out of there, the owner locked up the garage and said it would cost us one CUC.

Jesús and I returned to our room in the casa. I took a shower and was reminded once again that I had no comb to use, since my youngest son took it out of my travel bag before leaving and never returned it. That stinker! Jesús hooked up his mini DVD player to the back of the TV. To settle down for the night, we drank Havana Club 7 años rum, watched more Jeff Dunham recordings, and then finally went to bed.

Early the next morning, I was awoken by strange sounds. I lay in bed for a while, but kept hearing strange sounds, faint and continuing off and on. I could not figure out what it was as I lay there in bed. It turned out to be a turkey that these nice grandmas kept in their little open courtyard. At least this time it wasn't someone's intimate moment. So, right here in the middle of the city, in the middle of this house, was a turkey! It was a cute bird, a big fat one. The grandmas were keeping it until it grew big enough to be either eaten or sold on the black market.

They served our breakfast on fine china. It was truly a nice breakfast of eggs with vegetables and homemade cheese, fresh cut fruit, bread, and that wonderful Cuban espresso. After breakfast, we decided to walk around the town and did so for a couple of hours.

Compared to Remedios, where we had just been, Holguin felt modern; though the first houses here were built in the eighteenth century. Called the City of Parks, Holguin is known for its many town squares and plazas.

The area surrounding Holguin was the site of many battles during both wars of Cuban independence. The first war, from 1868 to 1878, is known as the Ten Year War. Antonio Maceo was a Cuban general who fought in the Ten Year War. A *mulato*, he was nicknamed "The Bronze Titan" for the many countless times he had defied death during battle. Upon hearing about the treaty with the Spanish to end the war, Maceo refused to surrender. The treaty was known as the Zanjon Pact,"and Maceo felt that it brought no honor to Cuba as it did not abolish slavery nor provide for complete Cuban independence from Spain. He refused to sign the treaty and regarded his peers in the Mambi army who signed the Zanjon Pact as sellouts. In Mangos de Baragua, a town not far from Holguin, Maceo made a famous speech called La Protesta de Baragua, or "The Baragua protest." On March 23, 1878, Maceo resumed fighting in hopes of restarting the war. But in May of 1878, the Ten Year War officially ended due to the Zanjon Pact. Maceo went into a prolonged exile in Costa Rica. Hearing news of the second war of independence many years later, Maceo came back to Cuba. The second war was from 1895 to 1898.

The largest brewery in Cuba, Cerveceria Bucanero, is located in Holguin. The three beers produced there are Bucanero, Mayabe, and Cristal. The town of Holguin is situated between two mountains. As we walked around, we came upon another book fair. It was in one of the town squares and the *policia* (police) had blocked off some of the adjacent streets. People were selling flowers and books, among other things. I walked down one of the streets and saw an old Russian box-type delivery truck parked in the street with its back doors wide open. Inside, I could see already plucked chickens hanging from the many hooks dangling from the ceiling of this truck. Soon the chickens were unloaded. Some were placed into open crates and taken inside the building nearby. There were many people standing there, milling around, and looking at the back of this open truck full of hanging chickens. They all stood around with their handbags in their hands, almost drooling at the sight of these birds, looking as if they hoped to get a piece to take home. I took a picture of them. Funny thing is I remember seeing this exact same scenario at other towns while traveling on this trip. An old 1950's Chevy was parked on the street. It was loaded with a lot of beer destined for either a party or a store. I noticed that the car had a great hood ornament, and I stopped to take a close-up macro picture of it. While I was looking at the hood ornament, in my own world, quietly with my camera—WHAAAHHH! The driver honked his horn. I jumped and about hit the Moon! I looked up at this guy sitting in the driver's seat, and he was laughing and laughing. I had no idea who this guy was, but he sure had a good laugh at me. I then gave this unknown comedic stranger a nod and a smile to acknowledge, *Yeah! You got me; you got me good.* What else could I say?

An old abandoned building with interesting composition caught my eye. As I was taking pictures of this building from across the street, this character whom I nicknamed the "Happy Bum" walked right into my shot. He carried a clear plastic bottle and cup, which I suspect were filled with *aguardiente*, which is a fermented sugarcane moonshine. The guy stopped, turned, and leaned against the wall. He stretched out his arms like he was Jesus Christ on the cross. So, I took the picture. And then he just continued walking, not breaking stride.

I got a chuckle out of that because it was so out of the ordinary. It was so out of character for a Cuban to do something like that. I decided that I better take another picture as a backup. I told Jesús to ask him to do it again.

"He's going to want a buck," Jesús said.

"I don't care," I said.

So the Happy Bum did it again. And then, just as fast, he came running over from across the street. I gave him the one CUC. And then, without any warning, he gave me a big hug, wrapping his arms around me, almost

knocking my sunglasses off. Meanwhile, Jesús, who was just laughing and laughing at this, took a picture of this guy giving me a hug. But before Jesús knew it, this guy turned around, grabbed him, and gave him a big bear hug before abruptly going on his way. Without looking at each other, Jesús and I instinctively and immediately started checking our shirt and pants pockets. We patted ourselves down, the sounds from our hands hitting our bodies playing in stereo. When we realized that we were doing the same thing at the same time, we looked at each other and started laughing, realizing nothing was taken. This guy didn't try to steal anything. He was truly a happy bum.

As we continued walking, Jesús told me about a boxing arena that was on the other side of the town square. He thought maybe we could get in free and take a look. We walked through the front gate and down a small, narrow tunnel that opened up to a full-size boxing arena. The small arena had a covered roof, except for the seats at the highest point, which were located amid a small ring of open air. Some children who were part of a boxing league and appeared to be about eight to ten years old were getting ready to square off. The stands were made of concrete and were only partially filled with people waiting to watch the fights. I took a few pictures, although, for some reason, I seemed to be attracting most of the attention.

Before we left Holguin, we drove to the top of Loma de la Cruz (Hill of the Cross). This small mountain is about 980 feet high and overlooks the city of Holguin, providing a panoramic view. The road to the top is at the back of the mountain, while on the front side there are about 475 steps leading straight up from the city to the mountaintop. At the top stood a cross and an old Spanish lookout tower. A Friar named Francisco Antonio de Alegria planted the cross there in May 1790.

While looking at the city from the mountaintop, I noticed an old lady sitting off to the side smoking a big Cuban cigar and taking in the morning view. Her skin was very dark; she was obviously of African descent. Her straight hair looked like it had not been washed in a few days. It was held back with a colorful four-inch-wide cloth that wrapped around from the top to the back of the head. Her hands looked extremely aged and weathered, showing that she had a very hard life of work. She was pleasant and minding her own business. I wanted to take her picture and had Jesús ask her for permission, since I felt that he could word it more eloquently than I could. I wanted to show her respect. She allowed me to take her picture, but she seemed happier to be chatting with us. I offered her one CUC, which she gladly accepted.

At mid-morning, we decided to hit the road, to make sure we had enough daylight to make it over to Santiago. Our first stop would be Bayamo. We would pass from the Holguin Province to the Granma Province.

In Cuba's lower plains, there are giant ceiba trees scattered about. These trees are revered by most Cubans and are considered sacred by the Afro-Cubans who practice Santeria. The giant roots of these trees rose and pressed out high and wide above the ground from the base of the tree. The trunks of these trees are about 10-feet wide, and rise up extremely high in the air before the first limbs start. The canopy is massive, and reaches out horizontally with overall vertical heights of 230 feet or higher. The trees have a prehistoric aura about them and almost look like they are defying physics. It's an unbelievable sight to see.

The road to Bayamo cut through field after field of sugarcane and bananas. The soil was dark red. From what I could tell, the whole area appeared to be a very fertile growing area. I thought back to my airport interrogation, and how angry El Comandante got when I spoke about this area. Along the way, I saw a number of abandoned railroad lines. We passed through beautiful countryside. Occasionally, I would see baseball fields, some of which were makeshift dirt fields. It was interesting to continually see the giant, beautiful Cuban Royal Palms. These trees were scattered alongside the road and up in the hills. I saw a few more of these Cuban Royal Palms that had been struck by lightning. They stood dead with no crown on top, continued products of some of the thunderous tropical storms and lightning that pass through.

All through here, people sold all sorts of things along the road, even tangerines. People were standing around doing their hand signals in hopes of catching a ride. *Where do they come from?* I wondered. Seemingly out of nowhere, many suddenly appeared. I saw big trucks loaded up with sugar cane. Out in the fields, the combines break up the sugarcane and spit it onto the backs of very old trucks. From the fields, the trucks head to the nearest sugar mill refinery. Small pieces of sugarcane fell from the trucks onto the road, predominately at stop signs, on sharp turns on the edges of the roads. It reminded me of the San Joaquin Valley in California, where it is common to see trucks piled high with tomatoes, lemons, and other crops, and with fallen fruit on the ground at these same types of intersections. I saw many interesting similarities here; like the same laws of gravity apply, no matter where you are.

On the way to Bayamo, we came across several police checkpoints. The first one was just outside of Holguin, and seemed to come out of nowhere. There were no signs telling us to slow down. I honestly didn't see any. I was going 80 kilometers per hour, or about 50 miles per hour. Jesús just happened to look up from the map that he was reading and saw the checkpoint at the last second.

He screamed, "Slow down! Slow down!"

I came right up on the checkpoint and slammed on the brakes so hard that the police blew their whistles and motioned aggressively for me to pull aside. The police were standing along the road watching the cars. As I pulled over, I could tell Jesús was getting nervous.

"Get everything ready," he said in a little higher pitched voice than before. "Your passport, your papers."

The officer came up to my window wearing a stern look. As I rolled the window down, he asked for my papers. I started to pull things out. My hands were beginning to shake just a little, as I fiddled with the paperwork. After the experience of my airport interrogation, I was nervous and more than a little gun shy.

At that point, Jesús opened his passenger door and jumped out of the car. He walked around the car toward the officer and began to speak. I had never heard Jesús speak so fast in Spanish as I did then. They bantered back and forth. Jesús later told me that he was explaining to the police officer that he was my tour guide and had been looking down at the maps.

The officer spouted back, "Why aren't you driving?"

Jesús responded, "I can't do two things at once." The officer was still not convinced. Jesús then told him, "Now, I've been watching this guy's driving for a long time. Did you notice that his wheels didn't squeal when he abruptly slowed down? He wasn't going 100 kilometers an hour. I've been watching him, and he's been around 80 kilometers an hour." At that point, the officer seemed to mellow. "OK," he said. He was convinced.

Jesús got back in the car. The officer turned, walked back toward me, and returned my paperwork. He said that I could proceed and abruptly gave me a crisp salute. I nodded very respectfully and was free to go. Man! That was close. I was beginning to learn that every time we entered a new province there would be a checkpoint.

We drove into Bayamo, and Jesús was trying to direct me to a parking area that would be close to the center of town and the historic town square. Amongst the many bici-taxis, bikes, horse buggies, and old cars on the road, it took awhile to finally find a good parking spot. As I got out of the car, an old mulatto Cuban approached me. This guy looked like he tipped the bottle a little too regularly. With a loud and gravelly voice, he adamantly tried to explain to me that he was going to watch my car.

He told me, barely understandable and slurring his broken English, "I watch your car. I stay right here, right here! And watch your car." He said this loudly while dramatically pointing to my car and the ground where we were standing. Other than thinking he was a scruffy little guy, I didn't think too much about it at the moment. We walked a few blocks to get to the town's main square.

Bayamo was founded in November 1513, making it the second-oldest city in Cuba after Baracoa. There was unrest with the Indians during the early years there, until European diseases took a toll on the native population. Then came the pirates. The most notable pirate was Gilbert Girón who was also the same pirate who frequented the area that was to become the Bay of Pigs. Gilbert Girón met his end in Bayamo—killed in 1604 by the freed African slave Salvador Golomón. His head was put on a stake and displayed in the town's open plaza square as a strong warning to future pirates. As time went on, cattle were raised in the area. Sugarcane grew abundantly, and was commercially farmed. The sugarcane crops made people wealthy, and the town grew. Lavish churches and fine homes were built in Bayamo. Because of the explosion of sugarcane crops, and the need for people to work in the fields, Bayamo became an important hub for the Spanish slave trade.

The people of Bayamo became fed up with the Spanish and their policies. In 1868, Carlos Manuel de Céspedes, a poet, lawyer, and sugar plantation owner, organized a revolt. From his sugar plantation, on October 10, 1868, he called for the abolition of slavery. As an example, he freed all his own slaves. With an army of supporters, Carlos Manuel de Céspedes took control of Bayamo and declared it the capital of the Cuban republic. His rallying cry for freedom and an independent Cuba was *El Grito de Yara* (Cry of Yara). This was the spark of the first revolt of the Ten Year War of independence. This was a moment of the beginning of the Cuban mind, and the love for their mother country.

The odds were against the townspeople of Bayamo. Soon they faced recapture and reoccupation by the Spanish troops. Rather than surrendering Bayamo to the Spanish army, the townspeople burned their whole town to the ground on January 12, 1869. They would rather see their own town destroyed than see it taken back over by their enemy. When Jesús told me this, I felt that there was a demonstrative level of anger and frustration these people had. I thought, *Wow! They had such intensity in their beliefs and held so true to their convictions that they were willing to take such a drastic course of action.* In a way, it had a similar intensity of feelings and convictions to the Jews under the Roman siege of Masada in ancient Israel.

Jesús and I continued walking and came across a small chapel, Capilla de La Dolorosa, which dates back to 1630. The chapel is dedicated to the Virgen de los Dolores (Virgin of the Sorrows); miraculously, only this chapel survived the fire of 1869. It has a *Mudejar* (Moorish) ceiling and a Baroque altar made of gilded wood. The original Cuban flag sewn by Carlos Manuel de Céspedes' wife is preserved there.

Some time later, we got ready to leave Bayamo and made our way back to the car. As we walked around the corner from where we were parked, I remembered the old scruffy guy. As I got to the car, I started looking around for him. I was waiting for him to hit me up for some money for supposedly watching my car. I didn't see him! But then I looked down and there he was, passed out on the sidewalk snoring away loudly, with his arms crossed over his chest. Our car was parked right next to a row of houses, and this scruffy old guy was leaning up on someone's doorstep, against the wall. I thought to myself with a laugh, *Yeah, you're really watching our car.* We slowly opened our car doors. I said, "Let's see how far we can go before he wakes up." It became a game to us. We got in slowly, and he was still asleep. I started the car. He's still asleep. We started to pull out and slowly drive, and he's still just passed out snoring away. Then we started laughing about how loud and adamant he was about watching over our car to make sure no one would take it. And here we could have been burglars stealing the car. We started making jokes about what he might say when he wakes up and sees that the car he was watching is gone. I'm sure that this is not the first time that this has happened to him. Jesús started doing great imitations of the guy, "Dang! That's the third one this week that I lost…. Another one got away from me!" Right then and there, the saturation point of watching so much of the black market recordings of Jeff Dunham on this trip hit us. Jesús had it down to a science and euphorically just started going off like Walter, one of Jeff Dunham's characters. Thus, marking the start of the Jeff Dunham one liners. That was especially humorous with Jesús's Cuban accent.

We drove off, and as I was looking for the main road to take us out of town, Jesús screamed out, "Stop!" My first thought was that I did something wrong. He exclaimed, "Pull over somewhere!" I did so immediately, and he explained that he saw a place where he could buy phone cards that Cubans were allowed to buy. Dodging the bici-taxis and old cars, he dashed across the road and disappeared into the building. About fifteen to twenty minutes later, Jesús came back holding four phone cards in his hands and a look on his face like he was a kid in a candy store.

Knowing that we were set for a while with cell phone minutes, I asked Jesús if we could call Pilo right now! I still felt bad about my last conversation with him in Remedios. I felt that I had rudely cut him off. I wanted to call Pilo and explain what had happened in Remedios regarding the cell phone conversation and make sure that he did not feel slighted. Pilo and I talked for about ten minutes, and I was able to clear the air. He was very happy and very understanding of what had happened. We made plans to connect when I came back to Havana in a couple of weeks.

Leaving Bayamo, the surroundings started to change, and the roads started to climb up the mountainous Sierra Maestra. We were going to pass through a village of El Cobre while making our way toward the city of Santiago, where we would stay for two days.

With some of the highest peaks in Cuba, the Sierra Maestra covered territories in both the Granma and Santiago de Cuba provinces. Its highest peak is 6,476 feet. Fidel Castro and *Los Barbudos* (The Bearded Ones) brought notoriety to these mountains. In the untamed jungles of the Sierra Maestra, they played cat-and-mouse games with the Batista army. During the late 1950s, Fidel Castro made this area his revolution headquarters and Ché Guevara even had a makeshift medical aid station there. Ché also used short wave radio from this area to transmit the propaganda of the revolution to the people.

The road was getting narrow, as the lush forests pressed against it. There were beautiful native wild orchids. I noticed one tree with beautiful bright red bark, and it looked like layers were peeling or flaking off the bark. I didn't know what tree it was, so I asked Jesús, "What is it called?"

He said calmly, "A tourist tree."

I thought to myself, and then I said, "Wait a minute, a tourist tree?"

And he said, "Yes, that is the only name that I know for that tree." He explained to me how they came up with the name when they were kids, "It has red bark, and it peels."

I looked at him and said, "You have to be kidding?" He was serious. As a child, he and his friends saw the Soviets and other European tourists with their sunburns from the hot, Cuban sun. Their skin would get red and peel, and the name has stuck ever since.

We dropped a bit in elevation, and the road started to wind a bit more. Off in the distance, a big church nestled in the dark, lush green jungles stood out, surrounded by the high mountains. It was the Basilica de Nuestra Señora del Cobre.

As I was driving on this winding jungle road, the bright red brick dome of the towering bell tower was the first thing to catch my eye. On either side of this bell tower protruded two smaller towers also capped with the same bright red brick.

The façade of the church is a light cream-colored shade of white. Further up behind the church was an open area of dirt that had been a copper mine. Mining began with the Spanish around 1530 and ended with the closure of the mine sometime in the year 2000. The word *cobre* means "copper" in Spanish.

We approached the turnoff to the church, and people started running out of the bushes. These people were in the bushes for the shade from the sun, and when they heard the sound of a car, they came running out. They had trinkets they were trying to hustle to anyone who happened to be driving by. The sellers aggressively pushed the trinkets, as offerings to the Virgen del Cobre whose statue is inside this church.

We continued driving and did not get more than thirty yards when more people started running out of the bushes. This pattern of people fervently coming out of the bushes continued. After a while, I thought, *You'd think these people would figure out that since I didn't stop for the last batch of people, why would I stop to buy from them?*

We hit the turnoff into the village, and then it became even more aggressive. People were selling all sorts of things. There were round, flat objects the size of a Frisbee covered with yellow sunflowers. People were holding many different types of trinkets up in the air. The idea was that you could choose a trinket based upon the needed offering. People walked out in the middle of the road, trying to make us stop and buy from them. I'd never seen anything so aggressive, never an onslaught of people like that. It was like they practically jumped onto the car trying to sell their trinkets. The best description I can give is like someone had just kicked a live hornet's nest.

I was able to make the turn to the church and drive up the road that winds up the hill and behind it. We got to the dirt parking area where an old man watched the cars. I had to pay him one CUC. Then we hit one last seller's gauntlet—a guy selling little pieces of stone, copper, or rock. We entered the church from the back rather than from the front door. At long last, we were no longer bothered by anyone. As we entered the church from behind, we walked into a room that appeared to be a visitor's center. Further in was a very large table with numerous lit votive candles.

There were many objects on this table that had been recently left for the Virgen del Cobre. These offerings were given either in thanks or for requests for much needed favors bestowed by the Virgen del Cobre.

To the right I saw that there was an open room. This room was called the Room of Miracles. When the table in the entry becomes too full, the not-so-recent objects and offerings are then moved to this room. These offerings are piled high; the more valuable items are placed behind glass cases. Some of these items in the glass cases include Olympic medals, Cuban baseball sports jerseys and team photos signed by the players, military medals, and an object left by Lina Ruz, Fidel Castro's mother, to protect her son during his battles with the Batista regime. Even Ernest Hemingway left his 1954 Nobel Prize for *The Old Man and the Sea*. Outside the glass cases were many pictures of anonymous people, and even a television.

I saw people going up the stairway to the top floor. Jesús told me that was where the Virgen de la Caridad was. We followed behind the people going up the stairs to a small half-moon-shaped sanctuary. The Madonna icon was in a large glass case facing this sanctuary room. An attendant was standing respectfully to the side, and she seemed to be very accommodating with my picture taking. She was attentive when I pulled out my camera and various lenses. Without even being asked, she opened or closed the blinds on the window for me, so that I could have the proper lighting for my pictures.

Sunlight colorfully shone in the room from brightly colored stained-glass windows. The statue itself was dark skinned and stood about fourteen inches tall. It was clothed in an elaborate yellow dress with brightly colored jewels. The Madonna was crowned with a golden halo and carried the infant Christ and a cross of jewels. On May 10, 1916, Pope Benedict XV declared the virgin of El Cobre to be the patron saint of Cuba. The Basilica de Nuestra Senora del Cobre was built to house the statue of the Virgen del Cobre. Construction was completed in 1926. In 1998, Pope John Paul II visited Cuba and ceremoniously blessed and re-crowned the statue.

The whole time we were standing in this small sanctuary and viewing the Madonna, I could hear a constant and harmonious chanting in an even tone that reverberated and echoed throughout the Church. To the side of the Madonna altar was an elaborate marble balustrade railing. I stepped over to it and was able to look down. I saw the main sanctuary area where the congregation sits for Mass. Down below were nuns wearing white robes with blue trim. The nuns were on their knees in the front pews, chanting in a loud cry. It reminded me of the Wailing Wall in Israel, though I have never been there myself. Those nuns were oblivious and unaware of anything else around them as they were doing their thing. It looked as if they had been there for a long time.

I turned back to where I was previously standing and saw Jesús on his cell phone. He was talking to his mom, letting her know that he was standing at this very moment right in front of the Virgen de la Caridad. He asked his mom if she needed anything, and if she wanted Jesús to say anything on her behalf at the altar. I was amazed at how intense and sacred this place was even to the point of being a major pilgrimage site for many Cubans.

As I looked around at this Madonna, I saw a mixture of the Catholic and African religions. I learned that this statue is associated with the Ochun goddess, an orisha, whose figure is represented by the color of yellow in the Madonna's clothing. These two religions seemed to be interwoven in this one icon. There appeared to be much affection, devotion, and belief in its religious powers. There did not seem to be any feeling of contradiction with the mixing of the two beliefs.

As we were making our way out of this area and down to the main sanctuary of the church where the nuns were chanting, I asked Jesús, "How did this all come about? I mean, where did the Madonna come from?"

Jesús told me that according to legend, three men sometime around 1612 were on the north side of Cuba along the coast of Bahia de Nipe. While in their boat searching for salt, they saw something floating in the water. It was the statue of the Virgin Mary with the inscription, "I am the Virgin de la Coridad." The men were caught in dangerous storms and felt they would have surely perished had they not found the statue and been saved by the Virgin Mary. In the very early sixteen hundreds, the statue was brought to the copper mine here in El Cobre.

When we walked into the main sanctuary, I was blown away at how large and beautiful it was. I could tell that a lot of love was put into this place.

The architecture was beautiful and majestic—large white pillars with rolling nave arcade archways on either side of the center aisle. A high rib-vaulted ceiling allowed for clerestory stained-glass windows that led from the back of the church all the way to the front altar. The ornate high altar is about two stories high, and appears to be of Baroque and neoclassical architecture. High above the altar, the ceiling transitions from the high rib-vaulted ceiling and changes to a large, round, cloister-vault ceiling with five large, perfectly round, clerestory stained-glass windows surrounding it.

The Virgen del Cobre is encased in glass and sits near the top of the high altar. I took a few pictures, and then it was time to start thinking about making our way to the car.

We left the church, got back in the car, and got ready to pass the gauntlet of people who were waiting for us to leave. We slowly came driving down the hill. At the bottom, we could see a high arching wrought-iron gate with a cross on top and a sign that said, "*Santuario*

Nacional de la Virgen del Cobre." Approximately 255 steps lead you from the gate straight up to the front doors of this church. Jesús told me that he's always wanted to get a picture of this front gate with the name and the church in the background behind it. But he was never able to do so because of the angle.

I looked at him and said, "That's easy! If it means that much to you, I'll get it!" Unfortunately, that meant I had to park and get out of the car amidst the throngs of people who were there hustling and selling their trinkets, offerings, and miniature Cachitas. I pulled out my wide-angle lens and took the picture that I needed. As I turned to go back and walk to the car, I was literally pounced on. This time my size did not help me out any. My God! It was like being a rock star! The only difference is they did not ask for my autograph, nor rip my clothes off. That is the only way I can describe it. I was finally able to get back in the car. I hit a boiling point, and I told Jesús what bothered me most about all this unbelievable onslaught of frenzied people here was their utter disrespect for their church. They claim that this church is a sacred place, yet many of these individuals appeared to have no respect for it. The only thing I can compare or parallel it to is about the story in the Bible of how Christ angrily turned over the tables of the money changers and chased them out of the temple. Just like the money changers, this intense aggressiveness at the basilica was turning this place of worship into a place of irreverent rudeness. My God, I could really see the visual similarities here. I didn't want to be so direct about this with Jesús. I was trying to be as respectful as I could. We finally got out of there. As we got further away, I started to calm down.

As we left El Cobre, Jesús told me that in order to run for political office in Cuba, a candidate first has to be elected from one of the country's many different municipalities. It was from this town of El Cobre that Fidel Castro was unanimously elected.

We were getting very close to Santiago, located only twelve miles from El Cobre. But we were not able to drive very fast because of the mountainous curves and poor road conditions. We finally came over the last hill and dropped down into Santiago. The city is surrounded by large mountains and is known to be one of the hottest areas in all of Cuba. I immediately noticed the energy level seemed to be much higher. Even the driving felt more intense, with loud noises from the cars and buses. The streets were throwing me off a bit. Thank God, I had Jesús to help navigate.

In Santiago, the buildings were set on crowded low hills. Some of the roads ended at the bottom of stairways that are almost fifty feet wide. Their steps lead you up to a whole different area. With its rolling hills, intermittent steps, and alleys, Santiago reminded me of San Francisco. And yet, the vibe and movement of life had a feeling of Rio de Janeiro. I will say, though, that out of all the initial chaos, my eyes were definitely stimulated by all the colors and different buildings.

Jesús said he knew of a good casa in the part of town by Parque Céspedes, the most historic square in Santiago, and close to the steps of Padre Pico. We drove over there through narrow streets only to find out that it was full. The people there told us about another casa a few blocks away that should have room. We drove to the next casa. There was a nice room available. "We'll take it," we said.

We unpacked the car and decided to take a walk before it got too dark. Before we could leave, the older lady who owned the casa asked us what we would like to have for dinner. Jesús talked to her in Spanish for a bit and then turned to me and gave me a short run down of the possibilities. Of course, I knew Jesús wanted pork.

Then he laughed at me and said, "I knew you wanted lobster, and I already told her to cook it." Well, what could I say to that? A thought

occurred to me, and I asked Jesús if they have a special way of cooking in Santiago. I mean, are there recipes and dishes that this area is known for? Since the lady of the casa did not understand English, she wanted to know what we were talking about. So Jesús told her.

She gave me a great big smile as if saying, "I know what to do." We told them we would be back from our walk in about an hour and a half. Dinner would be ready when we came back. As we left on our walk, the evening was starting, and we could feel the beginning of the city's energy level start to change and begin to come down.

4

FRICTIONS

BEFORE WE LEFT on our walk, I found out that we could go to the top floor of the casa for a view of the city. People went to cool off and catch a light breeze on the roofs of the houses. I went upstairs to look around and take pictures of the views. In one direction, I could see the Bahia de Santiago de Cuba, Santiago's bay, where big container ships were docked. The different ships' hulls were green, black, or red. Big shipping cranes were mounted on large decks along the shore ready to reach high and inside these boats. In the other direction, I could see row after row of old colonial homes with red tile roofs contrasted with crude and odd looking makeshift television antennas. Some of the day's bright colored laundry was still hanging, strung out in the open, in the late-afternoon air. Emerging from the rooftops of many of the homes were small, gray concrete, gravity-fed water tanks. Most of the tanks sat at the highest points of these homes, dotted about in no particular order. They cascaded along the endless contours of these buildings with varying high and low irregular rooftops.

On top of the existing structure of some homes were small, haphazardly constructed building additions. Rebar stuck out from the concrete and brick. There didn't appear to be many building codes in Cuba.

We went back downstairs and finally stepped outside for our walk. At the last minute, we remembered that we had to find a place for the car. At night, we had to be vigilant about finding a safe place for the car, and during the day, we had to be alert for potential causes of flat tires. As it turned out, these two conscious themes for the car were just things we had to be on top of at all times.

We saw a guy in one of the houses across the narrow street. He sat behind a simple window that only had wooden shutters and nineteenth century iron grilles.

"I will watch it. You can leave it right there for a peso a day," he told Jesús in Spanish. Since it was practically in front of where we were staying, I thought this was fine. This parking spot was more out in the open, and not as good as our previous parking arrangements. But it was the best we could do at the time, so we parked the car in front of this guy's house on that very narrow street. At least it was on a side street and away from the main city paths and traffic.

These neighborhoods had no sidewalks. Old colonial houses were built right up to the edge of the narrow curb. Houses here had red tile roofs and many were painted in various bright colors; although houses painted in white and cream were common too. Our casa was blue with white trim; in fact, it was the brightest blue I had ever seen.

The foundation had been built about eight feet above street level. The stairway to the front door was built up against the wall of the foundation and situated parallel to both the side of the house and the street. These types of steps are called *pretorios*. Very narrow half steps (definitely not OSHA approved) are prevalent in cities such as Santiago. As we walked on this beautiful night, we took in the sights and sounds of the area.

I was pleasantly surprised to find that the jineteros in this area were less aggressive than I heard they would be. I'm sure having Jesús with me helped a lot. Instead of hitting me up, most of the time they would go to him first and see if there was anything we needed. I told Jesús that I wanted to walk this way again the next day, in the daylight.

We were getting hungry, so we slowly made our way back to the casa. I remembered that lobster, pork, and of course, Bucanero beer were waiting for us. When we stepped through the front door of the casa, we could smell dinner cooking and saw a table nicely set for us. I heard a television in the background tuned to the world baseball games. Cuba was playing—now it made sense why we didn't see too many people while we were on our walk.

Jesús and I sat down to eat. We had a salad of thinly sliced tomatoes and cucumbers. The tomatoes were marbled red and green. Also on the table were black beans and rice, a thick soup, and the most beautiful plate of lobsters I'd ever seen. The lobsters were cooked in a dark red sauce with spices. *Holy Cow!* I thought. There must have been three or four fat lobsters in this dish. Jesús gave me a big smile, as he held his opened can of beer up in the air.

"Cheers," I said, as I took my first bite of that wonderful lobster dish. I then noticed the lady of the casa standing off to the side watching and waiting to see if I approved of this recipe that was cultivated in Santiago.

Wow! The sauce had a thick texture with a pleasant tang. Of course, since it was mixed with lobster, well then, thumbs up for me! I turned to look at her, and all I could think to say was, "Ole! Senora." At this, she gave me a big smile, clapped her hands high in the air, and left us to eat our dinner privately.

As we ate dinner, we looked at our maps and discussed what we might do the next day. I asked Jesús if he knew of any place that had Internet access, as I felt the need to get a note off to my wife and children to let them know I was OK. As it turned out, the casa had a computer for Internet access. For three CUCs, I could send an e-mail. That was great news! It sure saved us the big hassle of trying to find a place in town. The casa owner's daughter, who was probably in her late thirties, spoke English. While we finished dinner, she went off to fire up the computer and see if she could connect to the Internet.

We had another round of beer, and I was definitely slowing down on the food. Still, I kept finding more pieces of lobster in that thick tangy red sauce, and of course I just had to eat them. It took about an hour to get the computer up and connected to the Internet. The whole country is on dial up, which explained why it took so long. In the meantime, I kept eating. I was so stuffed from that dinner that I felt like I was going to have a baby! Jesús could not believe I had eaten everything on my plate. When I got up from the table, I moved very slowly to the couch, where I gently sat down and had to do a type of Lamaze breathing for a while. As I sat there on the couch waiting to send my wife an e-mail, I was trying to think of what to say to her. Thoughts of my detention and interrogation when I arrived in Cuba were still fresh in my mind. I was worried about what was going to happen to me when I tried to leave Cuba. In my mind, I saw the faces of my three children, and I started to miss them, even though sometimes they can drive me bananas! When they argue, fight, or try to kill each other, at various times I feel like I have become a referee in the brightly animated, melodramatic world of the World Wrestling Federation. But I still love them, and I knew that they and my wife needed me to get back home safely.

Abruptly, I heard, "Voila!" shouted from the other side of the room. The Internet connection was made, and Jesús was able to open up his e-mail account. He had it ready for me to write my letter home. I slowly rolled myself up off the couch and went to the computer. There were a lot of things I wanted to say, but I didn't want to scare my wife. I told her that I made it to Cuba and that I was safe, but that I got detained at the airport. I didn't go into detail about my interrogation. I told her:

> "I am fine now. Just please keep me in your prayers for on my way out of Cuba. Tell the kids I love them. I love you too. Your faithful husband. P.S. I will be in Baracoa in a couple of days. I was told there should be a place in Baracoa where I can connect to the Internet. I will be able to reply to you then. In the meantime, you and the kids can look on the Cuba map you have to follow along and see where I am."

I clicked on send, but it took fifteen to twenty minutes for it to finally go out.

After this, I wanted to retreat back to our room, rest, have a little Havana Club 7 años rum, and catch Jeff Dunham on the television. The older woman of the casa wanted to know when we wanted to have breakfast the next day—we figured around eight o'clock. Back in the room, we had a shot from our bottle of Havana Club, as I stretched out on my bed, had a good laugh, and relaxed.

The next morning, we ate breakfast at eight o'clock sharp. The eggs were cooked like a flat pizza with cut veggies and a little cheese thrown on top. There was a very dense, reddish-purple guava paste cut in thick slices and white cheese served on a side plate. By now, Jesús knew what I liked. He knew I loved that Cuban espresso. Even the other Cubans were amazed. They were used to people just drinking one. But me, I couldn't get enough of it. It was almost as good as the Cuban rum. I could hear a man outside yelling at the top of his lungs, as he walked up and down the narrow streets selling this morning's bread.

After breakfast, we left for the day's walk. I thought the morning light was perfect. We went about two blocks when we happened to pass two women. They suddenly stopped, turned, and stared at me. It was almost like they appeared to be smitten, that is the best way I can describe it. One of them made kissing sounds and gestures. I thought they might be streetwalkers and didn't want to entertain any trouble.

I said, "Come on, Jesús. Let's keep going."

Jesús said, "No, they're not streetwalkers." It became obvious that they were interested in being together at the same time! Well, after hearing that, I didn't know what to say. Feeling awkward and at a loss for words, I said, "Well, ah, well, tell them thank you and I'm flattered, but I'm married and have a family." Jesús mumbled something to them, but I don't really know what he said because I kept on going. Jesús caught up to me, and we continued walking.

We turned onto a long, narrow street called Calle Heredia, a famous street in Santiago where many of the amateur Cuban music bands play. During certain times of the year, music emanates day and night, and there is much dancing and parading in the streets. Street performers appear in bright colors, costumes, and many different kinds of paper-mache masks. A festive atmosphere, similar to Carnival in Rio de Janeiro, permeates the area. However, it is not associated with pre-Lenten festivities; the Carnival de Santiago is more to do with the many African cultures that settled in Cuba.

Since it was a Sunday morning, the area appeared a bit quieter with less activity on the street. But I saw children playing with small handmade kites. The kites were hexagonal with long tails of thin torn cloth and about ten feet of string attached to them. The children were running barefoot up and down the narrow, gravelly streets, as their kites were flying and weaving dramatically around in the air.

I walked by several old colonial houses that had been converted into makeshift churches. Music played and the doors and windows were wide open to invite people in. I was surprised to see that one of these churches was a Pentecostal church. The preacher shouted away in Spanish, as if preaching to a full house of people, but as it turned out, all the seats were empty except for one—one person sitting alone in the front row. Further along the street, many more people attended what I think may have been a Baptist church. They were dressed in their Sunday best. It was great to walk around and see the people.

Further down the road, I saw something in the middle of the street spewing orange flames and dark black smoke. As we got closer, we encountered a man selling a pig he had just slaughtered, right there on his front doorstep. He had a makeshift table set up with an old scale. I saw the fresh stains of pig's blood that developed from the slaughtering. A few pieces of piled wood were burning in the middle of the street, and above the fire sat an over-sized, black, cast-iron cauldron. In that hot bubbling pot, I could see a large vat of boiling lard or pig fat. I took a picture of the scene, then I innocently asked the guy, "Where's the pigs head?" He got a really excited look on his face and took off running into the house.

Jesús just started laughing and said loudly, "Chris, he thinks that you're going to buy the head. The head is the hardest part to sell."

Jesús started doing imitations, saying things like, "Honey, you sold the head!"

The man's wife was probably inside the house, and when she saw him running past her and outside with the pig's head, she would be saying, "Oh my, you sold the head. How great!"

Well, the man came out all smiles. He held the whole pig's head—eyes, ears, snout, and all high in the air. I took a picture of him with it.

"*Gracias!*" I said. He then gave me a funny look as if to say, "Ahhh-man!" realizing that I wasn't interested in buying the head. Jesús was laughing at all this and going off again imitating what he imagined was happening when the man took the pig's head back inside the house. His wife would probably say, "What!? Didn't you sell the head?" It was comical. It was interesting to see the everyday life innocently unfolding right there on the street.

We came to Parque Céspedes, an area considered to be the heart of the city in Santiago. The square itself is designed in a neoclassical style, and there was much history in the surrounding area. We took a break at an historic hotel known as the Casa Granda, which was built in the early 1900s. We went to the top floor to sit, get a cold drink, rest, and cool off in the shade. My back was wet with sweat from carrying my large, heavy camera pack.

From the open terrace on the top deck, I felt a cool breeze, and we enjoyed looking down over the entire area around the square. The first thing I saw upon entering this terrace was the yellow and white Catedral de Asuncion, which was originally built in 1522. The upper reaches of this beautiful church facade stood out right in front of us at eye level. Because of earthquakes as well as razing and looting by marauding pirates, this church was rebuilt several times over the centuries. A tall, marble angel with large open wings stood holding a brass trumpet on the apex of the triangular pediment between the two large front towers.

Viewing this church and the surrounding area from the top of the hotel, definitely gave us a different perspective on things. Looking to the north end of the Parque Céspedes, we saw a building called the Ayuntamiento, or town hall. On January 1, 1959, Fidel Castro appeared on the central balcony of this building to announce the victory of the revolution to the Cuban people. I took pictures of the people and old cars in the streets below us.

Sitting at our table with a cool drink, we enjoyed the view of the bay in the distance and looked over our maps. We stayed there for an hour or so, taking advantage of the light breeze from up high. It was interesting to learn that Graham Greene, who wrote *Our Man in Havana*, spent a lot of time at this hotel, and he featured the Casa Granda in parts of his novel.

When it was time to go, I bought a postcard in the lobby and wrote a note to my wife and kids. (It arrived at my house nineteen weeks later.) From there, we decided to drive to the Castle de San Pedro del Morro, which is about six miles from the city and sits on top of the cliffs of Santiago bay's narrow entrance from the Caribbean Sea. We walked back to our car and started on our way. I had to navigate while going through the gauntlet of Santiago's hectic traffic, which included honking horns, motor scooters darting around, and the uncertainty of pedestrians moving erratically. Driving through these hectic cities became like Abbott and Costello's "Who's on First?" skit. It was almost comical, after the fact, of course.

I would see a roundabout coming up and try to stay ahead of the traffic's confusion by asking Jesús ahead of time, "OK, which way?"

"Straight," he would reply. But the road would fork! So, which straight? To the left straight? To the right straight? Then Jesús would scream for me to watch out for something, like a car or a person, or he would tell me that I was driving wrong.

Question! why did it always seemed more difficult to understand his accent at these times? Jesús reminded me of Ricky Ricardo, on *I Love Lucy*. Once out of these crucial turns, all I could think of was to call Jesús a crazy jalapeño.

We got away from the more congested areas of Santiago and drove through the Vista Alegre section, an area of tranquil neighborhoods. Large trees cover the roads around these large neocolonial mansions built in eclectic architectural styles. Like the neighborhoods in Havana, these neighborhoods in Santiago once belonged to the people who fled Cuba and went into exile in the United States when Fidel Castro came into power. I noticed that some of these mansions were divided up for multiple-family residences, and some had become schools and clinics.

We reached the dirt parking area for the Castle de San Pedro del Morro. The castle sits up high on the cliffs above the entrance to the bay. Smaller fortifications were originally built in this area starting in 1590. Over time, a much larger fortress was needed, so a larger fortification was added. Construction started in 1638 and finished in 1700. These massive stone fortresses were built all around Cuba during the Age of Sail to repel and protect the cities from pirates and invading countries. Chief among these pirates were British pirates and the marauding French buccaneers from the sixteenth century. Christopher Myngs, the famous English admiral and pirate, pillaged Santiago and razed parts of the stone citadel while it was still under construction in 1662.

This fortress has many intricate levels, impressive parapets, prominent lookout towers, and a drawbridge leading over a dry moat. Cannons were in place, lain out and mounted in their battle-ready firing positions, as if ready to fire at a moment's notice, to fight, and to defend the city of Santiago and the entrance of the Bahia de Santiago de Cuba.

The large de Valliere bronze cannons had decorative Gothic designs embossed on them and had weathered to a beautiful green patina. The backs of the cannons were inscribed with the Latin motto, "Nec pluribus impar," meaning "not unequal to many." Below the motto appears the symbol of the Sun King, a face with large rays of sunlight. Further down is the Royal Crest of the house of Bourbon, also known as the Bourbon dynasty. Each cannon had a different figure covering the back end of the breach area, depending on the size of cannon ball used in that particular cannon. An eight-pound cannon ball had a monkey head; a twelve-pound ball had a rooster head; a sixteen-pound had a Medusa head; and a twenty-four pound ball had a lion head. I was looking at a 151 mm caliber cannon, which used the twenty-four pound cannon ball and displayed a beautiful lion's head on the back end of its breach area. An elaborate cascabel stuck out of the mouth of each animal. The cascabel was primarily used to attach ropes that secured the cannon during the recoil blowback that came from firing.

Two dolphins decorated the top of the barrel of the cannon, around the mid-section close to where the trunions are located. These ornate dolphin ornaments served as protruding handles from the cannon in the mid-area, leaving just enough room to run a rope through, so that the cannon could be lifted and maneuvered but kept perfectly balanced.

It was early afternoon. I was not used to the hot Cuban climate, and I was hitting that fall-off point. Jesús could sense it. He forced me to eat and drink something. I sat down to eat rice and beans and have a drink.

After a bit, it was time to head back to town. On the way, we stopped at San Juan Hill, the site of the famous battle in the Spanish-American War involving Theodore Roosevelt, which is also well covered in American history. I was surprised to see that people did not pay much attention to the area. We walked up the pathway toward the top of the hill. I found the hill to be not that big at all. I mean, after reading and hearing all the American folklore about Roosevelt and his regiment of Rough Riders charging up this hill, I assumed the battle that took place on July 1, 1898, was on a big and monstrous hill. While the Americans were battling for the high ground here at San Juan Hill, a Cuban general named Calixto Garcia and several thousand Cuban Mambi troops under his command were simultaneously providing an effective mobile artillery and ground support against the Spanish reinforcements advancing on Santiago.

Amid the large trees everywhere on the crest of the hill, I saw cannons left behind by both the Spaniards and the Americans. Mazes of trenches and foxholes were visible toward the flank side of the Spanish position. The American artillery cannons were still perched on their old-fashioned wagon-wheel frames rested untouched and rusting in their positions, as if the battle had just ended. I looked into the face of the barrels and saw the deep rifling spiral grooves inside. The one-and-a-half-inch thick barrels had the words "Watervliet Arsenal No52 D.A.H. 1892" stamped at the edge of the muzzles.

I continued walking on a concrete pathway that meandered to the other side of the hill. Off in the distance, I could vaguely see an amusement park through the trees. I watched as kids ran through here with their parents, and I began to realize that they see this as a common, open space—a "been here since I was a kid" place. This former battlefield has been here for more than a hundred years. Those cannons just sit there. Those trenches, still there. *My God, this is just sitting here untouched, as if it was just part of the furniture in a house!* That's when I started to recognize the abundant crossover between the history of the United States and the history of Cuba. So much history that appears untapped, overlooked, sitting everywhere—from my perspective, it was a raw reality.

I stood on my own, contemplating all this, when Jesús walked up to me and gently suggested in a soft-toned voice that I should look up the "Ripe Fruit Policy" when I got back to America. Then he stepped quietly away from me and said nothing more about this. We passed a few memorials here and there, as we made our way back to the car.

At San Juan Hill, there is a very large ceiba tree named El Arbol de la Paz, or The Tree of Peace. On July 17, 1898, underneath this very ceiba tree, Spain formally surrendered to the United States with an unconditional agreement, and the American flag was raised over Santiago de Cuba. Prior to this ceremony, tensions began to build between the US military and the Cubans. To the astonishment of the Cuban Mambi Army, these tensions culminated in the exclusion of Calixto Garcia and his troops from the ceremony that marked the end of the war. Additionally, no Cuban troops were allowed to enter Santiago. I was saddened to learn that US military officials enforced this exclusion. There were persistent rumors and immoral overtures that these altercations and exclusions were because Calixto Garcia's several thousand Mambi soldiers were black.

Around the time of its founding in 1514, and for many years after, Santiago was the main port of entry for African slaves brought to Cuba. These slaves came from many tribes and areas of Africa. There were the Kongo from Angola, the Lucumi from Southwestern Nigeria, the Arara from Dahomey in West Africa, and the Carbali and Abakua from Southeastern Nigeria. Also, smaller groups of slaves were sent to Cuba, which included the Mandinga and Malikes from Sierra Leone, the Macuas from Mozambique, and the Minas from the Gold Coast region.

The African slaves in Cuba were allowed to form associations known as *cabildos* (councils). Membership in a particular cabildo was based on the slave's African ethnicity. The cabildos provided a social network for the slaves and allowed them to maintain their African religions, traditions, and customs. Because of its history with the slave trade, Santiago is the Cuban city with the largest concentration of people of African descent. Quintessential Afro-Cuban culture is found in Santiago.

Over the years, Santiago became a mix of various groups of people. There were Spanish settlers from Jamaica, French plantation owners who fled Haiti after the slave revolt, Peninsulares who came directly from Spain, Criollos who were born in Cuba but were of Spanish descent, mulattos also known as *gentes de color* (people of color), who were a mixed-race people, and the black slaves from Africa.

The residents of Santiago today are the descendents of these various groups of people, and the resulting cultural mix has infused the city with its own unique culture. It is a rich culture, and its influence is felt throughout Cuba. Son, an original Cuban music, began in Santiago and is the precursor to today's popular salsa music. In Santiago, musicians are passionate and the arts thrive. French operas performed at theaters existed harmoniously with Afro-Cuban drumming and rumbas. The visual arts, literature, dance, and education all have a strong presence in Santiago. Although each area of Cuba has its own identity, it cannot be denied that a lot of the cultural influences from Santiago have spread to all ends of the island.

Driving back toward Santiago's city center, Jesús suggested we stop at the city cemetery to check out a few interesting things. This whole island seemed to be full of surprises, and I thought, *Why not?* We continued toward the Cementerio de Santa Ifigenia. The surrounding area became more industrial, the homes were smaller, and there were a few more horse carriages and bike rickshaws. I came up to a railroad track that stretched across the wide road, and Jesús began screaming out again to slow down and stop at the crossing. I caught it in time and thought to myself, *What the heck is it with these railroad crossings? They just seem to have it in for me! It's got to be a conspiracy I tell you! They're always popping out of nowhere at the weirdest times and places!*

Jesús saw a policia quietly off to the side watching. He blended into the landscape of people, but Jesús spotted him. I again looked straight ahead and just kept driving, acting like I knew what the hell I was doing.

We drove into the Cementerio de Santa Ifigenia. I could not help but notice a very large, tall hexagonal mausoleum to the left of the entrance to the visitor's center. This was the mausoleum and tomb of Cuban hero José Martí who lived from 1853 to 1895. The mausoleum featured a large tower that was intentionally built in the shape of a hexagon. Each one of the walls represents one of Cuba's former six provinces. The mausoleum sits on a large, elevated foundation. Each of the six sides had an archway at its base. There are two wide monumental stairways on opposite sides of the mausoleum.

At that moment, loud chimes sounded that could be heard everywhere. This was followed by music. Three honor guards in full military regalia appeared from the visitor's center carrying rifles with bayonets. The soldiers marched in a slow-motion goose step, swinging their arms in rhythm with each step. They marched past the eternal flame and toward José Martí's mausoleum. Steps lead underneath to the tomb, where other military honor guards stood in a complete motionless attention on either side of the entrance. The relieved honor guards made a calculated march out of the mausoleum. This elaborate procession to change the guards was every half hour.

Jesús turned quickly to me, "Don't stand over there when they're doing their thing," he said. "You cannot cross this area when they change guards."

I could see their big bayonets coming my way. "OK!" I said quickly. "Even better yet, with my luck. I think I'll stay way over here."

Once the changing of the guards finished, we were allowed to enter the mausoleum. We walked up the stairway and through one of the archways. Inside the mausoleum, we saw an open railing that encircled the area all the way around. From here, we looked down to the tomb below, where the military honor guards stood motionless at attention. A Cuban flag covered the tomb, which was graced with wreaths of flowers. Nearby stood a large, white polished marble statue of José Martí.

At the railing, I propped my right foot up on the stone coping on the bottom of the railing edge. Without any thought, Jesús slapped my leg down. That was the first time he ever did anything like that. But to him, this tomb is considered a deeply revered and hallowed place. I was not trying to be disrespectful. My bad knee was hurting, and I had set my foot there subconsciously to take weight off my knee. That's why I did it. I wasn't trying to be insensitive. "Oh, I'm sorry," I said when I put two and two together.

I was permitted to take pictures looking down on the tomb. We exited the mausoleum and continued walking through the cemetery toward a large, half-moon shaped, open-walled mausoleum standing about thirty feet tall with the words, "Martires Del 26 de Julio 1953," inscribed on it. This mausoleum memorialized those who died while fighting on the attack of the Moncada barracks in 1953 with Fidel Castro.

We walked further into the cemetery and saw the grave for Emilio Bacardi y Moreau, 1844 to 1922. His father, Facundo Bacardi, founded the famous Bacardi rum company in Santiago. Production of Bacardi rum began in Santiago in 1862. During the US Prohibition, Americans were invited by Bacardi to "Come to Cuba and bathe in Bacardi rum." Because of the 1959 revolution, the operations and trademarks of the Bacardi rum company were moved to Puerto Rico, where production has since continued.

The burial markers in this cemetery ranged from many, many monolithic structures to simple graves. The monolithic structures were in a neoclassical style, ornate and fascinating. They told the stories of people from a different time and place in history. It was like a last stand at immortality, showing what these people did long ago, their glories and their kingdoms here on earth. It was as if they were trying to extend their lives, grasping at it with these grand edifices. In reality, life continues to move, holding for no one. It was quite a contrast to the simple graves I saw further back in the cemetery for the meek and poor, the forgotten people, and those unknown by anyone but their God.

As I turned to walk on a different pathway, I was surprised to see a large rectangular marker embedded with a bronze guitar in the center. The marker stood about six feet tall. The neck of the guitar pointing upward, and a bronze hat was hung and resting over the top of the neck. Ninety-five bronze flowers that looked like tulips protruded out at a ninety-degree angle off the front face of the headstone surrounding the guitar and hat. The wording, "*Compay Segundo 1907 to 2003,*" of the Buena Vista Social Club was at the top of the marker. Beneath all the bronze flowers were the words, "*Las Flores de la Vida,*" or "The Flowers of Life."

As we were leaving, loud chimes sounded and music played, signaling the change of the honor guards. Being more alert this time, I was careful to stay out of the way, especially with those bayonets.

We continued our drive back to the casa, and since it was right there on the way, we made a quick stop at the Cuartel Moncada, the Batista's Moncada army barracks. Painted bright yellow with small decorative embattlements covering the horizontal cascading rooflines, the building had a strong horizontal massing, accentuated with many large and heavy vertical ornamental white pilasters. The whole facade was riddled with bullet holes, some big, some small. It was here on July 26, 1953, at six o'clock in the morning that Fidel Castro and his brother, Raul, led a group of approximately 120 rebels in an attack on this military garrison. The garrison held about 400 army personnel; Castro's group was severely outnumbered. The attack did not go as planned. A handful of rebels, including Castro, were caught, tried, and sent to the Prisidio Modelo. This isolated prison sits off from the mainland of Cuba on the Isla de la Juventud, or Island of Youth. The Isla de la Juventud is almost round in shape and encompasses about 930 square miles. After nearly two years in jail, Castro was freed as a political prisoner and exiled to Mexico. This attack became the underpinning of the Cuban revolution. After the revolution, this garrison and other Batista barracks across Cuba were turned into schools. To the revolutionaries, the Batista garrisons represented torture and death. Transforming these garrisons into schools utilized these buildings for a completely opposite purpose.

When we finished looking around the barracks, I was definitely tired from the long full day's activities. We drove back to our casa and parked the car across the street in the same spot on this narrow side street as before, in front of the house of the people I was paying to watch the car. Kids were running around having a good time playing and making do with the few things they had, things that really seemed to be of nothing at all. I was tired from carrying my big, heavy camera pack all day. Jesús went to take a shower, and I decided to go upstairs to the roof of the casa to sit down, have a beer, and just relax. I was feeling artistically drained and tired.

After his shower, Jesús showed up and sat down. We talked about what to do for dinner. He suggested a place not far away that served pizza and pasta. I left my camera pack in our room, and we walked up a small hill toward Santiago's famous square, Parque Céspedes. We reached the square, when out of nowhere this guy comes up to me and begins to tell me that he thinks I'm Osama bin Laden. I looked at this guy and could tell by the look on this guy's face that he was actually serious. Again, he adamantly said I was bin Laden, and he wasn't backing down. I know my face was unshaven for a few days and my hair was uncombed, thanks to my youngest son, but this must be the craziest thing I have ever heard.

I kept telling this guy, "No, I am not!"

After all the firm affirmations from this guy that I was bin Laden, Jesús, in typical comedic fashion, shot back, "No! He's not Osama bin Laden. He's Barack Obama!" The look on this guys face was worth it! I could not believe it.

He then said calmly, "Oh, OK!" For some strange reason, that seemed to satisfy him. He turned around and quietly walked off into the night. All we could do was shake our heads and laugh, as we continued on our way to dinner.

It was pretty interesting walking through the streets at night. A funeral was taking place. Jesús took a picture of it. I was not sure of the proper protocol, or what I should say, so I said, "Oh, man. I'm sorry to see this"

Jesús said, "Chris, there is nothing wrong with it." A lot of people were hanging around both inside the *funeraria* (mortuary) and in the streets outside the building. A few people were crying. Some people were just milling about. Most were in a state of quiet solace. I don't know who died, but I tried to show my respects as we walked by.

We turned onto a road that was just for pedestrians. This road had many different, interesting looking stores, open restaurants, and art galleries. Jesús found the place for pasta and pizza. We went inside and sat down at a table with a white tablecloth and candle. There were no tables left by the big open windows that faced out to the plaza of the pedestrian street, where the slight cooler air flowed in. Jesús and I had to sit a few tables back further inside the restaurant, away from the windows, where it was definitely warmer and felt a little like an oven in this typical tropical weather. I looked at the menu and had to have Jesús translate the pasta dishes for me. Although the dishes sounded interesting, I felt I couldn't go wrong with pizza. I had pizza with pork, shrimp, and chicken on it, and Jesús had just pork on his. I like our Americanized pizza better; this Cuban pizza was overly cheesy for my taste. It was extra thick and doughy. Maybe they did not have the right type of oven. But then again, it was not just at this restaurant that I noticed this. I noticed elsewhere on my trip that pizzas had three times the cheese and were very doughy, probably because meats are tougher to find and more cheese is used to compensate. I don't know. I decided to order a pasta appetizer along with another round of Bucanero.

After dinner, Jesús and I went back to the casa. I took a shower. We sat on our beds and talked about our plans for the next day. By now, I felt exhausted.

In the morning, I woke up pretty stiff. My shoulders were sore from carrying my heavy camera pack all day. As we came out of our room, I could smell breakfast and that wonderful Cuban espresso. Yeah, boy! After a few cups of that coffee, I didn't feel as sore anymore.

After breakfast, we packed up our things and got ready to hit the road. We were going to drive through Guantanamo and then to Baracoa. We paid our bill and said our formal good-byes to these nice people. *I really liked these people*, I thought. As we stepped outside to load up the car in preparation for leaving, the woman from the house across the street who was watching our car came over. She was happy and eager to be paid.

"No harm came to it!" she told Jesús in Spanish.

I looked at the car, pointed down to the tire, and said to Jesús, "You tell her one thing. If no harm came to my car, then how do you explain the damage done to my tire right here!"

Apparently, a stray dog came through and put his trademark on one of my tires. He nailed that tire good! The dog must have had a lot to spare in his bladder, because not only did it urinate on the tire, I could see the trail this dog made as it ran and flowed down the road like a river

When Jesús told her this, she looked mortified and didn't know what to say. I gave her a half smile and a wink. She started to laugh and was all smiles, as she went on her way to tell all her friends about it.

We drove off slowly, navigating ourselves through the narrow streets and merging with the morning traffic in Santiago. I wanted to make a stop at the Plaza de la Revolúcion, which is in the northeastern part of Santiago.

It sits high on a big, grassy knoll in the middle of many of the city's busy crossroads. I found a parking spot, and when I got out of the car, I was surprised that we had this place to ourselves. Jesús stayed by the car. I took off to look around, and nobody really bothered me. I did have one moment though when one of the guards at the monument walked up to me and wanted to know where I was from.

I paused for a second, then said, "Canada."

The guard nodded his head, "OK," and walked away. I could have said America, but then again, I didn't know how he would have reacted if I had told him America. I didn't want any trouble. I was just getting into my artist's mindset, and the last thing I wanted was another El Comandante moment like I had at the airport.

I continued walking around by myself, enjoying my time there. I was intrigued by what I had been hearing and all the history surrounding Antonio Maceo. At the Plaza de la Revolúcion, a monstrosity of a monument stood tribute to Maceo. The figure of Antonio Maceo sat high on a giant horse. Twenty-three massive iron machetes protruded, rising out of the ground. Some of the machetes were about one hundred feet high. Lined up in a long row, these massive machetes progressed from a horizontal to a vertical positions, symbolizing the consolidation of the Cuban nation. Each machete was larger than the one before it. They were impressive, and yet the way they jutted out of the ground was startling to my eyes. Having the appearance of a successive slicing motion one after the other, these machetes were almost lifelike, having fluidness about them.

These twenty-three machetes at the Plaza de la Revolúcion represent March 23, 1878. The Spanish had proposed a treaty known as the Zanjon Pact to end the Ten Year War. The Spaniards dictated the terms of the treaty, and as such, the treaty was more favorable to Spanish interests. Some of Antonio Maceo's peers were offered money to accept the terms of the treaty. Under these conditions, Maceo could not accept the Zanjon Pact. He strongly objected to the terms of the Zanjon Pact because he felt there were no concessions to free the slaves or to give Cuba its full and honest independence. To Maceo, signing this pact meant accepting defeat, when he did not feel defeated. Maceo fought in hundreds of battles with a machete in his hand. The machetes were used as working instruments until the beginning of the war, when they were used as weapons because of the lack of any other weaponry. On March 18, 1878, Maceo met with the Spanish under a cease-fire to discuss the terms of the treaty. This meeting is known as the Protesta de Baragua. Maceo was offered large sums of money to accept the Zanjon Pact to which he replied:

"Do you think that a man who is fighting for a principle and has a high regard for his honor and reputation can sell himself while there is still at least a chance of saving his principles by dying or trying to enforce them before he denigrates himself? Men like me fight only in the cause of liberty and will smash their guns rather than submit."

The cease-fire ended and Maceo resumed fighting on March 23, 1878. The significance of the twenty-three machetes is that, over the years, Maceo was proven to be correct in his firm stand against the Spanish, as the concessions in the Zanjon Pact never came to fruition.

I continued walking around this vast plaza. Off in the distance, I could see large Cuban flags and propaganda signs from the era of the 1959 revolution. In 1998, Pope John Paul II celebrated a mass here at the Plaza de la Revolúcion.

When I finished walking around the Plaza de la Revolúcion, we got back in the car and drove away. After a bit, I noticed a large stadium for

Santiago's professional baseball team, which was called Las Avispas, or The Wasps. These large baseball stadiums were a familiar sight throughout the different provinces in Cuba. Baseball is the national sport here. The first stadium was built in Havana in 1881. We stopped to take a look at the Avispas stadium. I was able to find a way to get part way inside and take pictures. *That was cool,* I thought.

We made our way out of town and drove through the Vista Alegre quarters again. Mile after mile, we drove on these wide streets past large homes. There were rows and rows of mansions. Although some of these upper-class neighborhoods were not holding up so well after all these years, they were still beautiful to look at. One can only imagine the heartache of the Cubans who abandoned these homes when exiling themselves to America during the revolution.

The scenery started to change rapidly as we drove on this rural highway road and got more into the country. Near an area called La Maya, there was a natural bypass in the road. Due to the poor condition of the main road, this bypass looked to be a good idea, and so we took it. The scenery on this detour was beautiful. Along the way, I took pictures of farming operations, banana plantations, and rolling hills with fields being plowed by oxen. I saw a baseball field for small children and stopped to take a picture of it. Again, Cubans walked by and gave me funny looks as if to say, "What is he taking a picture of an empty field?"

This area was beautiful. The morning mist was lightly lingering over the land. Large ceiba trees were completely covered with "air plants." These air plants were attached to the trunks and stretched all the way out to the furthermost tips of the trees' branches. We drove by a lake called Embalse La Yaya. It looked like it a good place to fish, although I did not know what fish might be in this lake. Cuba has thirty-six native species of true freshwater fish and eighteen other native species of catadromous or anadromous fish. Twenty-three species of fish have been introduced to Cuba, some of which are for recreational fishing, such as big mouth bass or the common carp. After we passed the lake, the terrain changed to high desert with a few pockets of tropical terrain remaining. I saw many horses, oxen, and sugarcane.

As we got closer to Guantanamo, I started to see an increasing number of large propaganda billboards along the road. One stated, "*Somos un pueblo de pelea y Victoria,*" or "We are victorious fighting people." Another proclaimed, "*Podran agredirnos pero ocuparnos jamas,*" or "They can attack us but they will never conquer us." To me, I took these as definite clues that we were now getting very close to the US Naval base, Gitmo. I stopped the car on the side of the road and stepped out to take a pictures of these

propaganda signs.

Out of nowhere, a Cuban military personnel in four-wheel drive jeeps drove out of the thick, brushy, vegetation and onto the road. They came from the direction of the US Naval base. I was given a few long stares while they were getting back on the main road. But that was it. They kept on driving.

Before we got to Guantanamo, Jesús told me, "Don't ask anything."

I had read about a Cuban man who works at the base. He is one of the last surviving Cubans who has worked there since the 1950s and supposedly still commutes there for work to this day.

I told Jesús, "Oh, it'd be great to get a picture of him."

Jesús cut me off, "No way! It would be interesting as you say, but you would draw way too much attention, and you would definitely draw a tail." Obviously, this was something I did not want.

We continued driving and finally reached Guantanamo. The city of Guantanamo was founded in 1797. However, Guantanamo Bay was discovered three centuries earlier, by Christopher Columbus, in 1494, during his second voyage to the Americas.

Upon arriving, the first thing we did was to look for a place to park our car near Parque Martí square. Guantanamo appeared to have a lot of things going on, yet it didn't feel intense like Santiago. On average, the buildings were one to two stories high, with a colonial architecture, arcades, and a few portico walkways. This city was nowhere near the size of Havana. Guantanamo appeared to be a sleepy town that does not get visited much by outsiders. It looked to me like people just passed through without staying and looking around. Although I will say, this area had the feeling of being on a tight lockdown.

As we walked down the streets of Guantanamo, a couple of guys made comments. They saw my large camera and were interested in it. They trailed us as we walked for several blocks, jockeying for the right moment to snatch my camera. Even Jesús sensed it, and he warned me to hold on more tightly to my camera. I did so, keeping the camera in front of me rather than carrying it in my one hand by my side.

Through the crowds of people, I saw a dark-skinned Cuban woman, about seventy-five years old, slowly weaving her way through the crowd of people as she walked toward us. She stood out, because on her head was a large, full, perfectly balanced burlap bag filled with things from the morning's street market. She balanced it on her head as she walked passed me. I turned back around to get a picture of her from behind as she walked. At the same time, right behind me, was one of the guys tailing me. He was about ready to make the move on me from behind to get my camera. I don't think he expected me to turn around like that, and for that matter, neither did I. It was just by chance that I got a photo opportunity with this old lady who walked by with a large bag on her head. I made eye contact with this guy, and his eyes grew big. He looked around as though he was looking at other things. The timing turned out to be good. The guy withdrew and disappeared, receding in the sea of people. However, he did get his few seconds of fame by chance, as he appeared in my picture, forever captured in the grains of my film together with this old lady walking with the burlap bag on her head.

We arrived in Guantanamo around noon and only stayed for two hours. We were heading to Baracoa, and I wanted ample time for the ride over the La Farola mountain pass, leading into Baracoa from the south.

When left the city of Guantanamo, the elevation increased, and we had better visibility of the US base. From this point on, the whole area was definitely locked down. I didn't see any skulls and crossbones around, but I got that feeling. Signs said, "No Pictures!" Propaganda billboards stated, "*Nuestro deber es vencer*," or "Our duty is to win."

After passing an area called Glorieta, we came upon a military checkpoint full of rows of razor wire gleaming in the bright, tropical sun and an entrenchment of large wooden hedgehog barricades. A fork in the road led to an existing Cuban military command post, Mirador los Malones, which is situated on high ground, about 350 yards up, for better observation of the US naval base. I heard that we might be able to go through this checkpoint and up the hill to look at the US base, but after my interrogation with El Comandante and the high-tension levels regarding the terrorist detainees at the base from the US war in the Middle East, we decided that it wasn't worth the risk.

Ironically, it was another war, the Spanish American War in 1898, and events occurring afterward, that led to the US presence at Guantanamo Bay. A joint resolution from Congress authorized the US to engage in the 1898 Spanish American War to intervene with Cuba's struggle for independence from Spain. This joint resolution included an amendment known as the Teller Amendment, which stipulated that the United States would not exercise or attempt control over Cuba upon the defeat of Spain. Cuba was to have its full independence with no strings attached. After being defeated, Spain left Cuba, and the United States continued to occupy the island. According to the terms of the Teller Amendment, the United States did not annex Cuba. In 1901, a Senate rider known as the Platt Amendment was attached to the Army Appropriations bill, which effectively overrode the Teller Amendment. The Platt Amendment established suzerainty between the United States and Cuba, with the United States acting as the suzerain. For the Cubans, their choice was to accept the Platt Amendment or have an indefinite US military occupation. Among the terms the Platt Amendment contained a provision that allowed the United States to lease Cuban territory. This ultimately led to the acquisition and establishment of the US naval base at Guantanamo Bay. This was consistent with the policies of then President Theodore Roosevelt. A self-proclaimed jingo, Roosevelt explained his view on the use of power when he wrote, "I did not usurp power, but I did greatly broaden the use of executive power."

In 1934, then President Franklin Delano Roosevelt, fifth cousin to Theodore Roosevelt, reaffirmed the original ninety-nine-year lease with a new treaty. The 1934 Treaty of Relations provided for annual lease payments of $4,085 and also stipulated that the lease would continue unless terminated by mutual agreement of both countries. Since both parties must agree to the termination of the lease, Franklin Roosevelt virtually ensured the indefinite permanency of the US Naval base.

After the 1959 revolution, Fidel Castro requested that the United States return Guantanamo Bay back to Cuba. The United States refused Castro's formal request. As an act of protest, Castro refuses to cash the rent checks and leaves them to pile up inside one of the top drawers of his desk.

We continued driving and passed by more sugarcane fields. Surrounding farms were burning off sugarcane in the fields. Other farmers loaded the sugarcane onto trucks for delivery to the mills. We headed toward an area called Playa Jateritas, located about twenty-eight miles east of Guantanamo. After a certain point, a sign in the road stated that it was now "OK" to take pictures. Driving beyond this area reminded me of driving on the Pacific Coast Highway in California, particularly of the Big Sur area, except instead of driving more atop the cliffs we drove down at the level of the ocean. This is where the Atlantic Ocean meets the Caribbean Sea. The water here was of a very deep, deep rich blue. My God, the colors in the water mixed with the white caps of the waves looked unbelievable. I got beautiful pictures of the arid shoreline and the water crashing onto the rocky coral.

We finally started our climb over the steep mountains to Baracoa. That crawl was intense at times. This was the area that Chiqui warned us about, where tour buses rip around the corners. Until the 1960s, vehicles could not pass the La Farola mountain range. In some areas, the road is literally carved into the mountainside and clings to the edges of the cliffs. Hairpin turns. I put it in second gear and putted along. We were in no hurry. I took in the beauty of it all.

In 1791, French refugees from Haiti fled to Cuba after the Haitian slave rebellion. These French refugees knew how to work the steep mountain

terrains in La Farola. They tamed these mountains and used other slaves to continue their farming operations, showing their great skill in growing coffee.

The area of the La Farola mountains reminded me of Las Terrazas in the province of Pinar del Rio. During my previous trip to Cuba, I saw the Cafetal Buenavista coffee plantation in Las Terrazas, an area with fifty-four other plantations. The Cafetal Buenavista coffee plantation was up high in the mountains at an elevation of about 790 feet. French refugees from Haiti built it in 1802. About 126 slaves worked there. I was able to look down on some of the old slave quarters. The roofs of the slave quarters are now gone, but the thick stone walls remained. The cells were six feet by eight feet and connected in a row. Plantation owners packed six people in each cell and locked them up for the night. Uphill from the slave quarters, I saw three very large, round, flat areas for drying coffee. At the top of the hill was the old grinding stone, known as *tajona*. The grinding stone was huge, and was used to break the coffee beans from their shells. Human power provided by the slaves pushed the wheel around in complete rotations.

Each year in February, the La Farola mountain range is the first stage of the "Vuelta Ciclista Cuba," or "Tour of Cuba." It is similar to the Tour de France and dates back to 1964. About six different species of bright, multi-colored, striped snails called Polymitas are found in this mountainous area. Their brilliant colors make them almost look fake.

When I made a stop on the side of this mountain pass to take pictures of the view looking out from the road, jinetero hustlers suddenly came up to us holding long multiple strands of Polymita snail shells.

"Don't buy them," Jesús said. Even though I wasn't going to buy the snails anyway, I could tell this is something Jesús felt very strongly about. He informed me that these snails are becoming endangered because people buy them from the jineteros. Despite my refusals, these hustlers were relentless, worse than a stereotypical used car salesmen.

After a while, the air grew cool and the road finally leveled to a plateau. The steep Sierra del Purial peaks reach almost 4,000 feet above the ocean. The residents had been isolated until this road was created. In fact, before that pass was made, the only way to reach Baracoa was by boat. When we finally reached the top of the mountain and dropped down into Baracoa, we could see the gorgeous Bahia de Miel.

Right when we got to town—WHAM! We got a flat tire. We pushed the car to the side of a guy's house. Although a fence encircled his house, he opened a gate for us. Sure enough, he worked on flats. Talk about timing. Fixing flats is big business in Cuba. With the road conditions being what they are, bikes and cars both get flats all the time. Still, that was some luck, and the guy was welcoming. The nice gentleman had a big pan of water. He submerged the tire and found a small puncture. He then pulled out a repair kit and told us it was hard for him to get this kit. The repair kit was the kind that uses a piece of rubber plug, which is pushed into the hole in the tire using a tool similar to a screwdriver. He twisted the tool and pulled it out, and the plug stayed in the tire. His was the only repair kit like this that I saw in Cuba. The gentleman felt proud to have it. He charged us five CUCs to fix the flat, and the patch held. I took a picture of the guy sitting with the tire and of people coming and going. Life just keeps moving, and we had to get over the Rio Miel. We drove slowly over a long, low bridge at the river where women did their laundry in the water.

We continued driving through the town of Baracoa. Jesús looked through one of our travel books to find a place where we could stay for the night. He called around on his cell phone. A lot of the places were full. After some time, Jesús found a casa. The guy he was talking to was a *maricon*. As I did not understand, he said, a *"cherna,"* which is a fish, a *"pato,"* which is duck, and a *"pajaro,"* or sly fellow. Seeing the confused look on my face, he then said very slowly in English, "The. Guy. Is. Gay."

"What?" I said, "How do you know?"

"Oh, I know!" Jesús said. After a long pause of silence, he turned his head slowly back at me and said, "You have no problems staying at a house where the owner's gay, right?"

I didn't have a problem, as I was not concerned. "It's fine with me. Besides, I think they know how to cook great!"

Jesús told me he liked the place because the description in the book indicated a balcony terrace looking out toward the ocean. After making our way around the one-way streets, we finally found the casa and parked our small tin-can car across the narrow street. The owner greeted us at the large front veranda of this attractive, old, wooden colonial house. We unloaded our things, entered the casa, and were shown to our room. The room had bright, fuzzy, pinkish curtains, very silky, bright red bedspreads, and was adorned with large vases of colorful, iridescent peacock feathers. It had the appearance of a Las Vegas honeymoon suite with a little bit of Elvis mixed in there somewhere. After spending a bit of time gazing about our room, our conversation turned to deciding who got what bed in this honeymoon suite.

I turned to Jesús with a half-grin starting to form on my face. As we were unpacking our things, I pointed my finger at him and said facetiously, "Hey! Now don't you be getting any funny ideas tonight!"

5

1511

AFTER WE GOT settled into our colorful honeymoon suite, Jesús and I decided to take a short walk around town before dinner. Before we left for our walk, the owners of the casa asked us when we wanted to eat and gave us a rundown on our menu options for dinner. Since Baracoa has been very isolated throughout its history, the area has retained many of its indigenous, pre-Columbian recipes. Whereas Santiago cooking is known for its red sauce, many entrees in Baracoa are cooked in coconut milk.

After finalizing our dinner arrangements, we set out for a walk around the beachfront. Many people walked about. Waves crashed over the rocks on the coral reef, and white ocean foam rolled up on the dark, sandy areas of the beach. A three-story home stood out from the other homes around it. This home was built in 1867. It once belonged to a Russian Princess, Magdalena Rowenskaya, who fled her country during the second Russian Revolution in 1917. Magdalena Rowenskaya converted the home into a hotel, the Hotel La Rusa, where she also had a restaurant and gave singing lessons. It is said that Errol Flynn stayed here. Years later, Magdalena Rowenskaya became involved with Cuba's revolutionary movement. Castro and Ché were known to occasionally stop over at her hotel when they were passing through the area.

As we walked further down the beachfront, we saw a large stadium built right up to the sand on the beach. It was definitely in need of renovation. An old Russian Lada car sat beneath the stadium sign, which read, "Estadio Manuel Fuentes Borges." The car had no tires, no engine, no interior, and no doors. I liked the composition of the car, isolated, rusting away there, and thought it made for an interesting picture. There were kids running around this area, most with no shoes. Some of them played baseball with a stick in a flat open area made of concrete.

My pack started to get heavy about the time we decided to loop back around to our casa. It was getting close to our appointed dinnertime, and I wanted to get the camera pack off my back. Just as we made our way back, we saw a place where we could access e-mail. I wanted to send an e-mail off to my family to see if I might have an e-mail from them. We decided we would take a short walk back this way after dinner.

Upon entering the casa, we saw that the table was set for dinner, so we washed up. We sat down at the table and dinner was brought out. First came Jesús's meal of pork cooked in coconut milk. I tried a sample of it and could not believe how good it tasted. Next came my plate of Dorado and shrimp, both freshly caught from the bay and cooked in coconut milk. As a treat, our hosts added a couple of freshwater shrimp from the river to my plate. They were cooked whole, including the shell, and were a good size laid out nicely on top of the plate, which made for a very nice presentation. Then she brought out tostones, black beans, rice, fresh cut papaya, and pineapple. Boy, that was a good meal! We had a round of Bucaneros. And then I did something crazy. I walked myself into something by not thinking about what I said. I asked the old lady who had prepared the food if I could take her home with me. When I saw the look on her face, I realized what I had just said. I meant to say, "You're such a great cook. Can I take you home to cook for me?" I didn't mean to imply that I wanted to take her and have her run off with me to America. Jesús had a shocked look on his face like, "*What the . . . !?*" He almost spat his beer out of his mouth as he took a drink. Then he realized what I had meant to say, and so he explained my gaffe in Spanish. She turned red and giggled like a young girl.

After dinner, we went out for an evening walk. I also wanted to check for e-mails from my family. I was feeling more relaxed than ever. While walking, we visited a few art galleries. Local artists were inside working on their paintings. There was a lot of finished work hanging on the walls. I thought some of this art was very impressive, and there were original styles of art. There were even musicians, *trovadores*, outside playing in the moonlit

portico walkways, which featured Doric columns. These trovadores played soothing and authentic Cuban music. It was quite pleasant. We then made our way to the place that had e-mail access, and I did in fact have an e-mail from home. I eagerly sent my family a reply, letting them know that I might get e-mail access again when we got to Trinidad in about four or five days. After checking e-mail, we returned to the casa.

We ended the day by replaying the Dunham recordings, watching in the confines of our small room and laughing incessantly before going to asleep.

Around five o'clock in the morning, I was slowly awoken by the constant sounds of loud, gaggling chatter. But this time, I knew what it was: chickens! Something we didn't realize the night before became very obvious to us during the night—everything cooked in coconut milk gave us gas. By morning, when it was time to roll out of bed, the room had been getting a pretty good fumigation. Fortunately, I could smell something better beyond this colorful honeymoon suite. It was that beautiful Cuban espresso. It was there waiting for me at the table along with the morning's fresh baked bread and cut up vegetables mixed with fresh scrambled eggs from the early rising, boisterous chickens.

After getting ready for our day of walking around, I went up to the top floor of the three-story casa to take in all the morning sounds and the view of the city from that vantage point. I got a few pictures of the morning view overlooking the city and a few shots of everyday life over the roofs of the other homes.

Once we were on our way, I saw that life was bustling. Many people rode Russian and Chinese made bikes. Occasionally I would see an old American one go by while several people rode sidesaddle over the bike frame bar off to who knows where. One guy pedaling down the road passed me with one arm on the handlebars and the other holding his arm out like a waiter, carrying a freshly decorated cake. The cake sat on an open plate, nothing more. I thought to myself, *Boy, I hope he doesn't hit a rock or a pothole because someone sure will be wearing that cake.* All the morning activity was interesting. Life moved at a different pace here compared to other cities. I'm sure it had to do with being on the furthermost eastern part of the island and with its long history of isolation. Baracoa was isolated from the rest of Cuba for centuries until the mid-1960s when a road was built. Before that, Baracoa could only be reached by boat.

Christopher Columbus discovered Baracoa on November 27, 1492, on his first voyage. Prior to discovering Baracoa, Columbus set foot on Cuban soil over by Gibara, which I planned on visiting later. Although Columbus

discovered Baracoa in 1492, the city was not established until August 15, 1511. The permanent settlement of the city of Baracoa marks one of the first cities established in the Americas—over one hundred years before the arrival of the Mayflower in Plymouth, Massachusetts.

As we walked through this city, I was struck by the architecture of the wooden colonial homes, the pastel colors, the red tile roofs and the multi-color, stucco walls, faded and worn with the age of several centuries. And the doors. My gosh, the colors of the doors were beautifully aged with time and history.

We continued walking through the neighborhoods, and I saw small mom-and-pop butcher shops on street corners. These wooden shacks measured about five feet by five feet with an open window-counter in the front. Hanging from little meat hooks inside the shack were pigs' heads and hind quarters with their curly tails still left on. Very aged and weathered old-fashioned scales with small rusted interchangeable weights sat on the counters. One even had a handwritten sign that read, "Punto de Carrneane," or "Meat Spot." A common theme around these butcher shops was the stray dogs hanging close by waiting and hoping for a handout.

The road came to a fork as it worked around the bay. We went one way, to what looked like a little industrial area. I began to notice a heavy smell filled the air. It was familiar to me from the years I spent working with people in the construction field—like the smell of galvanized steel after being cut or ground.

Not far past this area, Jesús pointed out the second terrace on somebody's house. On the terrace, I could see worn-out tractor tires that had been cut in half down the middle of the tread, creating two round rings from each tire. These old tires were four- or five-feet round. The resourceful Cuban people had cut tire rings, laid them down on their sides, filled them with dirt, and planted them for a garden. These four big half-cut tractor tires filled their patio terrace. Nothing goes to waste. They had grapes growing over trellises, which helped create natural shade.

That's when I got hit up by an odd guy. As I was taking a picture, he tried to ingratiate himself into my conversation with Jesús. He wanted my camera. "Let me hold it," he asked. I looked at him and said, "Yeah, right, sure. And I'm sure that will be the last time I'll ever see you again." This guy followed us for what seemed to be miles. Since he wouldn't back off, Jesús was ready to take a picture of him and walk up to him to say, "See, I got your picture. I'm going to let a policeman know that I have it." Jesús turned to me and said, "He'll run once he hears that." Before Jesús took his picture, he took off on his own.

We continued walking down through an alley area toward the dark, sandy shore. A small, makeshift marina opened up to a bay with fishing boats. People had pulled their boats onto the sandy shore to work on them. A man pounded a few eroded, intricate wood planks out of one of the small boats and attempted to insert the new individual planks back in.

As I turned around to look at something, I noticed that same guy following me again. When he saw me turn around, he got this look on his face like having been caught red-handed. With nothing to hide behind, stuttering a bit in his body movements, he abruptly turned and squatted down. He put his hands in this dirty, dirty sewage water and pretended that he was innocently washing his hands. The whole time he tried to nonchalantly blend in any way he could. He obviously looked like he wished he could disappear, though he kept rinsing his hands in that foul water. Jesús could not believe it. No one except this "knot head" would stick his or her hands in that sewage water. I had to laugh. This guy was trying so hard to be so inconspicuous, but he wound up drawing more attention to himself.

The area around the bay, Bahia la Baracoa, was idyllic. Coconut palms grew right up to the water's edge, and fishermen's small boats were pulled up underneath. Colorful clothes hung drying on clotheslines strung from palm tree to palm tree over the sand. At the mouth of the bay, we saw a large ship that was partway sunk and rusting away from the crashing waves. I took a few pictures of the ship looking like it had been there for a long time, and Jesús commented that he was blown away that it didn't get pushed around from hurricane Ike, which had slammed through here not too long ago.

As we made our way back around this shoreline and toward the mouth of the bay, we looked back to see the many surrounding mountains. One mountain in particular stood out. This mountain, known as El Yunque, or The Anvil, is the odd shaped mountain that originally attracted Columbus to this bay and which Columbus described in his ship's journal in 1492. The slopes of El Yunque were completely covered from top to bottom with dense, verdure jungles that thrive in this climate. El Yunque stands 1,885 feet high. The top of this mountain is flat like a table.

Because of adverse weather conditions, Columbus could not sail off and stayed anchored in the protection of the Bahia la Baracoa longer than he expected. He planted a cross at the bay's entrance and noted the following in his ship's journal:

Saturday, 1st of December 1492.

"Today I was prevented from being able to set sail again, anchored from with inside this safe harbour. Due to the continued adverse head winds from the east contrary to my plans of course and because of heavy rains I did not depart. I decided to set up a great cross at the entrance bank of this port on an out cropping of some bare rocks on the south-eastern side."

Columbus' adventures included other unforeseen layovers and delays, which prolonged his return to Spain. Because of these delays, he and his crew unwittingly became the first people to celebrate Christmas in the new Americas. Columbus constructed and erected twenty-nine crosses in the Americas. The cross in Bahia la Baracoa became one of the only crosses ever found, made of *Coccoloba diversifoia*, a native hardwood of the sea grape family that grows abundantly in Baracoa. Hence, the cross is named Cruz de la Parra, or Cross of the Vine. Parra, meaning "vine," reflects the type of wood from which it was constructed. Safeguarded since 1510, it sits in one of Baracoa's sixteenth century churches, Catedral de Nuestra Senora de la Asuncion, which I hoped to see on our walk back toward town.

As we made our way back, we came upon a building with a bakery in it. From the outside, it looked nothing like a bakery. A boy on a bike pulled up to the back door and started loading stacks of the morning's freshly baked Cuban Creole bread. The breads were in big, flat, square pans and were still slightly connected by their edges. They were stacked on trays about ten high and placed in a makeshift box on the back of this boy's bike. The whole thing was framed oddly over the bike tire, looking like as if it would flip the front wheel of the bike right up off the ground while the boy rode.

The owner of the bakery appeared to be really angry this morning. Things weren't moving as fast as he'd liked, and he was yelling at this boy. I thought the composition of trying to stack the buns on the back of the bike in this oversized square box was interesting. Through the open door, I could see stacks of bread on trays inside the bakery. The bakery owner had on a full apron, a white baker's hat, and flour all over his face. I got ready to take a picture. He took one look at me with my camera and started to wave his hands. He flapped his arms in the air and shouted in broken English, "No picture! No picture!"

I wish I had snapped that shot anyway because it was a moment I really wanted to capture. Jesús seemed to think that this visual street scene was intensely funny; he laughed and made comedic Jeff Dunham one-liners.

We continued walking and looking at the movement of life and the history of the area. There were horse carts and old cars going slowly by on the narrow streets. There were many colorful and old colonial wooden homes mixed with lush, green, jungle vegetation.

As we walked through the streets, I periodically noticed emblems above or to the side of some of the doors. They were Masonic symbols, and I remembered seeing some of the same relic symbols in Havana and a few other cities. They looked like they were from a different time period, but nonetheless, left tacked on these homes in a state of long forgotten awareness.

I also noticed different types of door knockers. They were mostly very small, and a lot of them had featured a hand or fist type configuration. Walking down an out-of-the-way side street, one in particular caught my attention. I saw a brass door knocker with elaborate detail engraved with the words, "*Recuerda El Aldabonazo.*" I asked Jesús what it meant. He gave me a quizzical look as he tried to explain the phrase to me. It turned out that the phrase has double meanings. Literally it meant, "Remember the knocking." Jesús told me that, remembering the loud knocking at the door, and the action of knocking, was to raise awareness and awaken consciousness for the need to keep fighting.

We came up to the Plaza Independencia, the city's town square—a small triangular-shaped city square with trees and park benches. School kids were taking a break for lunch and hanging around. They had differently colored school uniforms depending upon what grade the students were in. A few old-timers were playing chess. I could hear the faint sounds of the ocean waves in the background. At the far end of this square was the Catedral de Nuestra Senora de la Ascuncion. This church was built in 1512 and houses the Cruz de la Para, the cross that Columbus made and planted in the entrance to Baracoa's bay.

Unfortunately, when we got there, the church was closed. This church is old, and Hurricane Ike hit this area pretty hard. The windows were boarded up with plywood. In fact, from the outside, the church had the appearance of a condemned building.

"What's going on here?" I said to Jesús, "Why can't we get in there." I really wanted to see the cross.

I began to think that maybe we were just too early. As it turned out, we couldn't visit the church because it was boarded up due to damage, probably from the many hurricanes. We were now not sure what to do.

Nearby, in the square, we saw taxi drivers sitting on a park bench under a tree next to their old American cars. One of the taxi guys knew a little bit of English, and he could tell that I was upset about something. He perked up and started talking to Jesús. Jesús told him that I wanted to get in the church. That's when he responded by saying, "Hey, I've got a friend. Follow me." My first thought was, *yeah, everybody's got a friend.*

We followed him to a back door at the side of the church. The taxi guy started pounding and pounding on the door. I could hear the faint sound of someone inside. The man inside came to a little cracked opening a couple of inches wide in one of the corners of the plywood, just big enough for a finger or two. I could see our guy trying to say something to his friend inside along the lines of, "Hey, somebody would like to come inside and take a look at that cross."

The man inside came to the side door. It took him a while to open the locked and barricaded door. To my surprise, he let us in. I gave the taxi guy a couple CUCs as a thank you, and he went back to the park bench that he was sitting on in the square. Jesús and I continued on inside the church.

The gentleman was the only person in there. He was a caretaker for the church; even so, the inside looked like it was going to fall apart. I saw wood-pole scaffolding, little pieces of small, round tree limbs, hand lashed together. This scaffolding was used to steady the walls from the floor all the way up to the open cathedral ceiling. There weren't very many pews. Some were pushed to the side. A few were stacked on top of each other. The flooring was hit and miss. I saw little piles of rubble swept in certain corners.

The cross was in a glass case at the front of the sanctuary, to the left. It was a good four feet by three feet. While Jesús spoke with the caretaker in the middle of the church floor area, I moved forward to take pictures. I took my time and finally decided to ask Jesús a question that I thought was a total long shot, "Is there any way to ask this man if he can open the case? The glare on the glass from my flash is just . . . it's not working."

I figured no way. This isn't going to happen. But Jesús asked the gentleman, and he said, "Oh sure!" with out any hesitation.

He took out an antique key from his pocket, opened up the case, swung the door all the way open, and gestured with his hand, as if to say to me, "Here you go."

I could not believe I was given such uninhibited access. I was able to get many pictures. At one point, I even got one with my macro lens. I got within inches, capturing detail of the rough wood grains and the brass work, which I'm sure was added later sometime over the centuries. Then with my wide-angle lens, I took all kinds of other shots.

The reality of it all hit me when I was standing just a few feet away. This cross is so old. It is a part of history since it is one of the oldest religious symbols of Christianity in the Americas. Anything in the United States with this type of historical significance would be locked up in a museum. Theoretically, I could have stolen it. (I don't think I could have gotten it off the island though.) The caretaker told us that during the hurricane season, the cross is taken to a more secure building since the church might fall apart. Even in the church, it's not really being showcased. It is definitely not commercialized. It's just raw reality right there, and I got to have it all to myself. Wow. That was nice. I mean it was just like, Wow. It was a nice moment in time—history held still right there.

As I shot more pictures, I was thinking that I was so close to the cross that I could actually touch it. During this time, Jesús was talking with the caretaker at the other end of the church, and I had my back to them. Jesús did not know the thoughts that were going through my mind, but coincidentally, just as I realized how close I was to the cross, Jesús called out, "Oh, it is said people touch it for good luck. It brings good luck."

I slowly reached my hand forward to touch it. But then I stopped. *No!* I thought, *there is no way I will touch it.*

Even though he said I could touch it, I wanted to respect this historical object. Moreover, I personally felt that my fate does not rest in an inanimate object. This object, or any other for that matter, is not going to make my life any happier, richer, more famous, or whatever. Happiness and fulfillment in life comes from my simple trust in God. So I pulled my hand back. Right after I made this conscious decision, Jesús said out loud, "But! It has also been said people have touched it, and a lot of bad things have happened to those people." Aha! So it was a good thing I didn't touch the cross! I chuckled to myself.

According to Jesús, over the centuries, people have taken little pieces and splinters off the four ends of the cross for good luck charms, or worshippers kept pieces as relics. This is why the cross had pieces of metal wrapped around the four end tips. Jesús also said that carbon dating and other testing confirmed the age of the cross and the type of wood used to make it. I thanked the gentleman respectfully and shook his hand. He pulled his old-time key back out of his pocket, closed the case, and locked the case back up. We went on our way. I was truly in heaven.

Later, Jesús told me that he spent time chatting with the caretaker, who said he was really happy we came. The caretaker mentioned that people come but don't give a crap about him as a person. They were more of the Me! Me! Me! type of people. The caretaker told Jesús he felt happy, and that is why he opened the case up for me.

As we left, we walked by one of the three forts that the Spanish began building in 1739. Although these outposts in Baracoa are not as large and magnificent as the ones in Havana and Santiago, they are still very interesting. We stopped at the largest of the three forts, El Castillo de Seboruco, which has since been turned into a hotel. El Castillo de Seboruco sits on top of a hill and provides a commanding view of the city.

The hillside has stairs from the bottom all the way to the top, which Jesús and I climbed. From the top of the hill, I was able to get pictures of the city and the bay. I could see the sailors' maritime landmark, the flat-top mountain, El Yunque, or the Anvil, clearly standing out from the other mountains. After a while, we went back down the stairway on the hill and back to the casa to rest up for a little bit.

When we arrived back at the casa, there was fresh fruit on the table for a snack. The living room in our section of the casa was one of the larger living rooms in the house. I noticed a large, Paris *Match* magazine framed and proudly displayed. On the front cover, I saw a photograph of a woman and the name "Lucy." Lucy is the mother of the man running the casa. Looking back, I wish that I had found out the year the magazine was published.

Our hosts asked us what we would like to have for dinner and what time we would like to eat. Strangely off topic, they also asked for permission to use our living room to watch television. I didn't think much of it until I saw other family member's faces peering around the corner and through the other open doors. They were like little puppy dog eyes looking at us. Cuba has two national television channels, and it was apparently time for *Telenovela!*, Cuba's soap operas.

Jesús and I left them huddled around the small television set while we took another short walk toward the center of town. We walked back through one of the old neighborhoods with its wooden colonial homes and time-faded colored doors. Up the narrow street, I saw kids with their uniforms and packs walking home from school. Off to the side was an old, sun-bleached, colonial home. The centuries had worn into the accentuated wood grains. There was a political slogan painted in faded white paint on the foundation of the old house that proclaimed, "*Libertad Para Los 5 Heroes De La Patria Volveran.*" I was witnessing three levels of Cuba's evolving history—a many centuries-old colonial building, evidence of the twentieth century struggle for independence, and a new generation moving toward the future. We found the Internet place, and I was happy because I received a nice e-mail from my wife and family.

When we got back to the casa, dinner was about ready. Jesús had shrimp and I had lobster. Both dishes were cooked in coconut milk using the pre-Columbian recipes for which this area is known. We ate white rice, black beans, a salad of thinly cut tomatoes and cucumbers, red plantains, Cuban Creole bread, which was probably purchased from that infuriated and uptight baker I saw from this morning, and of course, Bucanero beer. What a feast to remember.

After dinner, Jesús and I discussed the next destination in our travels.

We looked at our maps and decided to turn back in a westward direction. Jesús mentioned a place he vaguely knew about called Saetia, which is an island where all kinds of African game animals ran wild. At one time, it had been a place where only high communist officials could hunt. I said, "Hey! That sounds like a very interesting place." And so it was settled, that Saetia would be our next destination, and we would head out for it tomorrow.

Jesús brought up the possibility of going to Biran after leaving Saetia, as we would be continuing back in the westerly direction. Fidel Castro was born and grew up in the small village of Biran. Jesús thought it might be a good idea to take me to Castro's house since we would be passing so close to it. I wasn't sure about going because of the interrogation I got from El Comandante. Of course, Jesús was concerned about my going there with my big camera.

I said, "Well, isn't it just a childhood home as you said?"

Jesús looked at me. "Chris, it's like the White House in your country. They've got military security all around there." I realized the gravity and suggested we still had time to mull it over some more.

We each took showers and retreated back to our room, the Las Vegas honeymoon suite with the silky, bright red beds and the red and fuzzy pink window drapes. And, no! We still hadn't found Elvis. Although putting black market Jeff Dunham on the television did just fine for us before we went to sleep.

In the morning, we got up, had breakfast, packed our things, paid our bill, and slowly made our way out. As we loaded the car, I noticed one of the tires that we had problems with before seemed to be low on air. We drove back to the place where we had our flat tire repaired when we first came into town. Our tire repairman checked it and checked it.

"Ahhh, I can't seem to find a hole," he finally said. But he did put extra air in the tire, and we went on our way.

About two and a half miles northwest of town, we stopped to look at a large chocolate factory amongst the many coconut palm trees. In front of the building, a big sign with Ché's picture read, "Fabrica de chocolate inaugurada por el Ché el 1st De Abril de 1963."

After the revolution, on February 23, 1961, Ché Guevara became the minister of industry. During his tenure, Ché inaugurated this factory on April 1, 1963, and chocolate production began at this factory due to the large amounts of cocoa tree plantations in this area that fueled production.

We drove past the chocolate factory. The dirt road was getting rough with potholes. We took in the breathtaking view of the completely natural state of the surrounding area. Grass shack huts known as bohios were nestled in the jungle. Their roofs were made of very thick layers of palm branches laid on top of each other with the sides sheathed in a plank-like form made from the bark of palm trees. A mother pig walked on the side of the road with eight piglets following behind her. I listened to her snorts. Then I looked down below and saw a woman washing her clothes in a small stream. She didn't see me take her picture, as she was all caught up, embraced in her solitude.

We continued driving and came to a beachhead near the area of Duaba. A monument marked the exact spot where Antonio Maceo returned to Cuba on April 1, 1895, following his prolonged exile in Costa Rica, where he had been since the end of the Ten Year War in 1878. Many attempts were made on his life during this time. The second war of independence against the Spanish began on February 24, 1895, and Maceo, after much coaxing by José Martí, returned to Cuba to help in the fight for Cuba's complete independence. Only after concessions were made to ensure that there would not be a repeat of something like the Zanjon Pact did Maceo come out of exile and return to Cuba.

The tropical and diverse stretch past Baracoa is where the largest and most remote rainforest in Cuba is located. As we were driving, Jesús heard something and screamed for me to pull over immediately. We heard it again, coming from the big Cuban Royal Palm trees, which were at least seventy feet tall. It was the sound of the Cuban parrots, *Amazona leucocephala*. I could see them too, but I couldn't get a tight picture. Jesús was very excited because it is very rare to see these parrots. They were once found all over Cuba, but now they are only found in small pockets of isolated, wooded areas and here in the Cuchillas del Toa biosphere reserve. Jesús told me that these birds are endemic to Cuba. It was good to see them, as they are becoming even more vulnerable. We walked off the side of this remote dirt road and stood in this lively jungle amid the numerous and different native flowering plants and fern species. We took it all in silently, listening and watching. This place has been isolated and has not changed since the beginning of time. There were no other sounds—no cars, no planes, no people. The birds flew to and fro, freely interacting, and loudly vocalizing with each other. We were existing as one with nature and time—the sounds, the sights, the birds. These birds were hidden and isolated from everything else in the world. Progress continues in the outside world. But to those birds, there is no other world that exists but here. This is all they have ever known. They have lived on this island for centuries in a state of timelessness, as the rest of the world moved on.

The Ivory-billed woodpecker was last seen in 1986 and 1987. Since then, some people claim to hear that distinct "double tapping" sound through some of these dense forests.

I made an off the cuff comment, "That would be kind of wild if I could get a picture of one."

Jesús looked at me and said, "You and a zillion other people want to be the first. You don't want to be that famous. Besides, this is such a desolate area all through here. Most likely there are secret military sites around here."

That's not the kind of trouble I wanted. I didn't want to go tromping through with my camera and American passport and stumble upon a military site. That's the last thing I wanted. I don't think I want to be that famous. "OK, scratch that idea," I said. "Let's just stay on the dirt road and keep going."

I continued to see more of the grass and palm shack bohio homes that dotted the areas. A lot of them were just boards cut from palm bark along with palm fronds laid and stacked tightly on top for the roof. Jesús told me that roofs made from the fronds of the Royal Palm lasted about nine years while roofs made from the fronds of the Palma Cana, which were normally seen in all the touristy areas, last about fifteen years.

"It depends on the moon," he said.

"What do you mean by the moon?" I asked him.

To which he replied, "I don't remember very well, but the farmers know by the phase of the moon when to cut the fronds to make them last longer."

I thought about the modernized world back home. These people had no streetlights, no cars, nothing. Yet they seemed to be happy, existing as one with their surroundings for the daily necessities of life. To them, time did not exist on a watch. Time existed around, was based on, and was marked by, the environment, darkness, sunlight, and the seasons.

As we continued across these disintegrated dirt roads and through dense jungle forest, I was surprised to learn about all the many native plants and animals in this area.

Suddenly, I began seeing military vehicles, which was really weird. At one turn in the rocky dirt road there was a turnout, and I saw a large Cuban military truck with a small radar device spinning around on top of the cab. I looked closer and noticed they had made a clothesline with rope and a makeshift A-frame tent with blankets. They had hung out laundry to dry in the sun. This led me to believe that they had been stationed there for a while.

As we traveled farther down this rough road, things seemed odd. I don't know how to explain it. Another twenty minutes later, we came around a blind bend in the road to find a makeshift military checkpoint right in the middle of nowhere. The soldiers had AK-47s strapped over their shoulders. Jesús thought it did seem a bit heavy-duty. We were stopped, and they ordered us both out of the car. They wanted to see everything. I started to feel a little uneasy and unsure of what was going on here. They told us to step away from our car. At that moment, I heard a small hand-sized motor start up, and they sprayed our car with so much white smoke that for a while we could not see the car. Jesús thought it was odd. The soldiers said it was for mosquitoes. After the smoke cleared, we were free to go.

From here, we filtered away from the dense tropical area and the terrain again changed, resembling a forest highland. Skinny, straight Cuban pine trees, *Pinus cubensis*, grew in abundance. Columbus noted that one of the ship's cabin boys spotted this endemic pinewood forest while they were sailing offshore. Columbus wrote in his journal that this forest would provide an endless supply of wood for future planking.

We came closer to Moa, an area of big industrial nickel mines— extensive excavation and open-pit mining for the large nickel deposits in the dense, bright red dirt. Thick plumes of orange-yellow smoke spat out from the silos. Water drew off some of the open stripped areas, which made for small runoff creeks that led out to the ocean. Workers drove large, heavy equipment. Everything was covered with the bright red dust. The red dust covered the windows and sides of the trucks.

Once past Moa, we turned inland toward a town called Sagua de Tanamo. Before entering this town, we came upon a wide river with a long and low bridge. I saw two huge oxen pulling a rickety old *carreta* (cart) in the middle of the river. The carreta had a big tank on the back. The oxen had the sharp tips of their horns cut off, and their noses had rings that were tied to a small rope leading to the driver. I pulled off the road and got out.

While the oxen were in the wide river, the farmer was sitting in his carreta on a wooden bench just above the water level. He was backed into the deepest part of the river filling this tank from the top of its opening with water. When the tank was full, he whipped the oxen and they pulled the heavy carreta with the full water tank out of the river over the smooth river rocks.

As the cart got further out of the river, I saw the tank's gravity-fed system. The farmer could lower a small hose connected to the bottom of the tank for water to flow out. When the hose was raised higher than the tank, the flow of water would stop. The carreta was set up so the tank could be taken anywhere—maybe somewhere on a ranch, his home, or his garden. This farmer lived in a natural state of working off the land—in sync with it, part of it. He evolved and adapted to his world and the daily conditions of the land. I thought that was neat, and I was able to get a picture of him and his carreta at the right time.

We got back in the car and drove into Sagua de Tanamo. As soon as we got into town—BAM! We got another flat, just like that! We put on the spare and drove around looking for a ponchero to fix our flat tire. We found one ponchero place, but the guy had just left for lunch. A local pointed us toward another guy down the road. Even though we were told that the other guy's repairs were not as good, we went anyway. This other ponchero had a ten-foot by ten-foot open metal cage for his workspace. The cage sat about fifty feet in front of his house, and he had it configured to lock up at night.

He took the flat tire off by hand and discovered that an old patch inside had come loose. He charged us five CUCs to repair the tire. When he finished putting the tire back on, he said, "You'll be good as new, OK?" We got back on the road and drove through town. It was interesting to see the many horse carriages being used like taxis to take people around and the many people on Russian and Chinese made bikes.

As we kept driving, we were figuring out how to (while not really sure if we could) get into the small island of Saetia, which is where we were hoping to stay. The only thing we knew to do was to keep driving through all these rough roads to get to the front gate of the island and hope that we would be allowed to enter. If not, well, it would be a long, rough road back, and we were not quite sure what to do for Plan B. Jesús yelled out when he saw the turnoff, and we drove a good way further until we had to stop at the front gate. At this gate, we saw an old kiosk, which looked like a remnant from the Cold War. It had a long, narrow, white bar across the road with a weight at one end.

As we pulled up, guards came out of a check station and I gladly let Jesús do the talking. Things seemed to go smoothly. We were told to wait while they radioed people further inside this island to see if they had room for us.

The island of Saetia is about sixteen square miles. It is connected to the mainland by the small animal-control bridge, which we were standing on. Beginning in 1980, wild African game animals were brought here to run free and for the hunting pleasure of top communist officials, who used this place as a getaway. In 2000, Saetia was turned into a natural park preserve. There are only twelve cabanas available for overnight stays. Prior to becoming an African game hunting ground, Saetia was primarily an area for fisherman and charcoal producers.

We waited a good half hour before we were told there was room for us. We were allowed to enter, and they raised the long, narrow, white bar for

us to pass. We got in the car, and of course, we thought we would be able to just drive off. But we couldn't. We had to go slow and easy while driving on the rough, dirt road. It took us a while to find the designated check-in area. We drove up on a grassy lawn area to park and got out of the car to check in at the main lodge. I noticed big, tall ostriches and a few wild turkeys walking about. We walked to the lobby, and I looked at all the old walls filled with animal heads and game skins.

I was struck by the contrast with many American game lodges and houses I had visited. In America, many people make their modern lodges or houses look old-fashioned. Here they didn't have to because Cuba is already held back in an apparent time capsule, and yet they were trying to make the lodge look modern.

We checked in, and I found out that we could take a late afternoon safari ride at five thirty. We dumped everything in our cabana and had fifteen minutes before the ride was scheduled to leave. This was the last safari of the day, for which I paid eighteen CUCs for both of us. I wanted to get that ride in and check this place out because we were not going to linger around too long the next day.

As it turned out, Jesús, the driver, and I were the only people on this big 4x4 vehicle with no roof. It was old. The windshield in the front folded forward, bolted to the hood. The vehicle had a roll bar in the back. Jesús sat in the front. I sat in the back on the elevated seat. As we started out, I sensed Jesús was telling the driver that I was an artist. The driver replied by saying that if I wanted to stop at any moment to get a picture of anything to speak out. "Bien," I said.

I had to put my camera on high speed, 1/1000 speed, because things were happening so fast. Warthogs with big tusks jumped out in front of us. A couple of them were covered in red mud, caked on them from wallowing in the ground in a mud hole. I could see their little piglets darting off into the thicker brush. All of a sudden, gazelles came darting out left and right in front of the jeep. Their horns were almost as big as the animal itself. Out in the open areas, I could see other herds of animals that looked like impalas. A few wild mustangs came stampeding through with zebras. We came up on big water buffalo that were chewing on the grasses. There were also other varieties of buffalo that had big horns with a curl to them.

I had never seen anything like it. With the high grassy fields, trees, and animals roaming around, if you didn't know any better, you would think you were in the middle of Africa. And, yet, here we were in Cuba.

The guide gave us an extra ride for our money. He took us around to areas that were really off road. Jesús turned to me and said it was because the driver wanted to get a good tip. We got to a spot where I saw a zebra in the distance among the wild mustangs. I made a comment to Jesús that I could not get the close shots that I wanted because the animals did not like the jeep. The guide asked if I wanted to get out of the truck with him, so we could sneak up on the animals. I got out of the jeep and Jesús stayed in. Of course, the guide didn't understand any English.

Jesús said, "He's really working for that tip, Chris."

I said, "Yeah, he's earning it."

This was cool. So here I was with my camera, ducking down in the low brush, stalking as if I were a hunter, I got about a hundred yards away from the jeep, hoping not to spook any of the warthogs. I took pictures and was able to get pretty close. After some time, we came back, got in the vehicle, and kept going. We got to a spot on a cliff that overlooked a beach. Our guide informed us that the beaches we were looking down on are the most virgin beaches here.

We came to an obscure, out-of-the-way monument surrounded by thick vegetation. The monument marked the spot where Fidel Castro landed on this beach one night in 1947. Castro had joined an expeditionary force training off this coastline. They intended to invade the Dominican Republic and to overthrow its dictator, Generalissimo Rafael Leónidas Trujillo. Castro and his group were aboard a boat out in the ocean when they were intercepted by a night patrol. Many shots were fired. It is said that Castro figured, "Sharks below me, bullets above me." Taking his chances, he jumped ship and swam ashore.

On the monument were several phrases, *"Al fracasar la expedicion a Santo Domingo"* (The failure of the expedition to Santo Domingo); *"Fidel llega nadando de noche en Julio de 1947"* (Fidel arrives swimming at night in 1947); *"A mi no me arrestan mas que nada por cuestion de honor"* (I did not get arrested it was more than anything a question of honor).

After the monument, we drove onto a small plateau. Through a cut of trees, we saw huge animals milling and grazing. They were antelopes of good size with horns that reached about six feet. So heading in that direction, we went further off road to get closer to these beautiful, large animals. But again, it was hard to get close, as they would run and dart off.

We came to another area, and there were five to ten buzzards on top of a dead animal. The deceased animal had obviously been there for a while. I got out of the jeep and walked right up to it. But those buzzards were reluctant to leave their meal ticket.

At the end of our safari, I gave the guide a nice tip. I made a point to look him in the eye and thank him. We went back to the cabana, took showers, and watched CNN Europe world news before going to dinner. The bathrooms in the cabanas were not modern by today's standards. They had the feel and look of the 1950s. It was like nothing had changed. But everything still functioned and looked to be in perfectly clean order. Cubans considered it to be quite nice.

We walked to the main lodge for dinner. Jesús and I, being the thirsty men that we were, sat down to have a cold Bucanero and check out the exotic menu. The food offered by the lodge was wild, literally and figuratively. We were like kids in a candy store. There was antelope game sausage, different meats cooked different ways, and appetizers.

"Jesús," I said. "This is once in a lifetime. Let's order everything!"

We pretty much picked everything that was on the menu, and then we had another round of beer. We were hungry. The only drag was the mosquitoes, which are bad all over Cuba, especially here. Of course, since I was wearing shorts, I somehow became their main dish.

After dinner and dessert, we went back to our cabana, hooked up the miniature DVD player to the back of the television to watch more Jeff Dunham, and pulled out a new bottle of Havana Club 7 años rum. Jesús, in perfect Cuban fashion and custom, opened the new bottle and poured the first few drops on the ground to give the first drink to the African deities or orishas, thereby asking these gods for their permission to drink from that bottle.

I crashed around eleven o'clock. Jesús stayed up watching television. He turned the volume off and read the Spanish subtitles. That's the thing about Jesús. He's a night person. He usually stayed up at night while I slept. I might wake up two hours later after falling asleep, and he'd still be watching the television. I kept thinking, *I don't know how he does this.* How he can go all night just like computer nerds, I just don't know.

Early the next morning, I woke up to sounds I kept hearing outside my window—weird sounds that I had never heard before. The sounds were persistent. Curiosity got the better of me, just like a cat. Wearing only my *choners,* (underwear), I got up and looked out the window.

Holy Cow! I could not believe what I was seeing. Camels! There were camels walking all around. "Where the heck did they come from?"

I quickly put on clothes and went outside with my camera. The camels were walking around our cabana and rental car. All the while, I kept thinking, *where the heck did they come from?* There was a mustang wandering close by I noticed, and one of the camels walked up to it. The camel appeared to be enamored with this mustang and kept giving it big, sloppy saliva licks, affectionately gumming the mustang's face. The mustang's response was like, "whatever," and it did nothing to fend off the camel. It was cute to see that contrast—a camel and a mustang just nose to nose, carrying on like that. I could now hear my daughter, Stephanie, excitingly saying, "Look daddy, they're married!" I walked around a little bit more. I saw ostriches and a whole gang of turkeys with baby chicks. A couple of mules came around with their big, long ears raised up high in the air. The outer fringe from their long ears was nicely highlighted by the early morning light. I was surprised by all the early morning activity going on.

Over breakfast, Jesús again brought up the idea of going to the village of Biran, Castro's childhood home. We needed to make a decision, as the fork in the road that led to Biran was past Saetia. I knew it meant a lot to Jesús to show me the childhood home where Fidel grew up and where he was born on August 13, 1926, and where his brother, Raul Castro, was born on June 3, 1931.

I was concerned about the military at the home and the attention I might draw with my big camera and small car rather than a typical looking tour bus. All they would have to do is ask for my passport and run it through. After what happened at the airport with El Comandante, who knew what might get kicked up.

I did not want to bring attention to myself like that, especially after Jesús told me about the tight military security. Sure, I wanted to check this place out and see it for what it was. I wanted to see it before Cuba opened up to the world, before the real cattle call of tourists came, and before everything started turning into a state of vogue. My other concern was for Jesús. Since he was with me, I did not know what problems this could potentially draw to him.

During breakfast, I made a conscious decision not to take the turn onto the dirt road to Biran, but to continue past it. Jesús seemed slightly disappointed, but he didn't argue. I know this was something he was excited about, proud of, and wanted to show me. I think, deep down he didn't want any problems either.

After making the decision about Biran, we finished breakfast and decided that we would go to where Christopher Columbus first set foot on land in 1492 in Cuba. We went to our cabana to pack up last-minute things and headed back to the lodge to pay our bill. We made our way out of Saetia for a full day of driving through the roughest, disintegrated roads yet to come.

6

ENCOUNTERS

WE LEFT SAETIA and found the road that took us in a westerly direction toward Playa Blanca, which is in the Bahia de Barlay, the bay where Christopher Columbus first landed. The roads were rough, but the scenery incredible. There were many little farming villages dotted about. These villages did not have any names. The homes had thatched palm frond roofs and were clustered in groups of two to ten homes. I was intrigued by the life that seemed to be moving freely at its own different pace, compared to a few of the other villages and towns we had been through.

As I was looking at these village homes, I saw a farmer standing on the ground holding braided ropes in his hands. The ropes led to two large oxen that were connected to each other by one large, wooden, and very weathered looking yoke. The oxen each had one small metal ring through the holes of their nostrils while going through and connecting between the fleshy part of their noses. The farmer held a rope that was tied to each ring. The farmer stood behind and to the side of the oxen; the ropes went over the top of the oxen's heads and horns. It was like a horse's rein that could be pulled as needed. Since an oxen's nose is such a sensitive spot, pulling on the rope controls those large beasts much like a small rudder controls a large ship. Another thickly braided rope ran between the two oxen, secured to the large yoke. This rope extended behind the farmer and was tied around a big Cuban Royal Palm tree, one of the larger and thick seventy foot trees, which lay on the ground. The farmer tried to get this fallen palm tree off the dirt road. He whipped the oxen with one hand while holding the reins in the other. He was able to get the oxen to move ever so slowly, as they dragged the palm tree down the village pathway between the bohio homes. Dust from the ground was kicked up from all the movement. I could see the oxen flexing their muscles like world-class weight lifters lifting at the max, struggling on the last bit of lift. As they leaned forward, pulling with the intensity and tension of a tug of war, cracks of the whip fell hard on their backs. Looking back, I could kick myself for not stopping to get pictures of that. I really wanted to, but by the time I was able to find a turnout, I was too far down the road. I found the whole scene to be very interesting. It was life happening. There it was. The farmer was doing what he had to do and nothing more.

We continued down this rough, potholed road. Occasionally, after blind turns, we would see one guy out in the middle of who knows where with two oxen pulling a full cart of red dirt. My impression was that this was a job—a government job for the day, or for however long it took to work a certain section of road. Each of these people would work with a single shovel. They took the red dirt off the cart and packed it into the potholes to fill them. These fills looked liked they would last through the hurricane

season. At the end of hurricane season, the dirt would be all washed out and the potholes would then be back to square one. Occasionally, I saw stretches of road where someone had filled the many potholes with dirt. When I saw this, I thought, *Great!* The road would be a little smoother, if you could call it that, and I could drive a little faster without worrying. But, inevitably, large potholes would start to appear again out of nowhere. I would have to slam on the brakes to slow down and begin going back to weaving slowly left and right to get around them.

I started to get fatigued from driving the bad roads and being the only one doing the driving. I had my left hand on the steering wheel. The hot sun beat down on my left arm through the window, making my arm hot and red. Many times, I had to put my right hand over my left arm to cover it while I drove.

Being in that sardine tin can of a car made my legs cramp. I was also getting tired from all the intense concentration required by the rough roads. The continued rough roads and the potholes meant I could not drive very fast. We still had another couple hours to go, given the speed we were able to travel.

We reached the turnoff to Playa Blanca. Playa Blanca is within the Bahia de Barlay, and is the exact spot where Columbus first landed in Cuba. It is located about nine miles east of Gibara. We were headed to Gibara for the night. Surprisingly, there were no signs or markings to help direct us to the site of Columbus's landing. We got lost. We had to pull over to the side of the road and stop to look at our maps. At that moment I looked up and saw this Cuban man out in the middle of nowhere walking down this rough road while pushing a wheelbarrow full of bright red tomatoes. He looked like he had been pushing this wheelbarrow down the road all morning long with no end in sight, heading to who knows where. This time, I didn't miss getting the picture. I seized the moment, jumped out of the car, and took his picture, as he silently passed by.

After looking at our maps, we backtracked on this remote dirt road and found the right road to Playa Blanca. We made our way to the beachhead where it is confirmed that Christopher Columbus first set foot in Cuba in 1492.

We slowly drove down a narrow, potholed road surrounded by lush vegetation. The road opened up to a small area where asphalt was torn up. Right at the water's edge, on the shore of the bay, stood a monument marker. I parked the car, and we got out to look around. There were no other cars and no one else in this remote area. As with the Bay of Pigs, I had pre-conceived ideas about Columbus, based on what I have heard in school and read in the past about him.

He had kept written notes that are documented in his journals where he describes the land formations of what is now Playa Blanca, his thoughts upon his first sight of land, and his thoughts upon actually landing:

Saturday, 27th of October 1492.

"Sailing south-south-west at six and a half knots on this course. I sighting land before nightfall. Lain off shore we spent the night on watch, there was much heavy rain all night. The vessels until sunset today made seventeen leagues on this south-south-west course."

Since it was too late in the evening to go ashore, Columbus did not set foot on actual land until the next day, Sunday the 28th. This was the furthest most point west in the new world. Columbus described it in his ship's journal:

Sunday, 28th of October 1492.

"I sailed and went for the nearest point of this island to the south-south-west course and I entered a very beautiful river with out danger of shoals or other perils. All along where I sailed was deep and clear bottom right up to the shore. The mouth of this river was good and wide enough for a vessel to tack. I anchored about inside the mouth of this river. I have never beheld anything so beautiful. All the banks of the river was fully surrounded by beautiful green flora all of them very different from ours, with each one having its own kinds of flowers and fruit. There were many birds of all kinds chirping and singing very sweetly. There are a great many numbers of palm trees of different kinds from our own, they are of heights and with out bark covering and the leaves are very large. The land is very flat. I descended from the boat and went ashore I came upon two houses which I believed to belong to those of fisherman upon seeing me the natives fled in fear. In one of them I found a dog that did not bark, in both the houses I found nets and rope made of twisted palm, fish hooks made of horn and bone harpoons. With many fires inside the houses I believe that many people live together in the houses. I gave orders that everything should not be touched, and so it was done. The vegetation was abundant. I went back and returned to the ship and sailed a good distance up the river. There was such great joy I felt to seeing these lush green flora forests and fragrant flowers, watching all the birds and hearing them singing that I did not want to leave. This land is the most beautiful that has ever truly been seen by any human eyes. It is full of good harbours, deep rivers and the island has very many beautiful mountains."

Jesús and I stood there for some time in silence, listening to all the natural sounds, the light breeze off the water and palms, the birds off in the distance. I could see the mountains and the other things Columbus described in his journal. And then the accumulation of the whole moment hit me. This was the western frontier at one time, the furthest-most edge of the known world. Right here. Right where we were standing. All these sites and sounds taking place right here as far as the eyes could see. There was still no development, no big structures, only a few small homes on the shore not far from the landing marker. We drove slowly on the potholed road; just before reaching the monument, we saw a few Cubans outside tending to their daily lives. Other than these few Cubans, we did not see anyone else.

It seemed no different than what Columbus had described about the natives he saw on the shore tending to their daily life except that these couple of Cubans didn't, as Columbus wrote, "run off in fear." I could envision his boat pulling in for the first time. I could imagine him and his crew first setting eyes on something so new—a beautiful little inward bay. I saw pristine water. It felt like a surreal moment, seemingly discovering it for the first time, seeing this place that he saw with his eyes. It was not commercialized here. In fact, there is only a mortared stone monument marker with a bronze plaque. It's not anything fancy. There were no signs, billboards, or flashing lights. Other countries would commercialize a place like this with an elaborate statue and a visitors' center. But here, everything has been left as it was over five hundred years ago, when first found, as if it was still undiscovered.

Marco Polo's thirteenth-century travels to the lands of Asia inspired Christopher Columbus. I thought it interesting that Columbus used Marco Polo's book, *The Travels of Marco Polo*, as a source. Columbus was in search of a new and quicker route to the Indies, the medieval name for Asia, to capitalize on the riches involved in the spice trade. Because of his geographical misunderstanding, Columbus reached the Americas instead. As he sailed along the Cuban coast, Columbus thought he had reached Cathay, or China. He searched for the magnificent Asian cities described by Marco Polo, but of course, did not find them. Columbus never realized his mistake. During his entire life, he believed the lands he discovered were along the east coast of Asia. The word "Cuba" is derived from the native Indian word, *cubanacan*, meaning "a central place." When Columbus heard the word "cubanacan," he thought the natives were referring to Kublai Khan, the great Khan. He now concluded that he had reached the kingdom of the Great Khan as described in the writings of Marco Polo. It is interesting that to this day, the native, indigenous people of the Americas are still referred to as "Indians" because of Columbus' geographical misunderstanding.

We left Playa Blanca, looped back around the bay, and made the drive into Gibara. We did not know where we were going to stay for the night, so we pulled over to the side of the road that surrounds and overlooks the Bahia de Gibara. Jesús was calling around on his cell phone and trying to line something up.

We were having a hard time finding a casa for the night. We called places listed in our travel books, and they were full for the night. Jesús said that he would keep trying to figure this out. Since we were pulled over on the road that surrounds the Bahia de Gibara, I chose to look around while Jesús continued to make phone calls to find a casa.

The further away I got from Jesús, the more the eyes of the preying vultures known as jineteros swarmed in. These jineteros were behaving as if they saw fresh road kill. I got hit up pretty good right there. A couple of times I said, "No, gracias. Yo bien. Gracias." I was hoping they'd take the hint and move along. But some of them wouldn't.

I kept walking and taking in the scenery. There were many small, differently colored fishing boats anchored out in the bay. I saw old, large buildings right up on the water's edge. Portions of these old buildings were even in a state of ruins. Fissures of the old walls were exposed. It was like peeking into the many different layers and types of materials used over the course of the building's history. Many different construction periods were reflected.

I took more photos and returned to the car. I saw Jesús talking to one of the local kids. He told me that this kid knew of a few places where we could go.

I looked at him and said, "Jesús, I'm feeling agitated about this place. I'm getting these jineteros coming onto me like vultures."

His response was, "Well, it's starting to get dark, Chris." Since we did not know where else to go, we decided to stay in this town and keep looking. The kid seemed OK. But, then again, he was all we had to go on considering that it was getting to be the end of the day.

Jesús, the kid, and I got in the car and drove off to places that the kid knew. At first it was humorous to have a third person trying to squeeze into this sardine tin can of a car. After a few choice words in Spanish between Jesús and this kid, we adjusted to having a third person, as we began to drive down the narrow streets of Gibara.

After driving five minutes, we pulled up to a casa. Jesús and the kid got out of the car. As it turned out, the casa was full. So, again, we kept driving and came up to another casa, which looked like a nice place.

I had a feeling that this place might work out, and Jesús agreed. He got out of the car to talk to the owners, who were standing outside in front of their house. Jesús felt good about these people and what they had to offer. He then motioned for me to get out of the car and come over. The owners of the casa also motioned with their hands, "Entrada. Entrada! Come. Come in!" they said. We went into the house because the owners wanted to show us the place, to see if it was acceptable. Jesús and I looked at each other and agreed it looked pretty good, until, well, until they opened the door to the bedroom. We saw that it had only one queen size bed. Jesús looked slowly at me, and I looked slowly at him. Then Jesús looked slowly at the owners of the casa who were all standing there, shaking his head with a half grin on his face—no. And, of course, the kid who was trying to make a peso by helping us burst out laughing. Obviously this was not going to work. We graciously thanked them for their time.

It looked like we were running out of options. The kid said he had one last place to take us. We headed out through the narrow streets looking for this abode; once found, it appeared to be a nice casa with two good beds. We decided to take it. I thanked the kid and gave him a pat on the back and one CUC. He left, happy to find his own way home.

The family was genuine. The man of the casa was a retired officer of the Cuban Coast Guard who, I believe, retired with the rank of Captain. He was very friendly, very cordial, as we made our introductions.

There were photos on the walls of different artists from around the world who had stayed at this casa. These artists mainly came to the town of Gibara to attend the annual Festival de internacional de Cine Pobre or International Low Budget Film Festival, or commonly known as the poor man's international film festival, which is held every year during April. Jesús told the captain that I was an artist. Upon hearing this, the captain really wanted my card to put up on the wall. He said there were a lot of people who came from all around the world and even from America. But these American producers came under different names, and sometimes in disguises.

After putting our things in our room, Jesús and I decided to take advantage of the last bit of daylight to see what we could of this fishing village. Before we left, the owners of the casa wanted to know when we would like to eat dinner and what they should prepare for us.

"What is on the menu?" Jesús asked.

"Pork, large prawns, turtle, and local fish."

I knew Jesús would like the prawns. Being the more adventurous type, and since I had never tried it before, I told them that I would have the *tortuga* (turtle).

We then set out on our walk through the streets of this seaside town to look around. Gibara was founded on January 16, 1817. At one time, this protected bay was a shipping hub for the export of sugar. Because many of the homes are painted white, Gibara has also been called La Villa Blanca, or the white town. The homes on the narrow streets of Gibara had wooden shutters instead of glass windows. They also had nineteenth century grilles over the outside of the windows. It reminded me of Remedios, except that it was more modern. There were homes with arched stained-glass mediopuntos, half moons, above doorways or windows to offer protection from the glare of the intense tropical sun.

A man came strolling down the middle of the street pushing a cart full of the day's catch of fish. They were huge Dorado fish, stiff and piled high in his cart looking like a stack of pick-up sticks, with their obvious protruding foreheads and brightly colored scales. The people here seemed very genuine and happy. I noticed there was less intensity in the hunter-gatherer attitude here, probably because food is more abundant in this fishing village than other parts of Cuba.

It was getting too dark for me to take pictures, so we went up a hill that overlooks the city. At the top was a Spanish fort called El Cuartelon and a small open-air cantina. The cantina was nothing fancy, a few tables and chairs, with a guy selling beer. We sat down. An old two-door car, a 1955 Chevy, was parked next to the cantina. It belonged to a gentleman patronizing the cantina. Music was playing loudly out of the car's open windows, but the speakers were distorted. It was the best this gentleman had, I suppose. To most Cubans, that would be considered top-of-the-line given what's available.

We had a commanding view of the whole bay. Way off to one side of the bay, I could see where the land came to a rocky point and where it jutted out. Two big ships had crashed into this rocky coastline sometime in the past and laid together on the sides of their bellies. The waves hit high and crashed on them. These were big, old, steel ships that looked half-cracked due to the weight of gravity once they were out of the ocean. They laid there in the distance. I took a picture of them. Beyond where the two half sunken ships lay on the shoreline and out and away from the bay's entrance, I could see six huge—and I mean huge—tall, white wind turbines. They were in a straight line right on the ocean's windy, rocky shoreline. I don't know how big they were, but they sure looked massive turning slowly in the wind blowing in from the ocean.

Unexpectedly, I kept hearing, "Psst. Psst. Psst."

I looked over in the bushes below and saw an old lady trying to get my attention, so she could sell stuff to me. She had sigua shells, a type of shell found only on the eastern side of the Cuban island. She had carefully cut the shells to make rings out of them. I normally don't want to patronize these vendors and get into the hustle of things. But after a couple of beers, what could I say? I was relaxed and told Jesús, "Tell her I'll take a look at it." Hearing this, the old lady gladly came out of the bushes and sat down next to us. She wanted to show us what she had. I looked at these rings and thought of my daughter, Stephanie.

"Well, I like these," I said. "But, they're too big. The size is for a man. Do you have any that are smaller?"

"Uh huh. I come back. I come back." She replied, in very, very broken English.

And *boom!* She took off. After another round, she came back. I bought two shell rings for one peso. The old lady was very happy, and I got something for my daughter, who loves jewelry. I suppose I could have gotten into trouble with US Customs though the shells could theoretically fall under "art." They were such insignificant items that I honestly forgot to claim them when I went through customs.

After that, we headed back to our casa to get ready for dinner. Gibara is known for great seafood and shrimp, and I was ready to eat! We sat outside in the back open courtyard on the veranda. With all the colorful and lush vegetation, it was quite pleasant. The first items our hosts brought out were a fresh salad of sliced tomatoes and cucumbers, a fruit tray consisting of papaya, guava, and pineapple, freshly baked bread, and of course, black beans and rice. Then the main course came out—a plate of giant prawns for Jesús, and a plate of tortuga, a large grilled turtle steak for me. And, oh my God, was it good. The taste was not what I expected it to be. When I first sliced it with my knife, there was a slight resistance, similar to the feeling of slicing a filet mignon. But the texture of the meat had an interesting feel in my mouth when chewing, consistent with a big piece of sushi, like the texture and feel of yellow tail or salmon. After dinner, we drank wonderful Cuban espresso.

After we reposed there for a while, the captain stepped out onto the veranda. He was happy to hear that I enjoyed the tortuga that he grilled for me. He invited us to sit with him in his living room. The television was on and the world baseball tournament was about to start for the evening. Cuba happened to be playing tonight. As we gathered in the living room to sit down before the game started, it became obvious that the captain was intrigued with our travels. He sat down in his easy chair and motioned for me to sit next to him on the couch. He seemed like a very sincere man and treated me as if I were his son in-law. He talked to me a little bit, and Jesús would say a few things. The captain spoke very little English, but I really felt at home. He asked me a few questions about our travels. We told him about traveling through Baracoa, as we made our way along the eastern side of the Cuban coastline, and how we saw a heavy concentration of Cuban military personnel. We explained that it was strange seeing this because we were on such a rough, dirt road in the jungle. The road was desolate and in an out-of-the-way place. The military personnel were camped out in different places along this road. We also told the captain how we had been stopped by the military in the middle of nowhere at a makeshift checkpoint.

The captain still had retained a few connections and much insight from his years in the Coast Guard. He soon solved the mystery for us of what the military was doing in the remote jungle location. The captain explained to us that big drug runners were caught a few days prior, and that 25 percent of the drugs had been recovered. This happened to be at the same time, unwittingly, that Jesús and I were traveling through that area. I wondered to myself how they knew it was only 25 percent. My next obvious thought was that the military interrogated the people involved and got the information they needed, probably a bigger interrogation than the one I got from El Comandante. I thought that it must have been a huge haul for the Cuban government to commit so much military to it.

The captain told us that, out in the waters of the ocean, the United States and the Cuban Coast Guards get along wonderfully—so well, in fact, that you would not even know that there is a conflict between the two countries. They have worked together out at sea giving and trading information back and fourth. He then mentioned that he wished that he had an American flag. I wished I could have given one to him, but I suppose a US flag would have been taken from me when I arrived at the airport in Havana.

We watched the Cuban team playing baseball on television. It looked like they were playing in San Diego, California. During a break in play, the captain turned to Jesús and me about a certain type of tomato. Someone had given him tomato seeds from America, which he planted and has enjoyed growing for some time. After hearing the description of the tomatoes, I figured out that they were Beef-Steak tomatoes. The captain seemed so proud of these tomatoes, and how great they were to eat. He appeared even happier to have finally put a name to them.

Because of driving all day on the rough roads, and because it was now late at night, I was starting to tire out. I was ready to go off to bed. Our hosts asked us what time to have breakfast ready in the morning, and we figured about eight o'clock would be a good time. I wanted to get a good start with the anticipation to see the morning life of the village's activities.

After breakfast, we went around town. There were a lot of people walking and a lot on bikes. People were trying to repair their old, broken down Cuban-American cars. I saw sections of old walls around town that were creating impressions and visual images similar to an abstract art form. I got great pictures of these old walls.

At that moment, people walked by with big buckets full of live prawns they had caught that morning. For sale, of course. A few blocks away, I could hear a loud, high-pitched, and ear-deafening sound. It sounded like bloody murder emanating from a few blocks away. It turned out to be a large pig with its four hooves lashed together lying on its side in the street on a scale being weighed before going off to slaughter. Three men picked this pig off the scale and put it on a horse cart to be taken away. All the while, the pig squealed loudly. Its long, curly tail hung over the back end of the cart, as the horse pulled the carreta slowly down the narrow street.

When we got back to the casa, I noticed a woman across the street. She was not bad looking, a bit older than me, with light-colored skin. She had her music turned up loud and looked like she was in her own world, cleaning house and singing to the music. Her front door and her wood-shuttered windows were wide open, so I could see the whole inside of her house. I was only able to see her from the waist up, as she walked back and forth. After some time, she stepped outside to sweep the front porch area, and I could see that she wore a pair of very short shorts. My eyes about popped out through my sunglasses when I saw her legs. This petite woman had the hairiest, blackest, woolly mammoth legs I had ever seen. They were shaven from an inch above her knees down. She had a perfectly straight shaven line around each leg. What made it stand out more was the fact that she shaved in a nice tight ring around each of her lower thighs. I have never seen a woman with such hairy, black thighs like that. If I had not known any better, I would have thought she was a man.

"Jesús," I said, "What! The heck is that?"

"Oh no, Chris," Jesús said.

He explained that he could tell by the music she was listening to that she was from a different generation. At that time, women did that. They would shave rings around their legs like that, and the men thought it was "Really Sexy!"

I looked at Jesús, and I said, with a stunned long pause, "Not a chance. No offense to this woman, but for me, not a chance. Why not shave the rest of her legs?" I asked.

"She's just living in a different time when that was the big thing to do, and she has never left it," Jesús said.

By now, it was getting time to say our good-byes to the captain and his family. As we were loading up our car, they stood waiting to see us drive away, to wave us off like we were family. I thought that they were a pleasant family. I hope to meet them again one day.

We made our way on the road out of town and headed to the city of Camaguey for the next night. Jesús asked as a favor if we could stop in the coastal village of Nuevitas, since it was not too much out of our way. Nuevitas is where Jesús grew up and where his family still lives. Apparently, it had been about nine or ten years since Jesús had been able to go back to Nuevitas and visit his family. It is not like in America where we can just hop in a car and go. Not everybody in Cuba has means of transportation. Jesús did not want to be presumptuous or rudely assuming. When he asked me, he said he felt like this was my trip, since I was paying for everything. But I could see the hope in his eyes.

Feeling that this trip is not all about me, I said, "No. No. Come on. Let's go. Who knows the next time you might be able to get by here again."

I figured I had to do that. I mean, I couldn't tell him no. Nuevitas was not too far out of our way. Plus, to me, I looked at it as another place to see. I had never been there. It was also the least I could do for him. Jesús got excited, knowing that he was going to get to see his home again. But he did not want to call his relatives ahead of time to let them know that he was coming. He said his aunt, who is like a grandmother to him, would probably get too excited and start fretting if she knew he was coming. Because of his aunt's age, Jesús did not want her to get all worked up.

Instead of taking the road down toward the Carretera Central, the central part of the Autopista Nacional, the Cuban highway, we tried to be creative and find wild short cuts to Nuevitas—across roads that more or less would keep us going along the northern side of the island.

Just outside of Gibara, there was a very small village called San Juan. If we took a right going west from that village and drove for about eleven miles, that would help cut across to another small village called Valasco. I saw that there was a small dotted line on the map, signifying that the road can be very rough and, at times, impassable by car. Not knowing what we were getting ourselves into—and oddly enough it just so happened to be Friday the thirteenth—we figured it didn't look that far to the village of Valasco. So off we went.

The road started to reveal signs of why it had a small dotted line on the map. But, by now, we were committed. The road disintegrated, and we could not go very fast. I tried to take it in stride. I will say that I saw incredible countryside. It was like a feeling of being lost in the middle of nowhere.

I stopped a couple of times to take pictures. Occasionally, I had to come to a complete stop to creep ever so slowly over potholes that were so large I could not even go around them. I came upon these potholes so fast that I almost did not have enough time to slam on the breaks. Jesús would get excited when this happened. He bantered to me that this is definitely not a place to get a flat tire.

To help him calm down and stop him from critiquing my driving, I reminded him that back in Baracoa, "I did not touch the cross!" which was a reference, of course, to the possibility of bringing bad luck.

With that, Jesús shot back, "Yes, but you definitely thought about it!" And then a relaxing smile started to come back on his face.

It took us about an hour and a half to cover about eleven miles. We finally reached Valasco and were able to get back on better country roads. The Jeff Dunham one-liners were flying, and I could tell that Jesús was getting excited, knowing that we were getting closer to his childhood hometown.

As we came to a town called Puerto Padre on the Bahia de Chaparral, we were able to drive a little faster. Puerto Padre is an industrial area known as the City of Mills. The town made famous by Teofilo Stevenson, a Cuban man who was born there and went on to become Cuba's heavyweight boxing champion in the 1972 Munich Olympics. Teofilo Stevenson repeated his gold medal performance in the 1976 Montreal and 1980 Moscow Olympics. It is said that Teofilo Stevenson was denied a possible fourth Gold medal in the 1984 Olympics in Los Angeles because of the heated Olympic boycott chess games of 1980 and 1984 between the United States and the Soviet Union.

Jesús looked at his maps again and determined that we needed to take one more dotted-line short cut once we got past Puerto Padre to get us toward Nuevitas. We had one problem with that: finding the road. Cuba is notorious for not having road signs. Usually, and most often in situations such as this, we only had descriptions to go on, like a certain tree, a boulder by the road, a ditch in the ground, and so on. After driving up and down this road for miles, we just could not figure it out. We drove up to a turn and were faced with five different choices. We didn't know which one to take and knew we could wind up on a road that goes nowhere.

Finally, I said, "We're on the road to hell!"

Jesús laughed.

We came upon a few people standing on the side of the road, hoping to get a ride. We were trying to figure out which person we should ask for directions. We didn't want a surging flood of people running up to our car in hopes of getting a ride. There was one kid we saw who was walking back from the road toward his school.

"Let's just ask him, all right?" Jesús said. This kid must have been thirteen or fourteen years old, max. He had a few pimples on his face and a crew cut. He looked like a junior-high kid, or what I more commonly call the pre-human stage. Jesús spoke to him in Spanish. The kid was helpful, as he knew about this one cutoff that we just could not find.

"Well, it's over there," he said, pointing to that direction.

The kid told us that he was out at the road hoping to get picked up for a ride home. He had been in school all week and thought maybe he could get a ride home to his parent's house for the weekend. He tried all morning, as it was heading into the afternoon and was not able to get a ride. He decided to remain at school for the weekend and was on his way back to his dorm room. Jesús paused for a minute then looked at me and asked if we could give him a ride since it was in the same direction that we were going.

"Chris, I think he'd be OK, giving him a ride," Jesús said in a reassuring voice. "He was helpful with the information, and he can find this road."

So, we took him with us on our journey to this mystery shortcut road. He threw his things in, got in the back seat of our car, and we took off toward the unknown.

Jesús put Cuban salsa music on the radio, and we started bantering back and forth with repartees, as if we were in our own private world. If I hit a pothole, Jesús would blurt out, "Chris, what the hell are you doing?" And I quickly retorted in my limited Spanish "*Silencio*, I'm just trying to kill you!" while pointing my finger in the air. Jesús would then throw out a quick jest about my driving, when I would ask if he had any idea as to the direction where we were going. He would then start shouting, "Left-hand turn! You're going to make a left-hand turn!" This was a reference that race car drivers only make left-hand turns on the oval speedway racetracks. After a good half hour of this back and forth bantering, I started to think that this kid must be wondering about us, like who the hell are these people? What planet are they from? And this oddball foreigner! Jesús and I were bantering away like we were Abbott and Costello. I'm sure that the kid did not know what to make of all this. It was as if he were being held captive in the backseat of this small car driving in the middle of who knows where and he can't get out. So I thought, *Well, maybe I better try and talk to him.*

So I turned my head, looked back at him, and said, "*Tu hablas Ingles?*" He looked at me with his eyes wide open. His head moved slowly up and down—yes. He then stopped for a second. Then he slowly moved his head side to side—no.

Jesús shouted out! I turned my head forward and slammed on the brakes. A big old crater in the road was right in front of us. We went in!

"You idiot!" Jesús screamed at me.

The kid was like, "Oh Crap!"

Fortunately, I was able to slow down enough to keep us from going all the way into the hole. I slowly got us out. *OK!* I thought, *No more discussions with this kid.*

From that point on, I spoke to Jesús and had him relay my message. I think this made the young kid feel a little more comfortable than having this *mucho macho grande hombre* American trying to talk to him incoherently in limited Spanish.

The roads started to get even more rough, so rough that they were designated as impassable during the rainy season. I felt so stressed trying to make sure we did not crash in these pothole craters. There started to be so many of them on the road that it resembled a war zone or a lunar landscape. I had to constantly slam on the brakes to prevent the tires from dipping into these craters. Then I would slowly drive around them.

As I was doing this, I worried we would get a flat in the middle of nowhere, with absolutely nobody around to help.

We definitely had to take our time going through here. We just had to. We had no other choice, especially in that small sardine tin can of a car. We were low to the ground with those eighteen- to twenty-inch tires, I was concerned that the rocks and broken chunks of road would kick up and tear off the car's oil pan from underneath the vehicle, then we really would be stranded.

There were big drop-offs on those roads. Sometimes I had to turn ninety degrees to get off the road and then get back on to avoid another crater. These craters were so big that they could literally swallow up the whole car. There was no cell phone service. Who knew when the last American, if any, ever came through here. In fact, I was beginning to think that I was probably the dumbest American to even come through here, EVER! On top of that, at any moment we were ready to become road kill and a three-course meal for all the buzzards I keep seeing all over this island.

Three hours and only fifteen miles later, we finally got through. We were coming up to a small town called Maranon Uno, characterized by a big, bumpy roundabout with three or four cutoffs stemming off from it. We needed to go one way and the kid wanted to go another, or so it seemed.

"*Bien aqui,*" he told us.

He then said it again with a little more urgency, "*Bien aqui. Bien aqui!*" (You let me out right here.)

I wondered if that was really his exit. I don't think he knew what to make of us anymore. I mean, with all our bantering and being held captive in the middle of nowhere in this small car, I think it was too much and too crazy for him. The way he asked to be dropped off sounded like he was saying, "Get me the hell out of here and away from this crazy American!"

We let him out and, of course, the other people who were standing close by on the side of the road came running over thinking they could get a ride with us. We took off quickly to avoid more people surrounding our car.

"That's the last time," I told Jesús. "I don't want to pick up anyone anymore."

To which Jesús replied, "That's OK, Chris, we got through that impassable road."

I was finally starting to feel a little relieved and more calmed down driving around the large roundabout. I turned to Jesús with a deep breath.

"OK, which way do we go now?" I said. Without missing a beat Jesús screamed out, "Left-hand turn! We're making a left-hand turn!" As if nothing had changed.

To which I said, "*Silencio,* or you're a dead jalapeño!" while pointing my finger in the air, as we continued driving down the road, bantering away as we went.

Journeying further along the road, it definitely started to get better. The surrounding terrain was flatter, and there were more cattle in this area. I got this crazy visual idea in my head while we were driving and looking around. I told Jesús, "If that El Comandante guy had sent someone to follow me, that person would really be hating us by now, after having to go through all the rough short cut roads we just took."

We finally got to the turnoff that would take us to Nuevitas. Jesús seemed to be getting happy. We neared the town and had to drive around for a while. It was obvious that Jesús had not been there for a long time, and things seemed a little unfamiliar to him. After a while, Jesús was able to refocus, the surroundings became clear again to him, and we finally found the right road. The road was next to a grouping of tall buildings that were built in revolutionary style architecture.

We rolled in during the afternoon. I was so exhausted from all that intense and exerted concentration on those rough roads. I asked if I could stay in the car. Jesús left to go visit his family. I told him to take his time, enjoy his family, and not to worry about me. I parked the car underneath the shade of a tree, rolled the window down, and rested my eyes for a while.

I must have slept for a good hour or more. The sound of Jesús and one of his cousins walking toward the car awakened me. He introduced her to me, and he said he wanted to keep visiting, but he didn't want to leave me alone the whole time. He invited his cousin to accompany us on our drive around to look at the city. That way, Jesús could still keep talking to her. Jesús proceeded to tell me that the aunt whom he considered to be like his grandmother was very surprised. She was very happy to visit with him.

Jesús was able to catch up on everything and everyone.

Apparently, there were many happy and festive things going on. Jesús's cousin had just received her certification as a specialist in general medicine. In Cuba, students studied at the university for six years to become a doctor. To become a specialist in general medicine or a family doctor required another three years. Now that Jesús's cousin finished her schooling, she and her fiancé were engaged to be married. Her fiancé had just graduated as a doctor too. Another one of Jesús's family members had spent the last five years working as a nurse and was preparing to take a big trip to Qatar.

Cuba takes pride in the education of its medical professionals. At the time of my visit, Cuba claimed that its citizens' average life expectancy was 78.3 years.

Christopher Columbus first discovered Nuevitas' large bay, Bahia de Nuevitas, in 1492, and the actual city of Nuevitas was founded in 1775. We drove around the city, stopped for something to eat, and continued to drive around, stopping when anything caught my eye.

Across the Bahia de Nuevitas was Cayo Sabinal, a flat island key covered with marshes and flora and inhabited by many types of butterflies. Cayo Sabinal was a favorite place for marauding pirates, especially since the inland city of Camaguey was not too far away.

North of Cayo Sabinal, there are more strings of small island keys. These keys are home to a wilderness of coral in bright turquoise waters. Thousands of flamingos live in these untamed, verdant sanctuaries. Ernest Hemingway spent a lot of time in the waters of these small island chains during World War II—hunting German Nazi U-boats in his thirty-eight foot boat, named *The Pilar*. The secret code name for Hemingway's covert operations was "Friendless," which he had coincidently named after one of his favorite, big, black, sassy cats. Hemingway's adventures and the time he spent here were the inspiration for his classic novel *Islands in the Stream*.

Hemingway started writing this novel in the early 1950s. He mysteriously set it aside, and it was not found until after his death. Mary Welsh Hemingway, his fourth wife and widow, discovered it. *Islands in the Stream* was posthumously published in 1970.

While driving down a street, I saw beautiful building walls. They caught my eyes, as I was drawn to the natural colors that were weathered over centuries of time and history.

Out of the blue, Jesús yelled out, "Stop!"

I thought I was about to hit railroad tracks that I couldn't see. Then I realized that Jesús wanted me to pull over.

Jesús got out of the car and quickly ran over to people he saw hanging

around on a street corner, talking. One gentleman in the group used to live next door to Jesús's family. At one time many years ago, he was a barman in one of the best *cantinas* (establishments) in Nuevitas. Apparently he was very generous and good to Jesús and his family and had helped them through tough and difficult times. Many years later, this gentleman was in Havana and ran into problems with his car. He needed to buy two new tires, but didn't have the money. Jesús wanted to help him and bought the new tires, so his old neighbor could make the 460-mile drive back to Nuevitas.

A few times later, Jesús ran into him again in Havana. The gentleman was not able to pay Jesús back. At the same time, Jesús did not care about the money; he cared about the friendship.

Apparently, this gentleman was having a hard time accepting the fact that he did not have the same access to money as he used to. He was feeling very ashamed about it; especially after all the things he had done for Jesús and his family.

Jesús returned to the car. We continued to drive around while Jesús caught up on things with his cousin. We drove back to the cluster of high-rise apartments built in the revolutionary style of architecture and pulled up to his cousin's home.

While she was getting out of the car, Jesús turned to me and quietly asked, "Can we give her money?" He looked at me with puppy dog eyes, like he really wanted to help out his family.

"Well, yeah," I said.

Then the light bulb went off in my head. "Oh! You need me to front? Now I get it. OK. Fine."

I pulled out twenty CUCs, and gave it to him on the side. Then he gave it to her. She was really happy and gave him a hug good-bye. In Cuba, even a doctor, is not well off.

Jesús was like a big brother trying to help as best as he could. Cubans have close families. I could see this at the airport in Havana. When one person is leaving, holy guacamole, the whole family shows up! Even at four o'clock in the morning. The family members show up at check-in time, and it looks like they are all leaving together on a trip.

"No. No. They do not all leave together," Jesús told me at one point. "When one person leaves, everyone comes to see them off and cry. That's how Cubans are." Then Jesús made some kind of joke about it.

Once Jesús finished with his good-byes, we turned around in our car and tried to find our way out of the maze of these high-rise apartments. The roads needed paving. I kept at least one eye on the road to look out for things that could cause flat tires. We came up on a near-feral dog that stood in the middle of the road. He ignorantly would not move, like a stubborn cow in the road. There are many stray dogs in Cuba. It was a common sight to see them wandering about on the road. These dogs always seemed to step out in front of the car, and I had lost my patience with this one. I honked my horn. A woman stood off to the side of the road and started profusely yelling at the dog in Spanish. Upon hearing this tirade, Jesús started to bust up, laughing hysterically.

When Jesús finally caught his breath, he said that the woman was cursing profusely at the dog, and she finished off her tirade with, "You stupid ordinary dog!" I'm sure it was one of those "you had to be there" moments. I'm guessing that this woman was running out of a rendition of curse words and was just grasping out in the air for anything left to say. It was a strange out-of-character ending to her tirade compared to what she had been saying before. When she had finished yelling at the dog, she walked off with a proud look on her face as if to say, "I sure showed that dog a thing or two."

We got on the main road and started backtracking away from Nuevitas, and toward the road that would take us to Camaguey. Jesús thanked me for taking the detour to Nuevitas, so that he could visit with his family. I could tell he really enjoyed it. I think it was good for him to go there.

We started to make up time on the road and went through a town named Minus. We didn't stop in Minus, but Jesús mentioned that it is known for manufacturing musical instruments, including violins.

We had last passed through the outskirts of Camaguey at night during our crazy drive on the dangerous Carretera Central highway road. This was earlier in our trip, when we were trying to continue on and make our way to see Chiqui in Holguin. Now I could see Camaguey during the daytime. From the outside of the city, it looked like an interesting place.

Jesús knew of a casa where we could stay. We tried to find this casa, but we found problems navigating the streets of Camaguey instead. We would go down a one-way street thinking that we could, then we would take another road to turn us back up to where we needed to go. That didn't work. We kept going down all the wrong streets.

"OK," Jesús said, "This road. No. No. No. OK. Maybe we'll go down left. Go down right. Hook around here."

We got off track every time, and I kept getting frustrated.

"What is this place? I can't . . . It just . . . nothing lines up the way it's supposed to," I said. There's a one-way street here, a one-way street there, or you turn right to go on the one-way up, and then that street is all of a sudden gone! Everything resembled a labyrinth. I kept thinking, *Hells Bells!*

What's going on here? It was the end of the day. People were behind me and in front of me. Motor bikes whizzed by, cars honked their horns, horses clattered past with carts, people rode by on bikes—all on these narrow streets.

I was tired from days of driving on the rough Cuban roads. I pounded my hands on the steering wheel and screamed out, "Just shoot me! Somebody just shoot me!" Jesús looked at me and started to laugh.

Yes, I was having a melt down. The confusion of streets was driving me nuts!

We drove around a few more directions, hooked back, and finally, we did it! We found the casa, but only to be told that it was full. The owner of the casa told us of another place that might have room. Jesús called the other casa on his cell phone, and found out that they did in fact have room. But then, we had the problem of trying to go out again and find our way to this other casa. Jesús got directions. So off we went progressing further up and down these streets again, getting lost here and there. Nothing made sense! These streets were so confusing that I was starting to think we were a couple of crazy lab rats in a maze with no cheese in sight. Something's not right. Something's just not adding up.

Out of nowhere, we finally and surprisingly found the casa.

"I don't care what it's like. We'll take it," I told Jesús.

I did not want to drive around this town anymore and get lost in these crazy streets again!

The house was beautiful inside. We were shown our room on the third floor. We unpacked our things and found a safe place to park the car for the night. That's when the mystery of the nonsensical streets was solved.

When the city of Camaguey was growing, there was a constant problem of marauding pirates who raided and attacked the city. To protect and defend themselves, the people of Camaguey intentionally laid out their streets in a confusing, irregular, and unorthodox manner to confuse the pirates when they entered the city. It helped to level the playing field, giving the townspeople a better chance to fight back and defend their city against the pillaging pirates. If these pirates were able to find their way out of the maze of this entanglement of streets, it was hoped that this would act as a deterrent, keeping invaders from coming back and want to take another chance.

I found it funny that hundreds of years later nothing has changed. These streets did and definitely were still doing what they were originally designed and meant to do—a great job of confusing the hell out me, and for that matter, any other outsider.

7

CLOSE
ENCOUNTERS

THE CITY OF Camaguey was established around 1515. It is known for its many large and historic churches. There are twenty-two in all. Camaguey is also referred to as the City of Tinajones. *Tinajones* are large earthenware pots, and the symbols of the city. For a time, they were used to collect rainwater and for food storage. Some of these pots are as tall as six feet.

After we unpacked our things, Jesús and I walked around town while there was still daylight. The streets are narrow and are pedestrian-only walkways during certain times of the day. We saw a lot of people walking about or sitting on their stoops watching the world go by. I was intrigued by the ease of the people in this city and by the movement of life filtering around and about. For a pretty big city, I found it to be a peaceful and tranquil place.

Jesús and I came up to industrial train tracks that intersected one of the busy roads. We continued walking and came upon the train station. A policeman stood in the middle of the road, amongst the train tracks. He was looking at me. Obviously, I was the minority there and stood out from the crowd of people walking about and riding their bikes past him. Not only that, I was taller than most people and had this big camera pack on too. I did not know what was going on in his mind, or what he was thinking about me. But I was definitely getting the once over. Without warning, he acknowledged me with a half salute, and I quickly gave him a respectful tip of my head. At that moment, the mass body of people started moving in earnest over these tracks. I was surprised that this body of individual people was able to instinctively pick up on the fact that a train was coming out of nowhere. As this train slowly, yet loudly, rumbled by. I took a few pictures. The train finally passed, and the mass of people that had bottlenecked at the tracks returned back to their seemingly normal rhythm of movement.

It was nearly time to make our way back to the casa for dinner. Jesús wanted to pick up a bottle of Havana Club 7 años rum, for later on that night.

"We're getting low," he said.

"OK. OK," I agreed.

Jesús is pretty good at negotiating. Being in his element, he naturally has a feel for where to go, and where not to go, for deals, the black market, and whatnot.

After taking care of the rum, we walked back to our casa. We found the table nicely set and ready for us to eat our dinner. As we sat down, a plate of pork was brought out for Jesús and a plate of *camarones* (meaty prawns) for me. Along with this came a large plate of black beans and rice and a bowl of some type of hot garlic soup. It sure did taste good.

She served a square side dish of dense guava paste. It was thick like fruit leather, but not too hard; it was like jello, but not translucent. The guava paste was always accompanied by small bars of white cheese. We had bread, a custard apple, and a round of Bucanero beer. The owners of this casa were old, so they hired a younger gal from down the street to cook and do light housecleaning for them. She sure knew how to cook a wonderful meal.

After dinner, Jesús and I went out for a little evening walk; it felt good to walk off that big dinner. When we returned to our casa, I took a shower, lay down on the bed, and started making notes about the places I had seen that day. I asked Jesús for follow up information on these places. I was tired from the intense driving all day, and I inadvertently fell asleep on my papers and notes.

In the morning, I felt rested. I found out that there was a big terrace toward the back of the casa that overlooked part of the city. I went to the third floor and stepped out on this terrace. As I walked out, the first thing I saw in the distance was one of the many churches in Camaguey, the towering Iglesia Sagrado Corazon de Jesús. This church opened in 1920 and was built in a distinct neo-Gothic style of architecture. It had three tall white spires, a red tile roof, and ornate stained-glass windows.

In the surrounding area, closer to the casa, were many rooftops and makeshift cubbyhole balcony areas that people used for hanging laundry at the upper reaches of their homes. I could see the bright, colorful laundry starting to be hung out on long lines to dry. It was time for breakfast and that wonderful Cuban espresso that I so loved. After breakfast, we decided to go look around at things and see what we could see. We walked through a couple squares, one was called Plaza de los Trabajadores, meaning Square of the Workers. Many, many bici-taxis buzzed about like flies.

High on top of one of the buildings was a large, completely square billboard in full color of Ché smiling with Cuba's flag in a waving motion behind him. Off to the side was another billboard of propaganda that said, "*Hasta la Victoria Siempre,*" or "Onward Victory Forever."

Once we were beyond these squares, I started to notice that the most common architecture style was neoclassical. Unlike many of the other places where we had been, there were no arcades from what I could see. I took a picture of a guy going down a narrow street on his bike. He sold brooms, and had ten to fifteen brooms bundled and tied onto the back of his bike. The brooms had short, stubby bristles and long, wooden handles. These handles were six feet long, and I could tell they were hand carved. The detail of the handles is what caught my eye. I could see the chip marks on the handles. It was as if someone had carved and tooled them down from a straight piece of tree limb. This guy had the middle sections of these brooms centered and perfectly balanced on the back of the bike, while the top and bottom ends protruded out horizontally on either side of his bike. As he rode down the street, his bike looked like a plane with wings ready for take off. I found it humorous because it appeared that he would not be able to get very far on those narrow streets that were full of people and cars.

Walking on, I thought it was interesting to see a lot of the old walls around town and how they were ravaged by history and slowly worn over time. In 1668, Welsh privateer Sir Henry Morgan arrived with a flotilla of ten ships and a mob of five hundred marauding pirates. They made their way thirty-one miles inland to Camaguey. Firing their muskets and wielding their naked cutlasses, the pirates captured the city. They plundered Camaguey for its riches and set most of the city on fire. By 1670, Morgan had terrorized and ravaged much of Cuba's coastline.

It soon became time to start making our way back from our walk and prepare to hit the road again. When we returned to the casa, I noticed that the older people who owned the place were all huddled closely around the small television looking as if they didn't want to be bothered. Then I noticed that they were all watching the *Telenovelas!* The funny thing about this is I recognized and knew that crazed look they had. My kids get that same look after watching too many cartoons on television. We packed our things, loaded the car, paid our bill, and said our good-byes. As we left, the older people of the casa quickly went back to watching their *Telenovela!*, so as not to miss a thing. Once we were on the road again, I had to reorient myself on how to get the hell out of this confusing network of irregular streets.

I came up to a stop sign that said, "*Pare!*" I pulled up to the intersection as far as I could go because the buildings and homes came right up to it, almost to the edge of the street. This made it very difficult to see up or down the cross streets. Cars, motorcycles with sidecars, bicyclists, and pedestrians all seemed to come out of nowhere fast.

"Chris, go!" Jesús blurted out,

"No! It says *Pare!*" I replied, as I looked left and right and back left and right,

"What are you doing? Jesús asked. It's only a one way street!"

He pointed to the little four-inch by eight-inch blue sign with an arrow. In every city, I struggled to find these signs. They were never in a designated spot. They might be tacked on a building, stuck to the side of a house, or fixed to a light pole. They could be far off to one side and not where they could be seen. It was almost to the point of playing *Where's Waldo?* Looking for road signs was something I had to be on top of everywhere I drove. This was especially true when the traffic became more free form and when there were many different people walking and traveling on bikes in the cities and villages.

I pushed through and continued driving. We were nearly out of town when I made a turn, and something caught my eye.

"I gotta get this!" I yelled out. I needed to pull over and find a place to park amid the confusion of the passersby and these streets. "It's just one of those things," I told Jesús. "I don't know how to explain it, but my eyes saw something. I have to go!"

I saw a connection of things in my head—a snapshot that I could not find the right words to explain to Jesús. I jumped out of the car with my camera and left Jesús while I went around the corner to get a bunch of pictures of it.

What caught my eye was a brick house. This house had no roof because Hurricane Ike had blown it off. I could partly see the thick brick and broken walls in the middle of this house. There was a room that looked like it had been painted over a few different times. I don't know how many years ago. There were objects purposely painted across the middle of one of the walls that looked like some type of hieroglyphics or contemporary art. They might have been paintings for a child's room, I don't know. I could see different faded patterns that depicted people doing things. Next to this wall, there was a large doorway opening that had a fluted, high barrel archway, supported by a respond pilaster column.

An old wooden door or window frame laid to the side along with little piles of rubble. Of course, no one was living there. I stayed only a few minutes, snapping off a few pictures, and then I went back to the car.

We continued driving and found our way out of Camaguey, heading west on the Carretera Central roadway. This was the same road we drove on that crazy night when we were trying to make it to Holguin in time to see Chiqui. Only this time, instead of the complete dark of night, I was able to see this roadway during the daylight hours. It was quite a contrast. All along the way, there were different fields and valleys. It was harvest time for sugarcane. Some areas had an arid feel, while other areas were tropical. Throughout Cuba, I noticed the white, tropical clouds of the typical Caribbean sky. They seemed ever present and always floating by so effortlessly.

The old road turned into long, straight stretches. Utility poles with wires ran alongside the road. They were cut from the rough, and not particularly straight, center trunks of the trees. I could see that a few of these poles had short cut-off stubs protruding from the tree from limbs that were lopped off from the main trunk. These utility poles made from rough tree trunks had a weathered and worn look. They were bleached gray in color, and looked very unlike the smooth, straight, black, creosoted poles we had in America. At times, on these long stretches of road, you might think you were on Route 66. That was, of course, until seeing all the huge Cuban Royal Palm trees scattered about.

After passing the small towns of Florida and Ciego de Avilla, I could not hold it any longer, I needed to stop as best as I could on the side of the narrow roadway. Nature called, and I ran into the sugarcane field about two rows deep. Feeling better, I walked back up the embankment to the car.

Jesús said, "Hey that's a good idea too." So off he went.

I got this funny idea for a prank: I looked around for big rocks that I could throw out in the cane field close to Jesús—so as to startle him while catching him in midstream, so to speak. Little did I know that while I was doing my business, Jesús got hold of the disposable camera in my bag and took a few pictures of me from behind. It was like Spy vs. Spy. I only found out that he ultimately got the upper hand on me after I was back home in America and had the pictures in the camera developed. I can just see Jesús snickering away, delighted, and fully reveling in the fact that I was now denied another chance to have a bite at the apple. He knew that he truly got one on me, and there was nothing I could do to get him back.

We were crossing back over to the Caribbean side of Cuba and on our way to Trinidad, where we would stay for two nights. But before going to Trinidad, we decided to stop at a town called Sancti Spiritus. Founded in 1514, Sancti Spiritus means Holy Spirit in Latin. This area was also known as the birthplace of the Guayabera shirt. As we entered Sancti Spiritus, we decided to go into the middle of town to the Parque Serafin Sanchez square.

Serafin Sanchez was born in Sancti Spiritus in 1846. He was a general in the Cuban military, and he fought in significant battles of the two wars of independence. He was killed in battle in 1896. The square was nice and had an abundance of trees and benches. Many buildings of neoclassical architecture surrounded it. I parked the car, and we got out to walk around. Right in front of me was an old, bright yellow theater built in an eclectic style of architecture. The building itself was built in the 1920s and was later turned into a cinema named Cine Conrado Benitez.

As I was taking a picture of the Cine, I was startled by the sounds of several cars honking their loud horns. Then an old, red 1950 Chevy Deluxe Convertible appeared in full view, as it came driving through the town's square. A bride to be was sitting atop the back seat over the trunk, waving her hand to anyone who was watching, even me as I took her picture. She was on her way to get married. Her bright white dress and train flowed lightly in the wind. The horns kept honking as other family members followed in yet more cars. Every spot on this American car where balloons could be tied, they had tied balloons. I could see the faces of the proud father and mother of the bride who were excitedly driving their daughter around town, making their way to the church. In America, a lot of times people will use old, restored American cars in their weddings to portray an aura or a coolness from the past. It is an interesting contrast to this Cuban wedding party I saw. In Cuba, the only things they have are the old cars. They were not trying to reminisce; they were trying to be modern, to go forward. These old cars are the most modern things they have.

Jesús and I continued walking toward the older section of town, which had cobblestone streets. We passed by an old, blue building with porticoes, which was built in 1839. It was the Teatro Principal. From there, at the Rio Yayabo—the river that winds through the town—was a bridge built out of clay bricks. This bridge was built in 1815 in a European style and featured five rolling arches over the river.

As we continued to walk through these cobblestone streets, I felt something was not right. I started feeling sick and then progressively worse. My head and the back of my neck got stiff, and felt like they were on fire. I started getting dizzy and my head spun. I was about to black out.

Jesús could see that I was out of character. He sensed that something was wrong, so he quickly got me to an El Rapido, a little government run mini-mart store. This particular El Rapido was an open-air store with chairs. It was the only thing close by that Jesús knew of. He navigated me through all the crowds of people, past the horse carriages, and around the bikes, as I was not able to think clearly anymore.

"Just sit down," Jesús said, as he got me in a chair. I was carrying my large and heavy camera pack, and my whole shirt was drenched from sweating. I collapsed into the chair and tried to hold my body up. Jesús rushed ahead of the line of people and ordered up, because he knew I had to get water in my body. He quickly came back with bottled water.

After a good thirty minutes and about three bottles of water, I started to feel like I was coming back to life. Jesús went back and ordered a couple of small day-old sandwiches. They helped.

That's when he gave me a stern talking to. "No matter what, we have to stop during the day to drink and eat something. You're not used to the weather and everything else here."

We stayed there for about an hour, as I tried to get it together. I could not just get up and go. I had to really be able to keep my head up—on the street and in the crowds. It's not as though bad people lurked at that very moment. Still, I had to be alert.

"OK, let's get in the car," I said. "I want to crank up the air conditioning, turn the vents right on me, and see if I can bring my body temperature down."

That definitely seemed to be working. As we got closer to Trinidad, I saw small rolling mountains. They resembled those in the California wine country. This area of countryside was called Valle de los Ingenios, or Valley of the Sugar Mills. As we passed through here, we saw a large number of old sugar mill plantations, many in ruins. Many of the plantations had been built in the 1800s; some of them were even older; some of them looked like old churches with their elaborate steeple-shaped towers. One tall plantation tower, standing 148 feet high dominated this whole area of countryside, as the steeple loomed over all these rolling hills. Some of the towers aided the landowners who could look out far and wide over the countryside to keep an eye on their slaves while they worked out in the fields. To the slave masters, these slaves were viewed as nothing more than cattle sprawled out across the rolling hills and endless fields. These towers and mills could be viewed as silent witnesses, reminders of the days when slaves by the thousands worked in these very same sugarcane fields. I thought the visual appearance of these slaves on the hillsides, all scattered wildly abroad, working in the fields could parallel what one might see today when driving through America's countryside where thousands of cattle can be seen dotted out on the far distant hills and valleys.

We finally reached Trinidad. Jesús said that he knew of a place where we could stay, and that this casa should have plenty of room for us. He directed me through the streets, as I drove to the casa. We checked in and unpacked the car. As we were stepping back outside, the owners of the casa asked us what time we wanted to eat dinner, and gave us the run down on the menu. Continuing on, we went to find an Internet place that Jesús knew about and to buy phone cards for his cell phone. I hoped there was news from home. Once we were inside, I could see that there were only Europeans and other foreigners sitting at the computer tables.

Even though Jesús was with me, he could not buy the Internet card. I had to be the one to buy it, and then Jesús could indirectly get on the Internet with me to go through his e-mail. Because of the dial-up connection, it took time, but I was able to see that I had a reply from my wife. I was happy to hear news from my family since the last time I was able to communicate with them was when I was in Baracoa.

My wife told me, "Everyone misses you, and the kids keep asking, 'Where's dad? When will he come back?' Garrett is really feeling sad about your absence and thinks you are not coming back."

I replied back to my wife that I missed her, and I tried to tell her that I was safe and doing well. I let her know that I would be back in Havana soon, and that I would be able to communicate with her then. "Please tell the kids everything is fine, and that I miss them and love them all very much! I will be home very soon. When I get back, we will plan some special and fun things to do."

After that, it was time to head back to our casa. I was starting to get hungry. Once we were back at the casa, we sat outside on the back veranda, to have a beer and wait for dinner to be served. A French woman who was also staying at the casa was on the veranda with us. She was actually pretty nice. It seemed she had been all over the world. She worked for a huge cosmetic corporation; her work may have involved writing. She told us she was on vacation.

The French woman spoke English pretty well. The conversation turned to philosophies and events going on around the world. Of course, as soon as anyone learned that I was an American, they wanted to know all about the United States. They were especially interested in American politics since my trip fell during a presidential election year. As the conversation went on, it got a little deeper as the conversation turned to the ramifications of things going on in the world.

At that moment, Jesús blurted out, "The only way to find world peace is through what's under the hood of a Cuban-American car!"

The implication being that the Cubans don't have the luxury of being able to get the exact same manufactured replacement parts for their cars. They have to cannibalize from other cars, and what they get is a mix of different foreign car parts. While creatively making do with whatever they have, inventing ways to make all the foreign parts fit, and come together, while at the same time being able to make the car work and continue to run after all these years.

After we had another round of beer, our dinner was ready to be served. They brought out a large plate of shrimp for Jesús. I had the fresh catch of the day: sawfish. There were side dishes of rice, beans, and fresh fruit. For desert, we ate *flan de huevos*, a Spanish caramel custard. Of course, we could not go without Cuban espresso. I thought the flan and the coffee went very well together, so much so that I asked for another round of dessert and espresso. Some of the older ladies preparing the meals seemed a little taken back at my appetite and consumption of the espresso coffee. However, they were quite pleased at my appreciation of their cooking. After dinner and a shower, I rested on my bed and went over more of my notes from the day's activities while enjoying a small snifter of Havana Club 7 años rum.

I woke up in the morning to the sound of chickens coming alive, making their rambunctious morning chatter. Once we were up, we made our way to the back of the house, toward the veranda. Surprisingly, I was presented with a double pot of espresso that was brought out to me, as I was given a wink and a smile from one of the older Cuban ladies who was getting breakfast ready for us.

After breakfast, and after finishing my high-octane espresso, and for that matter, most of Jesús's allotment of coffee too, I was like a rocket ready for take off. I was definitely wired and ready to blast off for our adventurous walk for the day.

As we were about to make our way out the door, I was asked if I had any laundry that needed to be done. To my surprise, I caught out of the back corner of my eye, Jesús smiling with big round eyes and nodding his head up and down to the lady. So, taking that as a very subtle hint, I said, Yes! I gave the lady my clothes to be cleaned, and off we went walking.

Trinidad was founded on December 23, 1514. There is much history here, and not much has changed over the years. The streets are still made of the original, tightly laid cobblestones. Old colonial homes were painted in various colors of pastels, and having eighteenth-century wooden Barrotes over the windows with wooden shutters. These homes had large central wooden front doors that all had smaller doors cut within them. These large doors were framed by pilasters with a Tuscan base and capitals, with varying ornamental motif designs in between. The roofs were covered with red terra-cotta tiles. The tiles were sun baked and had various shades of red intermittently mixed together, which had created natural faux looking patterns.

As the people walked by, or moved about on their bikes, I could hear the loud echo sounds of trotting horse hooves clip-clopping on the irregular cobblestones of these long narrow streets. After a bit of looking around, we walked to a large square, Plaza Mayor, with many Cuban Royal Palms, park benches, and white, ornamental wrought-iron fencing around it.

At the top of the square is a church called the Iglesia Parroquial de la Santisima Trinidad. An earlier church had been built here on this site in the seventeenth century, but it was destroyed by a cyclone that ripped through town in 1812. The later church was built on the foundation of the earlier church.

Inside, I saw an elaborately carved wooden neo-Gothic high altar and a long groined-vaulted ceiling that runs the length of the church nave. The church has clerestory rectangular windows, broken down into smaller geometric squares. Above them, I saw bright, colorful stained-glass mediopunto windows.

As I stepped outside the church and looked at its neoclassical façade, I was surprised to see a beautiful red 1959 American Chevy Impala Convertible. It looked like it was in perfect condition, with all its original chrome and trim still intact. I could not believe its beauty. I took pictures. The owner was proud of his car. Apparently he was hired for the day to drive for a *quinceañera* celebration, that was about to take place inside this church.

We continued walking and saw kids playing baseball in a small open dirt area, surrounded by old colonial homes. Most of the kids were barefoot, and they only had sticks to use as bats. But they all seemed to be having a good time playing.

One can only wonder how many marauding pirates had come through here centuries ago and battled on this same open dirt area along the adjacent cobblestone streets. There were probably many different raids on this town. How many stories remained untold? How many nameless and innocent residents died at the hands of these sword-wielding pirates right where we were walking and where these kids were playing ball?

With their youthfulness, these kids were only aware of the here and now at that moment in time. They were oblivious to the long-forgotten lawlessness of the past and unaware of the reality of the permanence of death. To them, this was just another open area where they had the freedom to play ball and have fun. Centuries ago, people fought for this land. They fought for the future, to tame this frontier so that the youth of future generations could live and play freely, just as these kids were doing now.

From where we were standing, I could see, way up on a hill, the old ruins of a building. A few people were sitting in the shade of it, looking out over the city.

"What is that up there?" I asked Jesús.

He told me that it was an old church.

"Let's hike up there and check it out," I said. So up we trudged, huffing and puffing, up this big hill. We finally found our way to the crest and came up to the ruins on a narrow dirt path. The church had been called Ermita de Nuestra Senora de la Candelaria de la Popa and was built in the 1700s.

Three old Cuban ladies were sitting on the front steps in the cool shade from the shadows of the old church. They were working on handcrafts. One was making a bag out of weaved palm leaves. The other two were threading beads to make necklaces and earrings. They were very friendly old ladies. One tried talking to me in Spanish, but I could not understand her, as she had no teeth. That didn't stop her though; she carried on talking. The gist of what she was trying to tell me was that the things she had made were available for sale—right now, today only of course, at a good price, for me only.

It was funny, because it reminded me of my last trip to Cuba—down below this hill, walking along these cobblestone alleys. This one area of the street seemed to be dedicated for a large handcrafts marketplace. They sold woodcarvings, ceramics, beadwork, and beautiful embroidered linens. There were tablecloths and many different kinds of shirts. I made the big mistake of stopping just a little too long to look at the different handsewn Guayabera shirts. By doing so, this created a scene of excitement, as the Cuban women immediately wanted to show me everything they had hanging in their makeshift stalls. They started pulling out all these shirts and tried to size them up to me. I kept trying to be as polite as I could. I told them, "*No gracias.*" But they were persistent, and I somehow relented to try one on. One of the women said, "*No. No. No!*" She motioned to me, "You have to take off your shirt first!" Now, how the hell they got me to take off my shirt and try on theirs I don't know!

I took off my shirt and handed it to the one gal to hold for me. Before I could get the other shirt on, all the catcalls started to come out from the Cuban women who were there selling. The women were watching me and laughing. One of the women reached out with her hand and rubbed my perspired belly in a circular motion, making a cooing noise and smiling. By now, my face was turning red with embarrassment, and I was completely speechless. So, I put their shirt on. Obviously, I was too big for what they had, so I quickly took it off. I really just wanted to put mine back on, and I reached out my hand to the one gal who was holding my shirt to get it back from her. She took a small half step backwards, clutched my shirt tighter in her crossed arms, and shook her head in very slow motion, as if trying to say no. The whole time she was smiling and staring at me, ogling, and looking up and down slowly, as if undressing me with her wide-open eyes. By now, I was speechless and red in the face. I did not know what to say anymore. All I knew was that I was feeling really awkward, that I wanted my shirt back, and I wanted it now! I never had anything like this happen to me before.

After a few more catcalls and laughs, I was finally given my shirt back. I guess she was done and had her fill of lustful looking. Once I got my shirt back on, the correct shade of color returned to my face. We said our good-byes, and all three of these playful Cuban women each gave me the customary Cuban farewell of the exaggerated sound of kissing two or three times while only touching cheek-to-cheek.

We spent time sitting up on this hill admiring the view, and now it was

time to make our way back down. As we started walking back through the streets, we walked up to the most recognizable building in Trinidad, the large double bell house tower of the Iglesia y Convento de San Francisco, which was built sometime in the seventeenth century. Before I walked in this building, I saw a dark-skinned Cuban man leaning up against the bright yellow pastel colored wall of the church. He had a large Cuban cigar in his mouth. It was as if he indirectly posed for me, as he stood there on the cobblestone street, leaning on the corner of this church. I took a picture of his silhouette; then, mysteriously he was gone.

I entered the church only to find out that it now is a *museo* (museum) that houses the actual fuselage of the United States U-2 spy plane that was shot down over Cuba, on October 27, 1962, by two Russian SA-2 surface-to-air Guideline missiles. At first, I could not believe it. I always knew about the U-2 spy plane that was shot down over the Soviet Union on May 1, 1960, during the cold war. But yet, here this one was on display, right in front of me, along with pictures and information. Tensions precipitated the plane being shot down. Tensions from the Bay of Pigs invasion; tensions from enacted embargos and blockades from Kennedy; tensions from the Guantanamo Naval Base; and tensions from the Soviet placements of nuclear warhead missiles in Cuba. These tensions came to a head in October 1962, which to the Cubans is known as La Crisis de Octubre.

The history of the Cuban Missile Crisis, which I learned in school and from the media, was pretty much that President John F. Kennedy stared down the Soviet leader Nikita Khrushchev. Kennedy's tough talk and stance during the crisis caused the Soviet Union to blink and to pull their missiles out of Cuba. The world came away from being on the brink of a nuclear war.

While I was tripping out looking at parts of this fuselage, Jesús mentioned to me that there was another side to this story. With Cuba's history of fighting for its independence, it needed to protect and defend its sovereignty from constant outside aggressors. Being allies with the Soviet Union changed the dynamics and put things in check. Instead of the constant harassment and prodding operations against Cuba, Cuba now had an equal deterrent. Because of nuclear weapons, this became an international conflict. The United States had nuclear missile sites in Turkey aimed at the USSR. As part of the conditions of the Soviets pulling out of Cuba, Kennedy had to remove all of those nuclear missiles out of Turkey and also pull missiles out of Italy.

As I was listening to what Jesús was telling me, I thought about it for a minute. I thought, *Hey! That sounds a lot like history repeating itself with President George W. Bush planning missiles sites in Poland and radar stations in the Czech Republic—despite the objections of Russian President Vladimir Putin.* Talk about déjà vu, a different time and a different place; same chess game, different round.

It was getting late in the afternoon, and I thought it would be good to make our way back to the casa, so we could kick back there with a cool beer on the veranda before dinner. When we got back to the casa, the ladies of the house were glued around the television watching *Telenovela!* As we entered, I told them not to get up, that I knew where the beer was, and we were going to go to the back to the veranda to sit down and relax.

A newly arrived couple came out to sit and have a drink on the veranda in the coolness of the twilight hours. After introductions, we found out that they were from Brazil, and the husband only spoke Portuguese. The wife could speak English and French. Her knowledge of English was almost equivalent to my knowledge of Spanish. Between the two of us, we tried to communicate. Jesús spoke in Spanish, and even used French to try and help clarify things. The wife translated to her husband in Portuguese to help keep everyone involved in the conversations. It was slow going, as we went from one translation to another. But, after all, we had nowhere to be and nothing to do other than having another round and enjoying the time.

Once we got past all the formalities and the new couple found out that I was an American, again, the main topic of interest was politics and what was going on in America with the elections coming up. After lengthy conversations about historical topics and subsequent discussions about the things that have been unfolding over the decades with these two countries. Then they asked when America might open up diplomatic relations with Cuba. Since the wall has been around this island, things have been always been muddled and unclear, wrapped in shrouds and layers of mystery, left to their distractions. But despite all these people's continued human endurance, wandering in its isolation, unbroken through the exposure of the desert experience, I found there to be a kind of floating consensus amongst a random few sincere Cubans. Alongside all the projections and rumors thrown about, there was a hopeful, underlying feeling, optimistically building, that something imaginable could conceivably happen in the near future. There were also rumors that Cuba's biggest concern about opening up is how to deal with the possibility of the mafia trying to get back in Cuba. But this time, it would not be the Italian-American mafias like before, as history tells us, but rather the possibility of Russian mafia trying to get into Cuba.

After some thought, I realized that Jesús was right. I remembered being at a couple of cabarets and seeing Russians in the audience. They had that stone-faced demeanor, and the way they were positioned around and carrying themselves you could tell to stay away from them! At one point, I said hello in passing. I got a look with no words, a death stare, in return. Before I realized who they were, it looked and became very clear to me that some of these people were to some degree Russian mafia. As the night wore on, I will say this—they sure knew how to drink! And drink that vodka they did. It got to the point that they behaved out of character, jumped up on the stage, and did a Russian polka dance with the cabaret dancers. They were acting like they owned the place. As for me, I just sat back and thought it was hilarious, and watched the double feature while I smoked the best Cuban cigars in the world—a Montecristo No. 2 and a large Romeo y Julieta. I will say though, that once Cuba does open, some of the best musicians in the world will be found coming out of there.

I have been very fortunate to have seen and heard these talented Cuban musicians. Being free of a lot of outside influences, their music is honed with the heart and soul of life on their island of isolation. As the Top 40 does not exist there, these musicians are not trying to fit a pop music format. Rather, their music has a true heart and a true feeling of expression.

The conversation on the veranda wound down, and we were ready to have dinner. Jesús had his favorite dish of pork, and since I can never get enough, I had a big plate of lobster. After dinner, we decided to take an evening walk around town to check out the quiet and tranquil nightlife. While we were out, we stopped at the Internet place, so I could send an e-mail home. I let my family know that I was still OK, and that I missed them and loved them all very much. I told my family that I would be home soon, and that I might be able to get access to a computer in a couple of days when we were back in Havana. After that, we walked around a bit more, taking in the sights and the night sounds of this old historical town. As we walked on the original old cobblestone streets, I reflected on the things that happened here hundreds and hundreds of years ago. I wondered what it might have been like for all the past generations of people.

By now it had been a full day, and I was ready for a shower and bed. Tomorrow was going to be a big day of driving. We were in Trinidad on the Caribbean side of the island, and tomorrow we were planning to cross back over again to the Gulf of Mexico side of Cuba. Jesús wanted to watch a little more of the black market recordings, so he connected his small portable DVD player to the back of the television in our room.

In the morning, I was ready for breakfast and my favorite rocket fuel for the day, the smell of that Cuban espresso and the feeling of it hitting in my veins. We left for the middle part of town to buy big carrying bags for Jesús's father in-law, Omar. Trinidad was known for its good carrying bags, which

were handmade out of palm leaves. The palm leaves are tightly weaved and can be turned into big sturdy bags with handles.

Jesús told me a story: "There are only four extremities to the basic human. The two arms and the two legs. But! To Cubans, there are actually five—two arms and two legs and a carrying bag!"

I thought about this and realized that he was right. When you look around, you do see a lot of Cuban's of all ages relying on those carrying bags. They have to be very inventive and creative in how they transport things around town. I saw bags hanging on bikes and horses. The bags are one of the only means of getting something around town or something home from a market.

While Jesús was looking for the perfect bag to buy, I walked around the older parts of the city. My eyes were stimulated by the old walls, the details left from history, and the color of time worn over them. I'm not sure why, but I found in Trinidad, like other cities we passed through, a connection of some sort. These walls kept catching my attention and stimulating my eyes. So much so that I kept taking pictures of them.

Out of nowhere, out from the crowds of people, I heard Jesús's voice shouting, "Voila!"

He came walking toward me with a smile on his face, holding two bags with nice patterns woven from palm fronds.

"Now," he said, "we can leave town."

Off we went! Our next destination was Mantanzas. We opted to take the rugged road that went right up over the Sierra del Escambray. This road overlooks Trinidad and continues through Gran Parque Natural Topes de Collantes, a nature reserve. The highest peak in the reserve is also called Topes de Collantes and it is about 2,625 feet high. The tallest peak in the Sierra del Escambray is Pico San Juan, which stands at 3,730 feet high.

While driving on this road, we saw much unspoiled landscape and dense tropical rain forests. There are many indigenous species of orchids and ferns in this area. The fern species were like palm trees, growing to heights of twenty feet. Although not endemic to this area, Cuba's national flower, Mariposa Blanca, or White Butterfly, *Hedychium coronarium,* grows here. Cuba's national bird, the Cuban trogon, or Tocororo, is endemic to this area and roams freely here. This area is also known for its many hiking trails, caves, and waterfalls with natural pools.

We wound around these steep roads and finally reached the area known as Topes de Collantes. There is a large building here that dates back to the 1930s, when Fulgencio Batista began construction. The building remained unfinished for several years. In 1954, when Batista was back in power, construction was finished and the building became a large tuberculosis sanatorium. After the 1959 revolution, the hospital went through many different changes, eventually becoming a mountain spa resort known as the Kurhotel. A large collection of original Cuban artwork by some of the most famous Cuban artists is amassed at the Kurhotel. The art is displayed throughout the many rooms and lobbies.

The road plateaued a bit, as we continued driving slowly, maneuvering around some of the larger mountains and lush verdure rain forest vegetation. There were some bad potholes in the road, although the potholes were nowhere near as bad as the ones on the road we had taken to Nuevitas. We got to an area of the road where there was a view looking out to the west. We pulled over and got out to take a quick look. Amid the high mountain peaks and deep jungle valleys was a large, long, narrow lake. The lake looked deep since it was snaking around the contour of the steep terrain of the deep, narrow mountain valleys.

Jesús corrected me, telling me that the lake was actually a manmade reservoir called the Embalse Hanabanilla. As I looked down further from where we were standing at the edge of this road. I could see red dirt trails

meandering down through the thick jungle on the steep hillsides. Bohio homes were dotted about. There were a few open patches of tilled ground, obviously farmland and obviously tilled by hand or with oxen. It looked like they were growing coffee and tobacco along with other food staples for their daily needs.

We started to drive again, and the road started to make a slow decline in elevation. Now that we had made it over to the other side of the mountain range, the road intermittently turned into rough dirt. As we progressed further, the road tended to be less curvy. We saw more tobacco and coffee farms. We passed the town of Manicaragua, known for growing distinctly flavorful coffee beans.

As we traveled further down this road, I noticed lush green fields of tobacco growing in massive rows. Some of the tobacco had already been harvested. The leaves were cut at the stems, bundled, and tied along the length of ten-foot long bamboo-type poles. These poles would be carried into large barns made of palm fronds where they were laid horizontally on racks with the tobacco leaves all hanging loosely and dangling downward, ready to dry, cure, and ferment. The entire western end of the Cuban island in the Pinar del Rio province is the predominate growing region for tobacco, where some say the best tobacco in the world grows.

Also within that western end of Cuba are areas known for having large limestone mountains called mogotes. These natural mogote formations are prolific here on this side of the island and are covered in thick dense green verdure vegetation that protrudes out high above the ground around the oxen tilled farmlands. Due to their distinct shape, if you didn't know any better, you would think you were in the middle of southern China where similar limestone formations exist. The difference is that in China, much of these formations are surrounded by bodies of water. In this case, Cuba's large limestone formations are surrounded by large swaths of deep red, fertile soil.

The scenery continued to change and became more of a wide, drier inland valley floor. We passed through Santa Clara again, but this time we crossed in toward a northerly direction. We were getting closer to the Gulf of Mexico side of the island. We passed through little villages, sugarcane fields, and people going about their business.

We finally came to the town of Sagua la Grande, which was founded in 1812. Sagua la Grande was made famous in 1962 as one of the medium-range ballistic missile (MRBM) sites set up by the Soviet Union. Upon reaching this sleepy small town, I was surprised to learn of its famous past, a time when the world was close to being brought to the brink of another world war. But this time the stakes were much higher because both players held the same cards—nuclear weapons. On October 22, 1962, John F. Kennedy gave a key warning during his public speech on the crises with Cuba. Kennedy gave a direct order raising the US military to DEFCON 3. On October 23, 1962, the United States reached DEFCON 2. This is the only time in recorded history that this had ever happened, and it happened only ninety miles from America's shoreline.

It had then dawned on me that we were not far from the village of Remedios, where I had seen those Russian MiG fighter jets screaming low and banking left and right across the Cuban morning sky. It made sense to me that there was a military base close by. I had not previously realized the historical significance of Sagua la Grande.

We were heading north when we entered Sagua la Grande. We drove part way through the city and turned west on the main road. We were traveling parallel along the length of the island, as we headed toward Matanzas, where we were planning on staying for the night.

The Gulf of Mexico was now in sight. We saw many sugarcane fields and passed through beautiful countryside with many little villages. We came to the large port town of Cardenas. Founded in 1828 on former swampland, Cardenas is known for its many bikes and horse-drawn carriages. Cardenas became widely known in 1999, as it is the hometown of Elian Gonzales, the five-year-old boy whose rescue in the ocean off the coast of Florida caused an international political custody dispute between Cuba and the United States for his rightful home. At the time of my visit, Elian Gonzales still resided in Cardenas.

As we left Cardenas, we were running out of daylight, and it looked like we might not make it to Matanzas by nightfall. Jesús decided to call ahead to a hotel that he knew about in Matanzas, but found out that they were fully booked. We did not want to drive around the city in the dark looking for another place to stay, so we decided to stop for the night in the next city in our path. That city was Veradero, which was located on the long, thin, and narrow Peninsula de Hicacos.

It made more sense to stop here for the night instead of pushing ourselves. In contrast to the normal daily Cuban life, this whole surrounding area here changed and transcended from seeing the many horse-drawn carriages that I had been seeing all over Cuba. Veradero was a resort area with large buildings and modern high-rise hotels standing on the sand of this narrow peninsula. Once we entered the Veradero peninsula, Jesús mentioned that he knew of some hotels where we might be able to stay. One of the hotels we went to was nice and not too expensive, but they would not allow Jesús to stay there. Jesús knew of another hotel a few miles farther down the road where Cubans were allowed to stay.

We finally found it and pulled into the parking lot, but Jesús's next concern was whether an American could stay there. He went inside to find out while I waited in the car. Jesús came out with a smile on his face and said that I was allowed to stay there. I had to show them my passport and papers when I registered. While we were checking in, the receptionist filled out the paperwork from my passport. Off to the side across the bar, I could see that they had on the television with European CNN news. I took a quick look at it, to catch up on what was going on in the world.

The great thing was that we didn't have to worry about securing the car for the night because the hotel had a twenty-four-hour guard for the parking lot. We grabbed our luggage and went to find our room on the third floor, which faced the ocean's turquoise water and fine, bright white sand. We got situated and decided to go for a walk and chose a restaurant. It was an open-air restaurant with no walls, just a thick thatched wide roof above made of palm fronds and plenty of chairs.

We sat down at a bamboo table where we could feel the light ocean breeze. We ordered a round of Bucaneros along with some Cuban *especial* appetizers. After some time of enjoying our drinks and the moment, we ordered our dinner. Jesús had the pork. I couldn't resist, and I had two big barbecued lobster tails. After that, we relaxed there for the rest of the evening.

8

BACK TO HAVANA

IT FELT ODD waking up in that hotel room after staying in so many different and unusual places. By traveling and staying in private casas, I had the sense of being lower to the ground, seeing life as it really happened. I was able to interact with the Cuban people, and felt like I was on a more equal level. But this resort town and hotel seemed to be so far away from all the reality of everything. It was isolated from the normal rituals of people going about their day. I woke up and did not hear any of the natural Cuban morning sounds—no morning animal noises, no horse-drawn carriages, no people on bikes, just rude Europeans in the morning buffet lines emanating their superiority, smugness, and cultural entitlements, as they continually cut into the front of those lines with no sense of respect. Jesús and I ate good food at the hotel's buffet breakfast. But I was turned off by the blindness of the other people in the dining room, and how out of touch with reality they were.

After we finished breakfast, we went up to our hotel room and packed our things to get ready to leave. While I loaded the car, Jesús mysteriously walked across the street to get something at a store. After a bit, he came back carrying a bag. We got into the car, and Jesús pulled a child's baseball shirt and cap out of the bag he was carrying. Since world baseball was going on at this time, Jesús purchased these baseball-related items from the store across the street. He told me that these were for me to give to my oldest son, Shane. Jesús was appreciative of the things I had brought from America for him and his family, and he was expressing his heartfelt thanks by getting a present for Shane. My oldest son also happened to be the same age as Jesús's oldest daughter. I was quite touched and thanked him. I knew that my son would be proud to wear it to school, as the boys in his class wear sports hats and shirts, and he would have something that nobody else has. All the while, it would also make him feel special that his Dad brought something back for him.

Once we were on the road, we decided to drive around a bit and take a look at the area. Veradero was a very beautiful place. Historical references to Veradero dated back to 1555, although the actual city was not founded until December 5, 1887. Veradero sits on a large sand spit. Its average width is about three-quarters of a mile, and its length is only about eleven miles. It jets out from the main island of Cuba in a northeasterly direction.

This whole peninsula is called Peninsula de Hicacos, and if I did not know any better, I would have thought that I was driving in Miami. Like Miami, Peninsula de Hicacos has waterway channels lined by palm trees, deep green, grassy lawns and exclusive hotels built right up to the edge of the beach. The sand on the beaches was a bright, pure, fine, white sand, and is just yards away from where the turquoise blue Gulf waters sit, calm as lake water.

Jesús mentioned that there were a few famous mansions that we could see before heading out to Matanzas. One of the mansions, in fact, was not far from where we were. It was the former house of Chicago Mafia boss Al Capone. Jesús directed me around the different roadways until we finally found it. I looked around the open area for a place to park the car. After parking, I got out of the car with my camera and began to walk on the immense, lush green lawn area that surrounded the whole estate. There were many tall coconut palm trees that encircled about randomly. About halfway up to Capone's house, a security guard came walking by. He gave me a glance. Since I wasn't sure what was up, I gave him a respectful nod of my head for good measure. I decided not to venture any closer, and I took a few pictures from where I was standing. As I walked away to leave, I gave this security guard another respectful nod as if to say thanks.

Capone's house was built in 1934, a beautiful multi-level mansion. The architectural style is a Cuban vernacular, an eclectic mix of Italian, Monterey, and Spanish colonial styles. Cut stonework wraps around the whole mansion in a coursed ashlars pattern. Over the tops of the windows, the stone had been cut in a flat arch pattern. All the stone looks to be indigenous rock from the area. The front entryway had a true stone arch. Rolling elliptical arches with thickly cut stones continue around half of the mansion and extends around to the veranda on the backside of the mansion, which faces the sea. The second floor has a wooden balustrade on the balcony with turned wood newels and matching wood spindles covering the first floor windows. The wood trim and windowpanes were highlighted with a deep, rich blue paint. The cascading roof was made of deep red terra-cotta tiles.

As we left and drove farther up the road, Jesús began to tell me about another mansion built by an American millionaire. Irénée du Pont, former president of the DuPont chemical Company, built his mansion between 1928 and 1930 as a get away home, a place to visit with and entertain guests. This immense estate was luxurious for its time. DuPont's alluring and enchanted dwelling was christened "Xanadu" after the palace that was built in the summer capital city of Xanadu in the thirteenth century by Kublai Khan, the fifth great Khan of the Mongul Empire and the grandson of the infamous conqueror, Genghis Khan. This mega mansion has four stories, eleven bedrooms, and three large terraces. A nine-hole golf course, coconut palms, and a private yacht dock surrounded it. The architecture is a mixture of traditional Spanish colonial and art deco, featuring Moorish balconies. The roof is covered with green ceramic tiles. After the 1959 revolution, du Pont never came back to Cuba. His mansion and everything in it was left as is and was taken over by the Cuban government.

By now, the time came to head out to Matanzas. We crossed over a few steel mesh waterway bridges, including one that was about to lift up for a boat to pass underneath. We made it back out and onto the main road. Then we headed in a westerly direction. It didn't take long before we caught sight of the very large, deep, industrial bay called Bahia de Matanzas.

Off in the distance, and across to the far side of this bay, I could see large, square, steel-framed cranes on the shoreline docks. Large container ships were moored sideways to the docks, as these cranes were reaching high up in the air over and into them. As we dropped further into the bay and drove around it against the long, curving shoreline, I again could smell that same heavy familiar odor like I did in Baracoa. It was a thick, heavy smell, and the scent was like that of galvanized steel after being ground or saw cut.

In the water's shoreline, I saw a few men with big, white, triangular shaped nets. These nets were made of a fine, cloth-netting mesh and were slightly rounded at the corners. These men walked very slowly in chest-deep water, swooping the nets downward and lifted them up over their heads. My guess was that they were trying to catch shrimp. I wanted to take pictures because it looked really cool, but I couldn't slow down. As we got closer to town, the traffic behind us was picking up, and there was nowhere for me to pull over.

The city of Matanzas was founded in 1693. Before that, in 1508, the Spanish explorer Sabastian de Ocampo sighted the bay. He is believed to have been the first person to circumnavigate the island of Cuba.

This bay at one time was a haven for many pirates. In fact, on May 20, 1628, the Dutch pirate Piet Heyn intercepted sixteen Spanish ships that were on their way to Spain in the service of King Philip IV. Twelve of these ships were taken at sea. The four other ships fled into and became trapped in the Bahia de Matanzas. All sixteen ships were easily taken over, as they were so full and heavily laden. These captured ships were carrying gold and silver bullion beyond anyone's wildest imagination.

Matanzas is surrounded by many big rivers that snake around and through the city. Eventually, they run into its large, deep, inward bay. As the city grew, bridges were built to connect the different sections of town and the outlying suburbs. Because of these many bridges, Matanzas picked up the nickname Creole Venice in the nineteenth century. Many artists, writers, and intellectuals lived here. Because many of these artisans contributed deeply to the artistic and cultural life here, the city of Matanzas also became known as the Athens of Cuba. Matanzas' role in the historical development of Cuba's arts, theater, music, and poetry rivaled that of Havana and even Santiago.

On January 1, 1879, Miguel Failde, a musician, introduced the Danzon, a musical form of ballroom dance with both European and African influences. This dance was interpreted for the first time at the Matanzas Lyceum. It is a dance of collective figures in which the couple executes slow, discreet, sensual, yet refined, movements. A wind orchestra played the music in an unprecedented manner. The title of the music was *Las Alturas de Simpson,* or *Simpson Heights.* The Danzon had become so popular that it became the Cuban national dance. Danzon developed from, and is considered, the legitimate successor to the music genre Habanera, a popular form of rhythm music that could be played, sung, or performed with dance. The Habanera, which was a creolized form, originated from the Contradanza.

Once we crossed over the Rio San Juan, the road turned and took us directly into town. We passed by one of Matanzas revered theater buildings, the Teatro Sauto. This neoclassical structure opened in 1863 and seats 775 people. The interior has a stately horseshoe-shaped, three-story balcony that is almost entirely covered in beautiful, elaborate wood paneling. This theater has superb acoustics and the ceiling in the main hall is graced with paintings of the muses from Greek mythology.

As we made our way through traffic, we finally found a good place to park, next to a town square called Parque Libertad. After grabbing my camera pack and locking the car, we took off to look around. We dodged around the main traffic coming through and made our way to an area of streets that were easier for walking, as it was not as busy.

I was very intrigued by the doors I saw through here. I saw some with small door knockers, a few more had Masonic emblems tacked above them that appeared to have been left and long forgotten over the last century.

Then something really caught my eyes. "Check this out!" I yelled out to Jesús.

It was a beautiful, old American car. The hood ornament was the most polished part of the car while the rest of the car was faded and looked like it had many layers of Bondo on it. As I was taking a close-up picture of the hood ornament, an old guy, the owner of the car, appeared from behind me. He spoke good English, with a deep, raspy voice. The tone revealed a longtime habit of enjoying Cuban cigars. In fact, he had a lit cigar in his hand.

"What year is the car?" I asked him.

He replied that it was a 1948 DeSoto. He looked as if he were reminiscing about decades back. "Ahhh, those were the better days," he said in his raspy voice.

Apparently the car had been in his family ever since. The old guy asked me where I was from. I caught a look from Jesús, and not quite sure, I said, "Canada." I sensed that if I had said America, the old man would want to get into a more in-depth conversation about America and really dig into it. I honestly didn't mind talking in depth with this interesting old guy. That was his freedom, but I subtlety picked up that something might develop. I guessed Jesús sensed something and felt that this guy might get pretty loud or passionate about things, and Jesús didn't want to argue or debate. The old guy was persistent and continued digging more, as Jesús tried to be friendly and chat with him.

I finished taking my pictures after checking out this old DeSoto. I shook the guy's hand, and thanked him for his time. Once we were further down the street, Jesús perked up and began explaining their conversation.

"This old guy was living in such the past." Jesús said, explaining that the old guy failed to understand that during the different time periods he was joyously reminiscing about, the United States was in a Great Depression while Cuba's sugar industry was booming. Not to mention that during Prohibition, everyone came to Cuba to drink, gamble, and spend money.

We came down along narrow streets that wound through town by the Rio San Juan. Small fishing boats were pulled up for repairs on the banks and on makeshift docks. The larger boats were moored in the river's brackish water.

As I walked, I noticed the old walls of the buildings, creating impressions and visual images that were similar to those in abstract art. The age-old colors were weathered over time.

It started to make sense to me why my eyes tended to be drawn to the old walls all over Cuba. Abstract art is something deliberately created. Throughout these cities, the evolution of these walls is on full display. Their history included centuries of deliberate events and the random collateral effects. Ravages of weather, hardships, and wars have left their marks of emotions on the walls. These old walls present history in its natural state as nonliteral, nonlineal, and unpredictable. They portray things that randomly and slowly evolved over centuries. In Cuba's old towns and villages, these old walls each have their own story to tell.

After a few hours of walking, we started to make our way back toward the car and away from the river. We came across a building with blue, arching

porticos where an art show going on. I walked inside to look around at the abstract and modern artwork. I found it intriguing and walked all the way through inside the building. As I came out, I was surprised to see a big, beautiful building of neoclassical architecture across the street. I was even more surprised to learn that it was a fire station; the Matanzas fire brigade had its headquarters here. I was blown away, as I realized that during my whole trip on this island, I had not seen one fire station or even one fire truck.

This historic building, the Parque de los Bomberos, was built in 1897. The front façade has smooth, uniform-cut limestone blocks laced with geometric motifs. A series of engaged ionic half-columns with fluted shafts and volutes on the capitals holds up a large, triangular pediment. Above the pediment is a hipped roof. A post-modern assemblage of fire equipment is configured into the letter "M," for Matanzas, and pin-mounted inside the pediment facade. Centered in the middle of the building, below the pediment and between the evenly divided engaged columns, I saw a very large passageway for the fire trucks to drive out. The header at the very top has a smooth, flat, stone arch that stretches across the top of the opening of the large doorway. Below the large header is a lintel that is inside the doorway opening, but still high enough for the fire trucks to pass beneath. The lintel supports a very large rectangular transom made of beautiful crystal glass, cut and separated into geometric patterns, with glazing bars in the glass providing the illusion of an arched mediopunto. I found this building was definitely pleasing to my eyes.

By now it was time to make our way back to Havana. Jesús was hoping that the timing would be such that we could arrive in Havana in time to pick his girls up from school. He wanted to be there when school let out to surprise them with his arrival.

When we got in the car, we realized we still had time. Instead of taking the more direct highway route to Havana, we decided to take a few backcountry roads instead. We did not realize how curvy the roads would be. Because of the continued lack of road signs, we got lost again. We were trying to head to the small village of Santa Ana, but we could not find the cutoff road that we were supposed to take. While we were driving aimlessly up and down this potholed road, I saw a dozen or so men riding bikes in a pack. They were riding slowly, but with obvious intent on their faces. Each of these men had large handsaws tied onto their bike frames. The saws looked to be about six to eight feet long, and they had very big aged wooden handles on each end. The men were riding their bikes with the saws sandwiched between their legs. The saws protruded about two to three feet past the front and back ends of their bikes. Those one- and two-man manual saws appeared to be very old. They had exaggerated large teeth on the blades and truly looked like something from a bygone era—from the old logging days at the turn of the twentieth century, before chain saws were invented. The men conversed with each other while slowly riding. There was a certain demeanor and camaraderie about them as they made their way, ready to go to work somewhere. It was as if they were saying, "We're off to battle!" I also found it odd that they were in the middle of nowhere with no large trees in sight. I had no idea where they were headed. But we slowly drove alongside them. Jesús rolled down his window and asked them for directions to help us find the missing road.

The directions one guy gave were, "Go down the road. There's a tree with a rock with a fence post. You got to take that. Go to the bigger outcropping to the right, and go to the left." We thanked them, turned around, and got back on the right road to cut across to Santa Ana.

After driving for a while on the road, I said to Jesús, "OK, you crazy jalapeño, do you know where we are?"

Without missing a beat, he went off and began mimicking one of Jeff Dunham's characters, Peanut, talking about Santa Ana, California. "OK. OK." I said, "I know how this conversation is degenerating."

After a bit of this comic relief from Jesús, we came up onto the main road again, and we started to make our way toward the Autopista Nacional motorway.

As we were driving up on an elevated area along these beautiful country roads, I could look down on this wide valley floor filled with fields of sugarcane. The cane fields were being harvested in large configured square sections, like a checkerboard. Some of the already harvested squares had turned brown while the other tight squares were green with tall fibrous cane stalks swaying in the breeze of these endless green fields. As we got even farther down the road, we passed a couple of men on a carreta, or cart, pulled by two slow moving black oxen just making their way slowly along the road.

Stalks of green plantains were piled high on the cart. They were cut, but in large bunches on big stems.

"Chris, stop the car!" Jesús shouted. I stopped fast, as we passed the cart and I put it in reverse. The guy driving the cart had a slightly concerned look on his face. I got out of the car with my big camera and took a few pictures, while Jesús walked up to the gentleman. It looked as though he did not know what to make of it all until Jesús opened his mouth and said, "Since the hurricane, we can't get fresh plantains in Havana. Can I buy some for my family?"

The man on the carreta relaxed. For two or three pesos, he let Jesús pick out one big bunch of green plantains on a large stem. It was about two or three feet long. Jesús said that these were the best plantains. He put them on the back seat of our tin-can car. We made like a banana and split. Jesús wanted to give those plantains to his family. I didn't realize it, but he was planning and wanting to host a big barbecue at his house. We drove onward and got closer still to Havana.

As we traveled, Jesús began insisting that I stay at his house, as I had two days before I was scheduled to check back into my hotel in Havana. He was very adamant about it.

"I can't do that," I said, not wanting to impose. But after much coaxing, I finally relented. After a moment of silence, the conversation became, "What bed am I going to sleep in?" Jesús insisted that I stay in his and his wife's bed

"No, I can't. I can't do that one," I said. For one, since he had been driving all over Cuba with me, he hadn't seen his wife for many days. I knew she missed him. And I knew what that meant.

"I can't get in the middle of you," I said. "I understand you guys are married, but . . . " Jesús cut me off, "No! No! It's OK, Chris. You stay at my house. My wife and I will sleep in the girls' room on the top of their bunk bed, and the two girls will both sleep on the bottom."

"No! I can't do that," I said.

But Jesús, again without missing a beat, responded with "Quiet! Or I will have to kill you!" With that one, he had me. Again, I relented. Jesús was happy that I was finally being reasonable and seeing things his way.

Later on, he had a good laugh at me, because I had to sleep corner to corner on his small bed. I banged my head and ankles on his hard wooden headboard and footboard all night. I was too big and tall to sleep any other way.

We reached the main Autopista Nacional roadway.

"We still have time," Jesús said. "Why don't we stop for a bit and check out the small town of Guines? It's close by here, on our way; it is an agricultural town in the La Habanas province."

We drove into Guines and parked across the street from the small town square. Most of the old buildings in the town were either one or two stories tall, and some had colorful arcades. I came upon a brightly colored old cinema called the Cini Mayabeque Teatro, and I took a few pictures. Across the square from where we had parked the car was a store with an open veranda. We decided to go there and have something to drink. We sat down in the shade at one of the tables. We talked about what we were going to do and where we could go to eat once we got back to Havana. That is when Jesús mentioned a place that served good beer in large tall glasses and *caballo carne* (horsemeat).

"That would be a good place to go once we've been back for a few days," he said.

Continuing the conversation, he mentioned going to the Chinese quarter, Barrio Chino de la Habana, the Chinatown of Havana. During my trip to Cuba the previous year, I remembered seeing the large Paifang dragon gate in Havana's Chinatown with its large pagoda roof. In 1847, a large number of Cantonese Chinese arrived in Cuba by boat as laborers to work on the sugar plantations. Although not slaves, they were treated as poorly as the slaves. A second wave of Chinese arrived later. Some came from California during the mid to late nineteenth century while others came during the early twentieth century after fleeing the political chaos in China at that time. Jesús told me that their food is a mixture of Cuban and Chinese cuisines. I thought that was interesting.

"We should go check that out," I said. "I'll treat your whole family to dinner there."

At that moment, Jesús unexpectedly jumped up from our table. He stood there in a fixated trance and continued looking out across the townsquare, gazing intently with a slight squint to his eyes.

"That man is washing our car!"

I did a double take like, *What the . . . ?* Sure enough, this guy had a bucketful of water, and he was splashing the water on the car. He splashed water on it and wiped it and doused it again. He was really doing it. This man had no shoes, and his clothes were hanging off of him. His pants had a tear up the leg, and one of his legs was slightly bandaged just below his knee.

Something was wrong with his leg, as it was badly swollen. The swelling made the leg big, almost round. The man had a slight limp. We never asked him to clean the car. Yet, he was working pretty hard at it. When he finished, he hung around there for an about an hour in the hot sun waiting, while we kept doing what we were doing. Obviously, he wanted to see if he could make a peso upon our return. At first, I didn't like it, because I resent being hustled to give somebody money. But when we were ready to leave and actually met the guy, he seemed kind and had a great humbleness to him and a real genuine, meek smile about him. He was an older man, probably in his sixties. He had no shoes, and his feet were the flattest and widest feet I have ever seen. The best way to describe how his feet looked is like a big triangle, like the triangle pattern of a duck's foot. So I gave him a couple CUCs.

He nodded happily and said, "*Gracias.*"

I gave him a pat on the shoulder, as I wanted him to feel respected. We got in the car and left for Havana.

"Well," I told Jesús. "We have a clean car to bring back to the rental agency."

Soon we were just outside of Havana on the Autopista Nacional motorway. Off to the side of the highway, I saw about six to seven motorcycles. But what really caught my eye about them was that they weren't just motorcycles, they were Harleys. And these Harleys weren't just Harleys; these motorcycles were vintage Harleys from the 1940s and 1950s. When most people think of Cuba, they just think of the old cars. But Jesús said that this area seems to have a high concentration of these old motorcycles. As I observed the motorcycles and riders, it was obvious that these people were not living in an alter-ego state. Many American yuppies with Harleys seem to be reliving and acting out something that they're not, cloning into a retro idea. Yet, these Cubans had the real machines and were living the life of many people's alter egos. Still riding, and still going on all the wide open roads, doing what they're meant to be doing, just living.

After passing a checkpoint and dropping under the mouth of the Bahia de la Habana in an eight-hundred-yard tunnel, we finally rolled back into Havana. The Trans-Bahia tunnel was built by the French company Societe des Grands Travaux de Marseille; it opened in 1958 to connect the outlaying suburbs and villages. As we came out of the tunnel, I entered a circular mixmaster of traffic. Jesús started talking louder and with more urgency, telling me to pull into the left lane and then pull over to that right lane, as we circled around. Once we were out of that cluster, we were now driving along the famous Av de Malecón, moving along and away from Old Havana.

This romantic seafront promenade was spectacular, with its waves periodically crashing over the walls of the Malecón and spraying high into the air and sprinkling out across onto the roadway. This whole dramatic seafront boulevard is lined with many attractive and strikingly colorful, historic, and eclectic buildings that accentuated the boulevard, as it curves along the contour of Havana's shore line. This road felt alive with the movement of all the old cars and the people strolling about.

This sensation I was feeling was that I could not believe I was actually driving along this famous and enchanting seafront boulevard that has been seen by many and is known the world over. I thought about that for a moment, as I drove and was in a state of speechlessness, but delight as I was taking it all in.

We continued driving along this iconic Av de Malecón, passed by the Hotel Nacional, and drove into the Vedado quarters of Havana. Jesús yelled out to get ready to make a left-hand turn. At first, I thought he was clowning around again about racecar drivers. But Jesús really screamed out with more urgency, "Make this left turn!!" Realizing that this was actually a "serious!" left turn, I quickly turned the wheel and we made it just in time, barely avoiding crashing into the oncoming traffic.

We drove into a residential area and wound our way to a market that Jesús knew about, passing a few streets up and a few streets that way before I was finally told to pull over. Jesús said that we were going to stock up on a few things for the party for the next day, and that he also needed pork for tonight's dinner at home. The market was inside an industrial warehouse. It was open, and it was not clean.

Immediately when we neared the entrance, some guys tried to approach me.

"He's with me!" Jesús said. They backed off a bit, and one of them said something in response to what Jesús had said. I did not quite understand.

I asked, "Jesús, what did he say?"

"Good luck."

I was a little bewildered, as I was not sure what he meant by that. We stepped up small, stone steps and went inside this old, open-air warehouse. Three or four people trying to get us to buy their meat immediately pounced us on. It got to the point that they were grabbing our arms and speaking over each other as they pointed us to their respective tables. They were really loud and very dramatic about it. Jesús acted like this was standard. It wasn't like they were being rude. To them, they were just saying, "Buy mine, not theirs! Mine's fresher! My pig's fatter!" It was the end of the day, and they obviously wanted to get rid of the last bits of their butchered meats. What was wild was seeing little metal tables and counters with blood all over them, and the pork sitting on top. I thought, *My God, it's been sitting there all day.* At least it was not in the full sun like I had seen elsewhere. Beyond these counters, I saw all the fruits and vegetables piled up. Many of the tomatoes looked and felt like they had been in the sun too long. Some were red. Some were green. Some were a nice marbled green and red, which I thought was interesting. There were squashes that had many, many different colors and shapes—big round ones. Some of them looked like pumpkins, but they were green. Some of them were yellow or red and had many different styles. That caught my eye.

I remembered my visit to the chef de Cocina restaurant the last time I was in Cuba. It was also in the Vedado quarters, housed in a beautiful peach-colored 1920s mansion that had contemporary artwork on all the walls. I had their squash soup, and wow, it was so good. The soup was thick, but also light with a very good texture. It was a bright rich yellow, with dark green parsley sprinkled on top and served from an elegant silver bowl on a platter. The servers ladled it in our bowls and added cracked pepper upon request. It was so good that I had to go back and get the recipe. I was able to talk to the chef, and he tried to write down the recipe for me:

Squash Soup (10 servings)
Ingredients:
1. 3.0 kg of Squash
2. 0.1 kg of Butter
3. 0.5 of Onions
4. Chicken or Curry Broth as you like
5. Parsley

What to do!!!

1. Wash and cut in pieces of the squash (do not peel the skin but do remove the seeds).

2. Salt the squash pieces and the onions with the butter in a frying pan. (Add more salt if needed).

3. Add the chicken broth diluted in water to cover the squash pieces; add powder curry if you like.

4. Cook until the squash pieces are soft.

5. Check the salt level, add more if needed.

6. Use a blender to mix everything.

7. Serve adding Parsley or very fine cut leek.

Back home, I had tried many times to make this soup. But after much trial and error, I've come to realize that the chicken broth at the chef de Cocina was most likely homemade. Having the authentic chicken broth, I believe, was what made the soup so good and what made it unmatched.

After Jesús and I picked out the best vegetables we could find for our meals, we had to make our way back through the gauntlet, where all the eyes of the meat vultures were watching us and lay waiting to see what last bit of their butchered meat they could get us to buy. Once we passed by their counters again, the frenzy began. Everyone started talking over everyone else as it got louder. Each man was grabbing our arms, pointing and pulling us toward their last bit of bloody meat. As Jesús spoke out, the loud exchanges abruptly stopped and the others walked back to their counters. The one who made the convincing sale was a Cuban man who had dreadlocks. He almost looked like he could be Jamaican.

We loaded the car and headed out of the Vedado quarters and back along the shoreline of the Malecón, then we continued back through the circular mixmaster again. We were getting ready to go through the Trans-Bahia tunnel at the mouth of Havana Harbor. I forgot to turn my headlights on. I didn't realize that in Cuba it was illegal to drive with headlights on except during foggy days or when going through a tunnel.

Jesús was looking at me and going off.

"Why didn't you turn on the headlights?"

I replied, "Well, I didn't know? What do I know? You don't even have a driver's license! You crazy jalapeño!"

At that moment, we started to sound like an old married couple again.

When we came out of the tunnel, there was another checkpoint, and we had to slow down. Security workers stood around looking at us, as we passed very slowly through the stalls that reminded me of a tollbooth. If the light stays green, you just keep going. Jesús was amazed that they didn't nail me on the headlights.

We headed a little further down the highway. The turnoff we needed to take was an exit that could take us toward Cojimar, the little fishing village that was the inspiration for Ernest Hemingway's 1953 Pulitzer Prize winning novel, *The Old Man and the Sea*. Hemingway also had his boat, *The Pilar*, named after the Patron Saint of Spain Nuestra Senora del Pilar. He kept it moored in the small Cojimar bay. *The Pilar* was made of mahogany, and Hemingway purchased it for $7,500. He picked it up in Key West, Florida, in 1934. Hemingway had bonded and became friends with the many local fishermen in Cojimar. Along with the village tavern, La Terraza, which was referred to in the story as "The Terrace," the village itself has not changed much over time from the setting described in *The Old Man and the Sea*.

After Hemingway's death in 1961, a monument to honor him was built in 1962. On this monument was a bust of Hemingway, which the fishermen of the village made by melting the oar rings and brass propellers from their boats. The fisherman did this for Hemingway because they felt he had done so much for them. Built in the neoclassical style of architecture, the monument structure is open sided like a gazebo, has no roof, and is circular like a rotunda. The bust of Hemingway rests on top of a marble rectangular pillar that is about five feet tall. The simple words, "Ernest Hemingway 1896-1961," are engraved on the pillar. The bust and pillar are encircled by this freestanding structure with fluted ionic columns that have volute capitals at their tops. The columns support a large, thick, circular entablature band at the top of the monument. It gives the illusion of being like a halo floating above this monument.

Across the street from the Hemingway monument is an old stone fort, Torreon de Cojimar, which was built by the Spanish in the mid-seventeenth century. Torreon de Cojimar stands at the edge of the bay's water. Instead of turning left toward the ocean and Cojimar, we went inland a little bit toward Jesús's house. Close to his house was the school where his wife worked. We drove up to the school and, of course, Jesús got out of the car. His wife came running out. She was all excited. The kids came running out. They were all excited. After they exchanged many long embraces, we all piled into this sardine tin can of a car. We had to reposition our luggage, the banana stalk, and the items from the market. It seemed as though we had to all breathe out before closing the car doors. We huddled tightly, and I drove them home being very careful not to hit too many potholes in the road. Once we were at Jesús's house, we unloaded the meats, the bananas and everything else to the happy sounds of his two children. Jesús had a small patio area surrounded by a chain link fence where we locked the car up. It was great not having to worry anymore about the car at night.

I then remembered that Jesús planned for me to sleep in his bed.

"Now, where are you going to sleep?" I asked again. He showed me a twin bunk bed in the other room, where the two kids slept. They would be in the lower bunk and Jesús and his wife would be in the top bunk together. This was even less space than that sardine tin can of a car of ours.

"No. No. I can't do this!" I told them.

"Chris, have a beer," Jesús said calmly.

Well, I couldn't refuse a Bucanero. After a few beers, the whole issue was decided.

"All right! All right," I said as I put my luggage in their master bedroom.

The next morning, Jesús was making scrambled eggs with cut up vegetables and coffee for breakfast. We discussed what places we might go check out today in Havana. After breakfast, we went outside to pull the car out of the fenced gate, only to find that we had another flat tire on the car. We put the spare on, and off we went to locate another ponchero to fix our flat tire, so we could be on our way again.

Once we were on the highway, we headed toward Havana and the Trans-Bahia tunnel. Before hitting the tunnel, we saw the Castillo de los tres Santos Reyes del Morro, also known as El Morro castle. It was a fortress built in 1589 to guard the entrance to the bay. It was to our right and sitting at an extremely strategic point on the bay. It has stood guard over Havana's harbor and shielded the city for more than four hundred years, perched majestically at the water's edge at the furthest entrance point of the bay.

We drove into the parking area ready to spend part of the morning walking around the grounds and the inside of the compound of the El Morro castle. We made our way past the high, imposing, and intricately cut impenetrable stone walls of this rampart, and we went down through walkways to the front entrance.

The many different levels of parapet walls on this stone fortress are dotted with turrets used by sentries in days gone by as lookout points. Many large batteries of cannons of various sizes pointed out seaward. This fortress was conceived exactly to the form of the rocky crag in which it is raised. It stood ready to defend against bands of invaders and, most commonly, the many different flotillas of raiding pirates.

I passed through an enclosed stone stairway that led up to more levels of massive stone walls. The rampart's salient walls faced out toward the seafront and away from the entrance to the bay. Batteries of cannons were lined up in offensive battle positions, as if they had the high ground. The impressive outer fringe walls of El Morro castle pointed out at dramatic angles, as if the fortress was deliberately built this way for defensive purposes to blunt the impact from opposing cannon fire. Because of the angles, a hit from the cannon fire during battle would be more of a glancing blow rather than a direct hit.

I came down an open stairway and continued along a few passageways to the famous lighthouse that stood within this fortress. Built entirely out of cut-stone block, this beautiful and yet graceful looking tower was constructed in 1844. At one time, another tower sat on its same foundation. This earlier tower was also used as a watchtower and was built to assist in the detection of approaching enemies. The British destroyed the earlier tower in 1762, when they attacked and captured Havana. Like its predecessor, the light of the current lighthouse was originally fed with firewood.

Britain occupied Havana until a year later. Like a world chess game, Britain traded Havana back to Spain in exchange for Florida in 1763, as part of the Peace of Paris treaty. This treaty marked the end of the Seven Years War, which in Europe was also known as the French and Indian War. The exchange of Havana for Florida allowed Britain in future years to consolidate its military operations in the part of North America that became the future United States. In addition to the Spanish flag, the other flags raised over the fortress Castillo de los tres Santos Reyes del Morro were the British flag in 1762, the US flag in 1899, and the Cuban flag since 1902.

I decided to go up this tall lighthouse. Upon entering, the stone steps spiraled up tightly like a corkscrew for a wine bottle. The higher I climbed the stairway, the narrower and tighter this stairway surrounding became. It had a dark, medieval feel. Just before reaching the last story, the steps turned upward in a vertical direction, and the walls and curved ceiling narrowed. It was increasingly difficult for me to get through because I was carrying my camera pack and because of my height and size. I practically had to lie on the steps and crawl on all fours to go up. I finally got through and came out of a hatchway that opened into a room with a large light centered in the room. The lighthouse keeper was there, off to the side sitting at his desk.

I wanted to catch my breath, so we sat down and talked to the lighthouse keeper for about thirty minutes. He showed us pictures of when Hurricane Ike had come through this area. The waves crashing on the lighthouse looked just as big as the lighthouse itself. I could not believe it.

I looked at him and said, "You were in here during that the whole time?"

"*Si!*" he said, nodding his head.

"*Mucho grande huevos!*" I said without thinking.

He got a chuckle out of that and started to laugh out loud. We continued talking with Jesús's interpreting to provide extra clarity. The lighthouse keeper was interesting and a nice guy.

I stepped outside on this narrow, circular catwalk at the top of the lighthouse tower. Holy Cow! What a tingly feeling of exposure to the elements I got as I walked slowly around in this open-air walkway. But what a view of the city! I could now see the reasons why the British destroyed the original tower. I definitely could see for miles out to sea. I was still feeling slightly queasy, as I was not finished walking completely around this open catwalk.

I then turned to look at Jesús, and off the wall, I said, "Do you want to get some lunch?"

The look on his face seemed to imply that he was thinking what an oxymoronic thing to bring up at this moment. After a slight pause, peculiarly, he turned and looked back at me again with a calm look on his face and said, "Yeah!"

We made our way out of the lighthouse, went back to our car, and got back on the highway. After going through the Trans-Bahia tunnel—but this time making sure I had my head lights on—into Havana we went. We drove along the Malecón again toward the Vedado quarter to the Edificio Focsa, a large high-rise building. The Edificio Focsa was built in 1956 and is an example of modernist architecture. The building has two wings that come together at an angle. It was surrounded by a mix of 1950's high rises, which at one time played home to the reigns of the many organized crime mafias, facilities for gambling, drinking, and prostitution, until those activities were kicked out by the 1959 revolution. The Edificio Focsa has 375 apartments on thirty-seven floors. At the very top of the building is a restaurant, La Torre, which provides a 360-degree view of the whole city. Jesús and I decided to have lunch there and enjoy the view of the city.

After we ate lunch, and after I took a few pictures, we decided to head over to Old Havana to check out a few more places, including the Batista Palace, now known as the Museo de la Revolúcion. We waited in line to use the elevator, which sure took a long time to get us down. This elevator seemed to be really slow and not working right. It took us a good twenty-five to thirty minutes, it seemed. When I got back to America, I happened to come across an article about an elevator accident at this building in 2000. One person was killed and three were injured when it plunged out of control. Apparently it was the same elevator that we were riding in at the Edifico Focsa.

Once we were in the historic Old Havana, we drove past the many people who were walking about and the old American cars. Finally, we were able to find a parking place, so we could get out and walk around here in the historic heart of Cuba. Havana was founded in 1514 on the south coast of the Caribbean side of Cuba and moved to its current location on the Gulf side of Cuba, on November 16, 1519. The first mass and the first city meeting were held in the area occupied today by El Templete, near the Plaza de Armas square.

We walked along the narrow streets that were a living community of colorful colonial street houses and elaborate seventeenth-century Baroque churches mixed with buildings of neoclassical architecture. We came up to a hotel called the Ambos Mundos, which was built in 1924 and made famous by Ernest Hemingway. Hemingway had only one room that he stayed in, room number 511, during a relatively lengthy period from 1932 to 1939. It was also in this room where Hemingway wrote chapters of one of his most famous novels *For Whom the Bell Tolls*, and also wrote contributions to the *Esquire* magazine periodical. This hotel sits beautifully right on a corner street. I could see why Hemingway only stayed in room 511. The location of the windows allowed him to look out, being able to see and feel perfectly the pulse of the activities going on below, and providing him with a beautiful view of Old Havana. Hemingway may have even been intermittently attracted to the beautiful views from these windows. These views possibly provided him with much needed mental breaks and temporary relief from the work of his writings and maybe even helped him to gather collective thoughts. The inside of the hotel had an eclectic interior that included an original Otis screen cage elevator complete with an operator in a suit. I was able to tour room 511. Everything in this room sits as Hemingway might have left it, along with his personal belongings. I even saw one of his Royal typewriters that he used when working in this room.

When not writing in his room, Hemingway was known to frequently haunt two of Old Havana's bars in particular. One of his favorites was the El Floridita. Hemingway liked to order his modified version of a daiquiri, a drink with white rum, grapefruit juice, lemon juice, cane syrup, maraschino syrup, and crushed ice, all well shaken. The other bars weren't interested in accommodating Hemingway's daiquiri request. Because the El Floridita was the only bar that would, this became the place that Hemingway continually patronized for his modified daiquiris. Today at El Floridita there is a statue at one end of the bar honoring the exact spot where Hemingway always sat. Down the street from El Floridita was another bar, La Bodequita del Medio, where Spanish immigrant Angel Martinez used to serve drinks and food over the counter. In the 1940s, Martinez decided to promote a bohemian scene for artists and writers. He used his home as a bar and featured the Mojito as the star cocktail. Ironically, the Mojito was originally a lowly drink favored by Cuban slaves. Martinez's house was the former coach house of the mansion next door. Later it became a *bodega*, a mom-and-pop grocery store. The name, La Bodeguita del Medio, means the little store in the middle of the block. It was odd to have a store in the middle of the block because, at that time, all business places were located on corners for maximum access to clients.

Hemingway only drank mojitos at La Bodeguita del Medio. Famous and not-so-famous patrons were known to write their names on the inside of the bar's graffiti-covered walls. The most famous graffiti writing belonging to Hemingway: "My Mojito in La Bodeguita, My Daiquiri in El Floridita."

In 1940, Hemingway moved out of the Ambos Mundos hotel and to a villa in the suburbs of Havana. Hemingway's villa was known as Finca La Vigia. It was built in 1886. Hemingway lived there until 1960. Since Hemingway's death, Finca La Vigia has been a museum run by the Cuban government. At the villa, everything sits as Hemingway left it. No one is allowed inside. You are allowed to walk around the whole outside of the house. All the windows are left open during the museum hours, and pictures can be taken through the open windows. The house is filled with mementos from Hemingway's travels. Even hunting trophies from Africa hang on the walls. Because his back hurt from time to time, Hemingway used to type while standing up. He placed a thick book underneath the typewriter so that he could get the typewriter set at just the right height. His Royal typewriter is still there today sitting on top of a thick book, which itself was on top of one of his smaller bookshelves. A wooden clipboard that he used for writing notes rests next to the typewriter as well.

Hemingway knew many people and was friends with Pablo Picasso. Since Hemingway enjoyed bullfights so much, Picasso created a round porcelain plate-like plaque for him that featured a bull motif. This original Picasso is still hanging on one of the bedroom walls of Finca La Vigia. In the bathroom, I could see evidence of Hemingway's obsession with his weight from the scribbles he left on the walls to record his daily weight after he weighed himself. On the shelves and counters of the bathroom, I also happened to see small jars of various sizes that held odd curious creatures preserved in alcohol floating inside. Outside there is a swimming pool. Ava Gardner used to visit Hemingway at Finca La Vigia, and it is said that she had been known to skinny dip while in his swimming pool.

One of the things that really caught my eye was the large collection of books that were stacked on the many bookshelves. As I looked at thousands of books, a thought came to me. All these books were from Hemingway's personal collections. It is what he liked and admired. To me, these books were like windows into his mind. I felt that they told stories and were like clues or puzzle pieces providing insight into Hemingway's thoughts. So I began to take detailed pictures of these full size bookshelves. I guess to some people, it would be just a picture of books. But to me, it became something a little deeper. I was able to see and read the names of those books on the pictures I took. Seeing the actual names of the authors and titles of these books gave a deeper meaning and dimension. Through the wide-range of books on Hemingway's shelves, some of them could be considered to be "B-grade" books. The wide range of books on the bookshelves shows that Hemingway was open to a variety of reading genres and did not limit himself to authors of a certain stature. These are a small sampling of the many different types of books that I personally saw and captured in my pictures:

A collection of poems by W. B. Yeats and Hart Crane.
Books by Robert Benchley, a great American humorist.
George Orwell's *Down and Out in Paris and London.*
Robert Trumbull's *Silversides*, an account of the patrols of the World War II attack submarine, USS *Silverside.*
Walter Van Tillburg Clark's *The Ox-bow Incident*, a 1940 western novel.
Theodor Plievier's *Moscow*, which provides a comprehensive view of life in the Soviet Union in its story of a German who fled Hitler's Germany and became an exile in Moscow.
Dillon Wallace's *The Lure of the Labrador Wild.*
Alfred R. Wallace's *A Narrative of Travels on the Amazon and Rio Negro.*
Kathrene Pinkerton's *Wilderness Wife.*
James Jones's *From Here to Eternity.*
Dawn Powell's *The Happy Island*, about the decadent life of a young playwright in Manhattan, and *Turn, Magic Wheel*. Dawn Powell was said to be Hemingway's favorite living author.
Budd Schulberg's *The Harder They Fall.*

Seward William's *Skirts of the Dead Night*, a mystery.

John Steven Strange's *Murder Gives a Lovely Light*, a mystery.

Training Your Spaniel.

Birds of the Pacific States.

John Hershey's *A Bell for Adano*, the 1945 Pulitzer Prize winning novel about an Italian-American officer in Sicily during World War II.

William Faulkner's *Sanctuary*, one of Faulkner's most controversial novels.

Joyce Cary's *The Horse's Mouth*, about a struggling artist.

Richard Bissell's *A Stretch on the River.*

William Albert Robinson's *10,000 Leagues Over the Sea*, a journal of circumnavigation of the world.

Nelson Algren's *A Walk on the Wild Side.*

Plato's *The Republic.*

Cyril Connolly's *Enemies of Promise*. Cyril Connolly was a contemporary literature critic of the time who recognized the writings of the up and coming Hemingway as being on par with the already established likes of James Joyce, Marcel Proust, and William Faulkner.

In addition to Hemingway's books, I saw a magazine lying on a small table next to one of the easy chairs in the living room. It was the July 5, 1960, edition of *Newsweek*, and the title on the cover said, "Can anyone stop Kennedy?"

Although Hemingway spent a good part of his life in Cuba, he stayed out of Cuban and American politics. Hemingway expressed approval for the overthrow of the Batista government, but only met Fidel Castro once, and that one time was at a fishing tournament in Havana. Hemingway did not get involved with the conflicts between Fidel Castro and John F. Kennedy. But because he was living in Cuba, Hemingway had a front row seat to the events that were unfolding. It was a perfect storm that had him caught between two worlds. It is interesting to me that Hemingway did stay informed by using contemporary periodicals as his eyes to the world's current events.

Once we finished walking around Old Havana, we decided to head over to the Museo de la Revolúcion (the Museum of the Revolution), formally the Batista Palace. We drove through some of the busy streets being careful not to hit anybody, and came upon a parking area close to the museum. We walked over to the museum and spent time walking around the grounds.

An SU-100 tank destroyer that Fidel Castro used during the Bay of Pigs battle in 1961 sits in front of the this former palace. Close by is a small portion of an old stone wall that used to be part of Old Havana's city wall. Upon entering the building, I was awed by its beauty and lavishness. With its neoclassical elements, the palace is elaborate and has great detail. It was constructed between 1913 and 1920, and Tiffany of New York decorated the whole interior.

The grand reception ballroom has beautifully painted frescoed ceilings and terraces. The foyer of the main entry had a grand and monumental staircase. Both the staircase and walls are made of marble. As it leads up to the open second floor, the elegant and open staircase splits in two and veers off to the left and to the right. At that juncture, I could not help but notice something. On March 13, 1957, university students stormed this building, spraying gunfire in wave-like patterns, as they made their way up this very elegant open staircase. It felt surreal and somber to me, as I slowly walked up the staircase and saw the different spraying patterns of the bullet holes that riddled all through the marble walls. The individual bullet holes were now a permanent part of these walls. I was able to put my fingers inside them, as I made my way up these stairways, moving in the same direction as those students did years ago during the heat of battle.

Each floor presented a different time period in Cuba's history. Cuba's historical struggles for independence, from colonial days to the present, are prominently featured. While we were touring this museum, Jesús told me that most outsiders thought of the revolution as just one day in 1959, but Cubans viewed it as ongoing throughout their history and enduring still to this day. Next to the Museo de la Revolúcion was an old church, Iglesia del Angel Custodio. This church was built in 1869 in the neo-Gothic style of architecture. In the center was a large, tall, rectangular-shaped steeple and bell chamber. Decorated crockets highlight a broached spire and sit atop the steeple and bell chamber. The front façade is decorated with many levels of blind arcades with lancet arches. Three large, open arched entryways lead into the church. The top of the cornice surrounding the whole church building is adorned with many small, rectangular Gothic pinnacles all highlighted with decorative crockets. It was documented in the church's records that José Martí was baptized here on February 12, 1853.

After touring the Museo de la Revolúcion and admiring the Iglesia del Angel Custodio, we walked further up the street. I was very careful not to step in the foul water that was flowing lightly across the whole road, as it bubbled out from underneath a covered manhole in the middle of the road. Something on the house up and across the street caught my eye. I was able to get around the foul water by trying to find the least shallow areas across the whole street and by walking over to this house. It was a simple, square, two-story white stucco house with two balconies and a red terra-cotta tile roof.

The house sits on a street corner and has a large, multi-trunk tropical palm tree next to it. Two sides of the house have a door. There is one large rectangular window that is covered with painted wooden shutters and a simple eighteenth-century iron grille. At first glance, the design painted on top of the shutters appeared to be two Cuban flags displayed side-by-side. I noticed that one of the flags had a star with five points while the other flag had a star with six points, which signified that the owners of this house were Jewish. I was surprised because I did not know that there was a Jewish history here in Cuba. I mean, I knew of Catholicism and Santeria and figured, at the most, that would be it. I had to take a picture of this house. There was just something about it that my eyes were drawn to.

I later found out that there were thousands of Jewish people in Cuba before the 1959 revolution, and now there are only about nine hundred left. Most of the remaining nine hundred live in Havana, followed by Cienfuegos, Villa Clara, and Santiago. Many Jews started to migrate to Cuba in the late nineteenth century. The year 1906 marked the founding of the Cuban congregation. By 1914, a gathering of these immigrant Jews banded together and built Chevet Achim, the first synagogue in Cuba. Now closed and very much deteriorated, the building that housed Chevet Achim appears to be almost forgotten and caught up into obscurity. I did learn that there are still three other synagogues operating in Havana, all built in the 1950s. But what took me by surprise was to find a kosher butcher shop in the most out-of-the-way place. The shop had rustic black bars across the front and two good-sized Stars of David affixed to them. This butcher shop was established in 1936, presently performing as the only one in all of Cuba still open and functioning to this day. Instead of pork, which is the staple meat for other Cubans, this kosher butcher shop is given an allotment of different meats, prepared in the ritually proper way. The meat is then rationed by these remaining Cuban Jews amongst themselves.

By now, it was time to start thinking about heading back to Jesús's house. We had to get things ready for Jesús's big family party. Just before we got to his house, Jesús yelled out, "Pull over here!" On the side of the road were groupings of things that looked like metal shipping containers. The containers were open from the side to display items for sale. They were just sitting there on the dirt in no particular order. One person was selling

beer and Brazilian vodka, which Jesús said we needed for the party. I still was not sure who would be coming to the party, but it looked like we were going to have a fun time!

Once we arrived back at Jesús's house, we parked the car in the patio area with the secure chain link fence and gate. As we unloaded our things, I asked Jesús if I could try to send an e-mail from his house to my wife and kids to let them know how I was doing. After about an hour or so, we were finally able to make a connection through the dial-up, and my e-mail was sent out. Jesús's wife was busy preparing the plantains that we had purchased in Cuba's Habana province and brought back on the last leg of our trip. She was making tostones by cutting the plantains into two-inch pieces, frying them in a pan of hot oil, pressing them into a patty, and frying them one more time.

By now, family members were beginning to show up. Jesús's mom went into the kitchen to help. His sister went too, but not before filling up on a glass of Brazilian vodka. As the people spilled out through the open front door, neighbors came by. I could tell what they were thinking, *Oh, party, food!* Food, in general, was not overly abundant. Jesús was trying to keep a tight lid on the situation with the uninvited guests, "Hey, only one drink apiece." Otherwise, that vodka was going fast. Jesús's brother in-law was a stallion when it came to drinking the Brazilian vodka. I was impressed! He kindly tried to get me to have some, so that I would not feel left out.

I said, "OK, just a small one." When I did, Holy Cow! It was not what I had expected. I knew right then and there that this could be dangerous. It had a little kick to it. Whew! So, I stayed with the beer, because I knew that was safe. Safe, meaning, I knew my limitations with the beer versus that particular vodka that I had never had before.

By now, the whole house smelled of great food being cooked. After a few bottles of the Brazilian vodka had been drunk, the chatter around the house picked up and became more excited.

After drinking the vodka, I thought maybe I'd better sit down on the couch and repose for a little bit. At that point, mysterious people knocked on the door. There were two people, and they had a backpack with them that they seemed to be oddly clinging very tightly to. Jesús told them to come in and made sure that the front door was closed behind them. Once inside, they pulled out big cuts of meat that looked like ham and large cans of tomatoes from the backpack. While they talked in hushed tones, Jesús turned to me.

"You got some money, Chris?" he asked.

"OK, fine, I'll pay for this." I said, without giving it much thought. I think I gave him about ten CUCs.

And then, just as mysteriously, they left.

Everyone watched quietly. All their eyes were on me.

Jesús blurted out loudly, "Great, Chris, you just participated in the black market. You're going down!"

Everybody started laughing at me. It seemed funny to me later. But at the time, it caught me off guard. I was like a deer caught in the headlights of a car. I thought something had seemed rather sneaky. And then, of course, I'm told after the fact.

By that time, we were called to dinner. We all sat in the back room, where the table and chairs were all set up. All the food was on the table. There were main dishes of pork and fish and side dishes of the squished fried tostones, black beans, rice, squash, and salad. It was wonderful. We all ate and passed the food around, and everybody was having a good time. I then noticed that Omar, Jesús's father in-law, seemed slightly bummed, as he was the only one not drinking. Apparently, Omar could not drink until sometime the following week because he was taking an antibiotic for an infection. Omar felt really bad about this, because he loved to drink. And without thinking, again, I opened my mouth.

"Well, we're just going to have to make you the designated driver!" I said.

Jesús couldn't contain himself and did a very rapid and quick translation to everyone. There was a slight moment of delayed silence. Everybody went crazy and started laughing hysterically because the reality was, no one, young or old, who was sitting at that table, ever had owned a car. And with that, another round of drinks was poured for everyone! Well, everyone except poor Omar.

After a wonderful time at dinner, we stepped outside to catch cooler air. I met the neighbor who had been able to get the copy of the Jeff Dunham recordings. I became really curious, like a cat, as to how he had acquired them. I almost asked him, but refrained since apparently they were from the black market, and I was not sure about what would or would not be proper protocol to inquire about it. Although, I will say that everyone thought that the recorded shows were hilarious as the Dunham animated banterings were being kicked about that night.

It was getting late, and Jesús's family needed to make their way back home to Havana on the other side of the bay. We said our good-byes around eleven o'clock or eleven thirty, and the house quieted down. I was definitely feeling tired and ready for sleep, and I was careful to lie in my bed from corner to corner.

9

❧❧❧

REALITY'S
REALITY

I WOKE UP the next day with a knot on my head from hitting it on the edge of the bed's headboard. After getting out of the shower, I was reminded again of my youngest son, and how he had taken my comb from my travel bag. When I dressed and emerged, Jesús had breakfast ready. I could smell that wonderful coffee. We discussed the places that might be interesting for us to check out for the day. Finally, we talked about when I would be checking back into the Hotel Vedado, as I had prepaid for a room ahead of time before I left for Cuba. Since Jesús and I finished up our road trip up a couple days earlier than expected, I still had about four more days left on this island before I was officially scheduled to leave.

My mood began to grow more serious, as I came to the realization that the dreaded day was approaching, the defining moment when I would probably have to face El Comandante once again at the airport. I did not know what would be in store for me. I started feeling uneasy, as I thought back to that first encounter, and that long intense interrogation I went through when I entered this island.

I asked Jesús if we could check e-mail before we left for the day. I wanted to see if I had any news from home. I thought that might make me feel better. So Jesús fired up his computer. It took a while, but we got our dial-up connection. I was happy to see that there was an e-mail from my wife and kids. In my wife's e-mail, she said that she was happy to know that I was still safe, but that my long absence was starting to take a toll on the family. My youngest son, Garrett, now believed that I had died and would never be coming back.

It broke my heart to read that e-mail, and I did not know what to say or do after that. I tried to send an e-mail back to reassure my family, to calm the waters. I told them to keep things in perspective, and I reminded them that it would only be a few more days until I returned home. Because of Cuba's slow dial-up connections, it took about an hour to get that e-mail out. I felt like my hands were tied, due to the height and thickness of the wall that's between our two countries. Penetrating through it created challenges that go beyond the general embargo. I tried to keep it at bay in my mind and not let my emotions get to me. After all, this was all I could do.

With that, I told Jesús, "Let's head out."

I loaded the car with my camera pack and off we went. As we drove slowly through the gravelly streets of Jesús's neighborhood, I noticed that there was a lot of dirt covering the roads. It seemed odd. I could see dirt and mud washed all over the potholed, gravelly blacktop. I asked Jesús about it as we drove up and over mounds of dirt.

"A water main had broke last night," he said.

Jesús went on to say that once his family had left the party the previous night, they were walking to an area where they could possibly find a taxi to take them home. But instead of being able to find a cab, they happened to get caught up in the mess and chaos of the broken water main. They had to wait about two to three hours before they were able to pass through the area. There was no way to walk or otherwise get around it. They could do nothing except wait it out since it was so late at night and dark from having no real streetlights there. They probably did not get home until early in the morning. It was not like the United States, where we have streets lined with lights.

It was about midnight. I wondered why they didn't just walk back to Jesús's house. Then I thought, *that just seems to be life for them—adjusting, evolving, having to ride problems out.*

At that point, I didn't know what else to think. I guess standing around allowed them to have more time to catch up and chat amongst themselves. I felt bad for them. It showed me that life for them moved at such a different pace. You have to have a different perspective about it. We take so much for granted in America. I was especially thinking of how we could just hop in the car and go here or there, thinking nothing of it.

Once we were past all this, we drove through the suburbs, outlying villages, and outer industrial areas of Havana. We came up to the industrial port town and fishing village of Regla. It was across the bay from Havana and sat on the eastern shore of the Bahia de la Habana.

Regla was founded in 1687 and is known for Santeria and other Afro-Cuban religions. During the 1800s, many freed slaves settled there, maintaining their strong, rich culture. Long before the town was called Regla, it was known as Hato de Guaicanamar. According to writings dating from 1573, this area had a grouping of aboriginal houses, and the people here were advanced in the areas of pottery and agriculture.

Jesús and I parked the car and got out to walk around. As we looked across the bay, we had a stunning view of the Havana skyline. It definitely was a different perspective. On our side of the shoreline, there were many shipyards and multiple large docking cranes. It reminded me of a child's erector set, like one that I had when I was a young kid.

I stood there at the water's edge and watched the boxy, blue ferry boats take people across the bay. I turned around and looked back and saw that there was a modest church with a ceiba tree in front.

This church was named the Iglesia de Nuestra Senora de Regla. Placed in the ornate high altar inside the church is the icon La Virgen de Regla. This black Madonna with parted hair was robed in bright blue and holding a white Christ child. The stories of the origin of La Virgen de Regla are many and varied and appear to be a mix of history and legend. It was said that La Virgen de Regla was brought here in 1694. This Madonna was associated with Yemaya, an orisha deity. She is the patroness of the ocean, which was represented by the color of blue. She was also the protector of sailors and fisherman.

It has been said that people invoked the protection of the Virgen de Regla while they are attempting to cross the ocean in rafts to the United States. On a seat-wall outside of the church were a few Santeria priests, or *Babalawos*. They were dressed in all white clothing, and armed with seashells, stones, seeds, and coconut shells, which they used for their divinations. I did happen to see a few Cubans receiving advice.

I heard a loud motor revving up from one of the ferryboats at the small dock in front of us. The boat was about to take off, and one person on the boat was going through and checking everyone's bags.

I asked, "Jesús, why are they doing that?" I asked. "They're only going across the bay."

Jesús old me that there have been several times that these passenger ferryboats here in Regla have been hijacked. The last time was by about ten people who wanted to be taken to the United States. The hijackers carried weapons and took hostages. The hijackers were caught, and three of them were put before the firing squad for committing acts of terrorism.

A thought occurred to me regarding these hijackers. I noticed that the ferryboats that are docked right in front of this church happened to be blue. And the church itself houses the icon of the saint who is the protector of sailors and fishermen; the icon was robed in blue. I wondered if there was any correlation or connection with the hijacking? Did the hijackers think the Virgen de Regla would protect them on the blue ferryboats?

From here we decided to continue along the shore of the bay to Casablanca, another fishing port located not too far away. The village of Casablanca has always been tied to Regla. It was named after a large white warehouse that was built in the village in 1589. Those people traveling from Havana to the other side of the harbor requested that the boatman take them to the "white house." For as long as anyone can remember, this big building has always been white. Hence the name *casa blanca*, meaning "white house." Between 1596 and 1598, a sugar mill was built in Casablanca. The name of the sugar mill was San Pedro de Guaicanamar, and it was the first mill on the Cuban island to stop using slave labor for the use of turning and rotating the mill in a large circular motion. The slaves were replaced by animal traction, and the milling was done by turning three large wooden cylinders that rotated around simultaneously using gears. As these gears turned, they squeezed the harvested sugarcane as it passed through extracting cane juice.

Casablanca's most recognizable landmark is a large statue of Christ, El Cristo de La Habana. It stood on a hill 259 feet above the bay, overlooking the bay and the city of Havana. The statue was 59 feet tall and is carved from Italian Carrara marble. It was created by Cuban sculptor Jilma Madera and finished in 1958.

After parking the car, Jesús and I walked across a large grassy parklike area to see the statue and get a view of the city of Havana from the high hill. The thick, uncut grass moved with every step I took, like a ripple effect, like water. As I planted my foot, the grass moved away from my step. So I stopped, squatted down, and looked closer. I realized that mixed in with all this thick grass was a low-growing plant called *mimosa pudica*, more commonly referred to as "sensitive plants." The plant is so named because it rapidly reacts when touched or disturbed. Its leaves fold up and inward, and its small branches droop and retract downward. Here they grew like weeds. In America, I would never see these plants growing wild like weeds out in the open landscape. I was tripping out, touching and poking the plants. I was having fun! It reminded me of going to the beach with my children at low tide, and how they would poke all the sea anemones in the tide pools with their newfound sticks.

I heard a loud clearing of the throat, "Ahem!"

As I looked up, Jesús was standing there giving me a look like, *anytime now. This is kid's stuff. What are you doing?*

To Jesús, this weed was an everyday normal, run-of-the-mill thing he sees. Then I realized, *hey! I guess that I react sometimes the same way to my kids with all the sea anemones around in the ocean's tide pools.*

Once my adultness and maturity returned to me, we continued to walk over to the tall, white marble Cristo de la Habana statue. The statue stands there like the Cristo del Corcovado statue in Rio de Janeiro. But instead of outstretched arms, like the statue of Cristo del Corcovado, the hands of this statue are in front, and they look as if they are blessing the city from across the bay. There are rumors and legends that Marta Batista, wife of President Fulgencio Batista, financed the construction of the Cristo de la Habana statue. At the time she vowed that she would build a large statue of Christ if her husband survived the attack on the presidential palace by the students who stormed the building on March 13, 1957. Of course, Fulgencio Batista had a hidden door next to his Presidential office that led to a private elevator, aiding him and buffeting him from the students' attack.

The Cristo de la Habana statue was completed in 1958 and inaugurated on December 24, 1958. Eight days later on January 1, 1959, Fidel Castro gave his victory speech of the revolution from a balcony in Santiago. Castro made his triumphant entry into Havana on January 8, 1959.

As we continued on this high hill along the bay's inward channel, I could see another fortress, the Fortaleza de San Carlos de la Cabaña. This stone fortress is more commonly known as La Cabaña, and it stretches all along the high hill line. It was financed by King Carlos III of Spain and completed in 1774.

Before the La Cabaña fortress was built, this was the area where the British outflanked the Spanish. The British landed up the coast at Rio Cojimar. Since Castillo del Morro was too fortified to attack by sea, the British crossed on land flanking behind the El Morro fortress to gain entrance into Havana. The British, seeing a weakness, set up their cannons and attacked Havana in 1762. British cannonballs were soon lobbed from this unprotected high ground, violently falling like iron-rain from the sky over the narrow inland channel and over the city walls that surrounded Havana. Thick smoke filled the bay's air from the gale of the ceaseless and unending cannon fire. The Spanish soon surrendered.

The British occupied Havana for a year until it was traded back to Spain in 1763 in exchange for Florida. After the British capture and occupation of Havana, the Spanish realized the need for additional fortification on the whole high ground of this hill that overlooked the city. Construction thus began in 1763 on Fortaleza de San Carlos de la Cabaña.

Twice a day at four thirty in the morning and eight o'clock at night, a cannon was fired from the mother ship anchored in Havana harbor. This was to announce the opening and closing of the city gates. Simultaneously, the harbor was also being opened and closed by a massive floating brass chain that was stretched out across from Castillo del Morro to Castillo de San Salvador de la Punta, at the front entrance of the harbor. The cannon firings were then moved from the mother ship to La Cabaña when construction was complete.

The city wall that surrounded Havana before modern times had many doors that served as gates into the city. Each of these gates had their own individual names. Construction of the city walls began in the sixteen hundreds. Over time, most of the walls and historic gates were knocked down as the city later grew and people felt more secure.

Few of the doors and walls still stand today. One recorded door called the Puerta de Tierra, or Earth Door, has a lion headstone at the top and an inscription in Latin which clearly says, "*A Solis Ortu Usque Ad Occasum.*"

This translates to "From the rising up of the sun unto the going down of the same." This inscription accurately describes and confirms the twice-daily cannon firings that announced the opening and closing of the city gates.

The twice-daily cannon firing continued until the first United States military intervention in Cuba. During the time of the US intervention from 1898 to 1902, the cannon firing was changed to only one shot fired, and the time was moved to nine o'clock at night. After the US intervention, the cannon firing became a tradition and continued until 1942, when Cuba was allied with the United States in World War II. The suspension of the cannon firing did not sit well with many of the people of Havana. During this time, Cuban General Manuel Lopez Migoya told the people that it was wartime, and that Cuba needed to save the gunpowder. A further explanation was later given in a press release: the suspension prevented German submarines from detecting the geographical position of Havana. The tradition continued after World War II.

At the time of my visit, the cannon firing still continued with only the one firing at nine o'clock at night and is ceremoniously performed by soldiers dressed in eighteenth-century uniforms. It could be seen and heard every night at La Cabaña.

La Cabaña fortress also served as a prison for the Batista regime. After the revolution, it was taken over by Ché Guevara, who used it as his house, headquarters, and military prison. During this time, the elements of the political landscape changed across the country because of the triumph and the euphoria of the new government. In this fortress, Ché Guevara, energized by the racing of adrenaline and the newfound forces of victory of the revolution, oversaw the tribunals and executions of those deemed to be war criminals, along with those who happened to be innocently caught up in the intoxicating frenzy.

After we finished touring La Cabaña, Jesús and I walked back to the car. Jesús sensed that something was on my mind. I was still having a hard time with the news contained in my wife's e-mail about what was happening at home with my children, and how my youngest son was thinking that I am now dead and never coming back. I was also wrestling with the reality of the lingering uncertainty of what was going to happen at the airport. I knew that I faced a good chance of being detained again by El Comandante at the Havana airport on my way out of Cuba.

Jesús tried to console me a bit as we walked. We decided it was probably time to head over to the Hotel Vedado for me to officially check in and unload my luggage. We drove up and around a few one-way streets. Once in the Vedado district, we passed by the Universidad de La Habana.

The university was founded in 1728. A broad granite stairway built on a foundation leads up to the University's neoclassical complex.

We made our way up and around these one-way streets and found a parking spot on a side-alley. After jaywalking through the crossing traffic that was rumbling and speeding by, we made our way into the Hotel Vedado lobby. My prescheduled check in time was three days before my prearranged departure date. After checking in, I quickly went up to my room on the fifth floor, unloaded my luggage, and went back down to the lobby. Jesús was waiting for me, as he was not allowed to go up to the room. We stepped outside along the busy one-way street. I could not stop thinking about my wife and kids.

It came to me, "What if I leave early?" I said.

Jesús told me that the airline had a ticket office just down the street; We could go over there and find out my options. At the airline's ticket office, we waited in line. When it was my turn, we spoke with the lady at the counter. She gave me the flight options about leaving Cuba, but could not change any flights or give me any information about traveling from Mexico to America. I would have to figure that part out on my own in Mexico. I thanked her for her time and told her that I needed to think about this a little more.

Jesús and I stepped outside to talk about it. And it hit me. Why didn't I think of this sooner? I needed to leave earlier to get back home to my family. By doing that, I would outflank El Comandante, who had already written down all my departure and personal information along with taking my laptop.

Now it started to make sense. El Comandante knew I needed to come back to retrieve that laptop. The laptop was being held as bait. Once he had me, he could rummage through all my things again and could theoretically take my forty rolls of spent film. I remembered back to El Comandante's interrogation of me. After relentlessly railing on me, why did he become friendly to me, then out of character suddenly take off five days on the daily fine he assessed on the laptop? At the end of the interrogation, he had given me a stern and loud warning: do not lose the paperwork needed to reclaim the laptop on my departure date.

Then everything came into focus. "I'm just going to let him have the computer. I don't give a crap. I won't claim it. It's not worth it. Let him have it. Besides, there's nothing on it," I said to Jesús.

At that moment, I could see the look on Jesús's face as he said, "Oh." I could tell he was still hoping to find a way to get the laptop. He did not want anything to go to waste, and it would have been a great asset for his family. I would have loved to give it to him and his family, but I knew that I could not take the risk. It was crystal clear to me that I needed to leave now. In doing so, I would most likely sidestep another interrogation.

Jesús and I walked back to the airline's ticket office. I changed my airline ticket from leaving Cuba in a couple of days to leaving the next morning. After paying an additional one hundred CUCs, I was set for my new departure date. I had to be at the terminal the next morning at four thirty in the morning to check in three hours before the scheduled departure time of my flight.

Once that decision was made, I got word to my wife about the change in my travel plans. I let her know that I was going to be leaving earlier than expected. I explained that I could not change my airline ticket from Mexico to the United States. She would have to do it from the American side of the wall. I asked her to see if she could have the new ticket waiting for me at the airline counter in Cancun. Even if that meant having to buy a whole new ticket, "Just do it!" I said. I would have to just cross my fingers and now hope for the best.

After this was set in motion, I told Jesús that we needed to turn the car in today, a day early, and not take a chance on doing it tomorrow. That early in the morning, I did not want to take the chance of anything going wrong and crossing over on my new flight time. If there was going to be a problem with the inspection of the car, or additional paperwork to complete, I wanted to deal with it today. It just made more sense to me to deal with it now even if it cost me more money in taxi fees. Jesús did not think that there would be any problems with returning the car early the next morning. But since he sensed my anxieties about my family and El Comandante, well, off we went to return the car.

We drove through the busy one-way streets again and made our way to the rental car agency at the airport. We drove past the Plaza de la Revolúcion, a large 86,000 square yard open area city square that stands on the highest ground of elevation in all of Havana. On an elevated area of the Plaza de la Revolúcion square was a 358-foot narrow tower that is formed in the shape of a star as it rises skyward. A 59-foot high white marble statue of Cuba's national hero, José Martí, was at the base of the tower. The statue depicts a contemplative Martí squatting with one arm resting on his knee. It almost looks as if Martí is bowing to his country, the Cuban nation, the land he loved, and the people he served and whose freedom he fought for.

For decades, history has recorded Fidel Castro standing at a podium here in front of the Martí statue delivering his long, fiery speeches, and rallying the crowds of people standing in the plaza. Scores of military parades and official celebrations have taken place through here as well. Standing across from the Plaza de la Revolúcion is the Ministry of Interior building, or Ministerio del Interior. Pin-mounted to the front façade of this building is a five-story steel outline sculpture of Ché Guevara. Written in cursive underneath the Ché image are the words "Hasta la Victoria Siempre" or "Until the Victory Always."

From here, we continued to make our way past the city to terminal two at the José Martí airport. We went through a big industrial area, and even passed by a very large and colorful propaganda sign on top of a building. The sign showed an outline of Fidel Castro defiantly raising his one arm high in the air, with his fist clinched tightly. The slogan below was in big bold letters and said, "Socialismo o muerte!" or "Socialism or death." I wished that I could have taken a picture of it, as I liked the contrast of the sign against all the industrial buildings and cars that surrounded it. But there was nowhere for me to pull over in the tight traffic.

Farther down the road, we finally pulled into the terminal two area and found our way to the right rental car kiosk. We had to maneuver around a few people in the terminal as well as a few Russian and old Cuban-American cars. Once we arrived at the rental car kiosk, the gentlemen whom we had dealt with originally came out to greet us. I extricated myself out of the sardine tin can of a car for the last time.

I still remember his last words to me before we left with the car.

"Good luck," he had said.

Boy, if he only knew the places we went to and the stories that could be told. I did tell him that we got three flats on this trip. He just replied with a smile and a half laugh. It seemed to be something that he was not too surprised to hear about.

After settling up the paperwork and getting final approval on the inspection of the car, we found a taxi to take us back to the Hotel Vedado. The fare for the taxi ride back was pretty reasonable. My next concern was how to coordinate the logistics for leaving the hotel at four o'clock the next morning. Jesús lived way out in the suburbs and there are no random taxis out there. I would be at the hotel. I was thinking of how I would get to the airport on time. I also felt the need to have Jesús there with me at the airport to make sure that I get in the right line. It could be confusing at the airport with all the extra people coming to say good-bye to their family members. The other reason that I wanted Jesús there was in case I ran into any problems, or wound up being detained while trying to leave the country. Maybe he would be able to help in some way or, at the very least, get word to my wife at home.

When we got back to the hotel, it looked like the taxi guy had given us a good price. I was still concerned about tomorrow morning, and not sure how I was going to get to the airport at that early time in the morning.

I had Jesús ask the taxi driver how much he would charge to pick up Jesús and drive to the Hotel Vedado to pick up me at four o'clock to take us both to the airport tomorrow. I felt a little committed to this guy since he had done us right so far.

"Sixty CUCs," he told Jesús.

Jesús felt that sixty CUCs was too much money. Knowing that the taxi driver didn't quite know English, Jesús turned to me and told me in English,

"Just shake your head, like no," he said.

This way Jesús could save face with the taxi guy and turn back around and make it look like I'm the one watching my money. In other words, Jesús was watching out for me. And so, for my one minute of fame, on location in the streets of Havana, I performed my best Academy Award winning acting job.

"Nah, nah," I said, as I shook my head no. I also added some last minute acting skills by combining a little hand motion in there as well, just for good measure. With that, Jesús turned around to the taxi man, who was still in his car, to tell him through the open window that I did not like the price and will look elsewhere. The taxi driver drove off, and that was it. Jesús said that somehow he would figure it out and be here in the morning at four o'clock to pick me up. I wasn't sure how, but that was Jesús. I've learned that he's able to wheel and deal. If he says it will be, it will be. Knowing that gave me much comfort. I don't know how he does these things. I'm sure even he doesn't know. He always finds a way. He has that will to survive, which is something I understand so well from my own life.

I gave Jesús money for a taxi, so he could get a ride to his home, and I thanked him for all he had done for me. As I reached out to shake his hand, I realized that soon I would not be around my good and faithful friend anymore. Our time was coming to a close.

As I watched him get into another taxi to leave and go home to be with his family, I took one last walk around the streets of Havana. I was having trouble, as I could not relax the thoughts in my head regarding all the potential unknowns that lie ahead for tomorrow.

I walked down the street toward the Malecón and came upon the beautiful Hotel Nacional. This luxurious hotel opened on December 30, 1930. It's beautiful eclectic architecture blended art deco, neoclassic, and neocolonial. Doric columns in several areas of the hotel support lines of arches known as arcading.

As I walked past the front of the hotel, there was a line of many old American taxi cars. Some of them were in beautiful shape. Many were convertibles. The owners quietly stood there next to their cars, patiently waiting to give someone a ride. I walked through the front doors and was awed by the open-air feeling and the elegance: brightly colored fresco tiled walls, hanging chandeliers, and the pure, natural elegance of its time in this place.

I soon learned that during the week of December 22, 1946, a "Mafia Havana conference" had taken place right here at the Hotel Nacional. Meyer Lansky, Lucky Luciano, Frank Costello, and Santos Traficante attended. Later on in this conference, Frank Sinatra was brought in by the mafia and served as the entertainment. Throughout the years, many famous people have stayed at this hotel including Errol Flynn, Marlon Brando, Marlene Dietrich, Rocky Marciano, and Winston Churchill.

In the back was a patio and large grassy area with lush green palms. A long veranda provided a place to sit and enjoy the ambiance and view of the garden. The entrance to the veranda is accentuated with arcading supported by Doric columns. This hotel sits upon an elevated, yet small hill that overlooks the Malecón and out toward Havana bay. I stayed for a little bit, looking around and listening to the sounds of a small band playing Cuban Son *musica*. The hotel patrons had their drinks from the open-air bar and were mingling about the garden. The scene was probably no different from what it looked like when this place first opened.

I continued down to the Malecón and walked in the opposite direction away from the entrance to the Bahia de la Habana. I came up to, and was walking alongside, another building. I remembered that the last time I was in Cuba and walked through here in this same area, I was not allowed to walk on the sidewalk where I was now standing. For that matter, I was not allowed to walk on any sidewalk around the whole city block surrounding this building. This building happened to be the site of the former United States Embassy, which had been closed since January 3, 1961.

The last time I was here, there were Cuban guards standing every fifty feet around this entire building block. The guards were carrying AK-47s, and some of them had headsets on. As I approached the outer perimeter of guards, I was pointed and motioned to stay across from this building on the other side of the street. They did not want to talk. They pointed very sharply to me, "Go across the busy street. Now!"

I thought it to be really odd at the time. And strangely enough, while I was in the airport in Mexico and boarding the flight to Havana for that particular trip, I saw what appeared to be five high-level US officials with passports also boarding the flight. I only found this out because the man at the ticket counter who was dealing with my paperwork for my flight and verifying my passport told me that before me, those five particular men came to the counter and presented him with the highest level of official government passports that he had ever seen.

I gathered with the other people from my tour group. But these American officials stayed away from us and did not want to dialogue with anybody. On the plane, they sat near the front. When we landed in Havana, I noticed Cuban military personnel standing around the outside of the plane, guarding it with dogs. There was not a first-class section on this flight, but before I knew it, these American officials were out of sight and gone.

I thought it was strange, but didn't think anything more of it at the time. After I had returned from the trip, I read a newspaper article about an agricultural trade delegation from California that went to Cuba for four days of meetings in 2008 to discuss future sales of California food products to Cuba. As I read this article, I remembered the high-ranking Americans who were on my flight to Cuba. I find it interesting that there may be more official American meetings in Cuba than we know about. American officials having unofficial meetings? At any rate, something was going on in the old, allegedly closed American Embassy.

From there, I continued further along the Malecón and came up to an open space of patchy, un-mowed grass and dirt. There was an uneven dirt track that encircled in this open space. This area was called the Estadio José Martí; it was an old sports field. A small section of cement bleachers stretched across the length of one side of the field, facing out toward the ocean.

The bleachers were built in a modernist style of architecture with elegant abstractness to it. The structure is supported by about thirty evenly spaced cement columns behind the bleachers. The columns alternate between red and white. They rose up high, became wider, fanned out, and connected at the top. As the columns rose up, they arch and curved, leaning and extending over the concrete bleachers to provide a type of artistic shading. The way the columns leaned and bowed over the stands looked abstract, sustaining a rolling scallop shape when viewed at the right angle. They reminded me of Japanese folding fans.

I saw people jogging around the rough dirt track. A bunch of kids were learning the finer points of playing baseball. All appeared to be having a good time. I turned onto a main street called Avenida de los Presidente, which had a wide, grassy pedestrian median separating the two directions of traffic. I passed by the Hotel Presidente, the vermillion and beige colored hotel built in the 1920s. It rose ten stories, and a large veranda surrounded the first floor.

I continued walking through these Vedado neighborhoods. There were large cement and brick houses and mansions built in eclectic styles of architecture. The mansions were two or three stories high, and had been divided up into smaller quarters to provide living accommodations for multiple families.

While I was walking, I found it interesting to watch the comings and goings of the people as they tended to their daily needs. I noticed that the needs of the people living in the city varied considerably from the needs of those living in the country. These city people carried a much different demeanor, which I could see in the general pace and movement of their lives.

I came to another intersection and turned left onto another busy street. Not far from the intersection was an old cinema, the Riviera. I got a picture of this *cini*. The building was painted in a deep, rich, bright blue. In very large, graceful, white italic script was the word "Riviera," written high across the front façade. I got a bunch of funny looks from people as I walked around to take pictures from different angles of this building. But it was worth it.

The intensity of traffic and people on this road started to pick up and get more active, as I began to make my way back toward the direction of the Hotel Vedado. I came to the Habana Libre. This hotel opened in March of 1958 as the Hotel Habana Hilton, and was operated by the American Hilton Hotels chain. Conrad Hilton, the founder of Hilton Hotels, was present for the opening.

This modern hotel was built on a full city block and, depending on what side of the building you were facing, was twenty-seven to thirty floors high with 630 rooms. The building is set back from the actual entryway to the hotel. The entryway is a one-story structure and the setback provided by the entryway helps the hotel blend in with the surrounding neighborhood. It was designed by the Los Angeles, architectural firm of Welton Beckett & Associates. This firm designed many of Southern California's well-known buildings, including the Capitol Records tower in Hollywood and the Beverly Hilton in Beverly Hills. At the time, the Habana Hilton was one of Havana's most symbolic hotels.

The building is graced with many decorative elements that were added into the architecture. On the protruding façade, above the entryway, is a very large and vivid ceramic mosaic. This mural is known as La Fruta

Cabana and was completed in 1957 by the Cuban artist Amelia Pelaez. The mural has waves of blue shades and is reflective of the avant-garde generation to which Amelia Pelaez belonged.

On January 8, 1959, after Fidel Castro reached Havana, he triumphantly entered the city. Shortly afterwards, it was here at this hotel where Castro entered, took over and set up his administrative office and headquarters for his revolutionary government. The hotel's name was changed from Habana Hilton to its new revolutionary name, Habana Libre, or Free Havana.

By now, I was ready to go back to the Hotel Vedado. Fortunately for me, it happened to be right around the corner. I took the elevator from the lobby up to my room. I was ready to take a shower, but first I turned on the television to check the world news on European CNN. Since I had been in Cuba, I hadn't concerned myself too much with world news.

The headline news story was about an unfolding terrorist attack on the

Sri Lankan national cricket team's convoy in Pakistan. After my shower, I felt a little better, but I needed to get dinner. I had to wait a little while for my hair to dry, so I could comb it with my fingers to make sure that it would stay down. I thought, *I'm going to get that little boy of mine for taking my comb. Oh, how I miss my family. But, I'll be home soon. And as for tomorrow, I just have to get past this wall that's between our two countries.*

I wanted to stay inside this hotel for dinner. My stomach felt uneasy, and I didn't feel like eating much, but I knew I had to get food inside me. Tomorrow would be a long day, and I would not be able to eat again until noon, when I arrived in Mexico. I needed to do everything I could to be on my toes for a possible rematch with El Comandante.

I sat down at a table and forced myself to eat. It was a solitary moment, as I realized that I had to ride out this holding pattern, when I could get it on and face my fears.

I did not sleep well that night. It seemed that I was looking at my alarm clock every hour. Finally, it was time to get up, grab my bags, and go downstairs. Sure enough, after about fifteen minutes, there was Jesús getting out of a taxi in the dark and coming in to get me. I turned in my hotel key, and we left. On our way to the airport there was not much talking going on between us. It took a lot longer this time even though there wasn't any traffic.

Jesús made three sandwiches for me to eat since he knew that I would not be able to get any food until much later in the day. I thanked him for thinking of me, but told him that I would take only one sandwich because my stomach was not agreeing with me. When we finally arrived at the airport, it was packed with people. Most were hanging around to see family members off. It was a little confusing to me to figure out which long line I had to stand and wait in. Jesús seemed to have a good idea about what to do.

We stood in line for an hour or more. Thoughts kept going through my head, as I did not know what was going to be in store for me. I noticed that way up at the front of the line, many officials were milling about.

It turned out that they were having mechanical problems related to checking in baggage. The lines of people waiting to check in had come to a standstill. Officials began to walk along these stagnant lines looking for people who would not be checking in any baggage. A call came out from these officials, and since I only had my two carry-on bags, I was able to jump ahead of all the other people at the check-in counter.

I was asked to present all my information. All the while, I was holding back the paperwork about the laptop computer that El Comandante had taken. The officials pushed me through, as they were frustrated about the baggage problems. They needed to address the backlog it was causing. The official gave my ticket and passport back to me. Feeling that all the commotion with the baggage problems could be a blessing in disguise, I went to the other counter where I had been directed to pay the twenty-five CUC departure tax.

I had to get a special stamp on my airline ticket to prove that I had paid the tax. At that point, there were a few more gauntlets to pass. There was a painted line on the floor that Jesús could not cross. That meant Jesús could not walk any further with me. I could see a line of doors ahead. I would have to pass through one of these individual doors by myself, so that the eyes of Cuban immigration on the other side could inspect me.

I was about to start the transcending process of passing through to the other side of this big wall that's between our two countries. As we stood at the line in silence, it became a sad moment for Jesús and me. We looked at each other before I crossed the line. I gave Jesús a big hug and thanked him for everything, and I promised him that I would be back.

Jesús said that he would wait around for a while in case anything happened to me after I went beyond these doors. I thanked my good and trusted friend again, picked up my two carry-on bags, and waited until the Cuban official told me to go through one of the doors. As I walked toward the door, I turned and took one last look back at Jesús, who was standing across the room on the other side of the line. I could see the look on his face, as it carried the feelings of losing a good friend, as mine did too.

I told him out loud, "I will, we will, keep in touch."

Once I walked through the door and it shut behind me, I was asked for my passport and the tourist visa I had filled out when I entered Cuba. The Cuban tourist visa is something you do not want to lose. I was told to look up at a camera that took my picture. The image was transferred to the immigration officer's computer screen. All the while, she kept looking at my passport and matching it up with the picture on her computer. I noticed that her eyes kept moving back and forth and then back at me. I was waiting for a red flag, some information that would pop up on the computer screen. I didn't want to appear nervous. After some time, I heard the buzzer in the other door. I was allowed to continue on, and I walked through yet another door. I came up to the table flanked by inspectors. I had to pass everything through the X-ray machine. I kept thinking that, at any moment, someone would be coming up from behind me, grabbing my shoulder. Trying to stay calm, I walked through as my carry-on bags moved along the conveyer belt. After a few glances, I was given the go ahead. I was starting to breathe a little better. I thought, *My God, maybe I'm going to be OK*. I found my gate number, sat down, and waited until boarding time. I passed the time filling out customs and immigration paperwork that I would have to present in Mexico.

At that moment, I realized I was supposed to meet with and spend a few days with Pilo! I felt so bad; once again, we would not be able to meet and to spend any time together. I remembered my phone conversation with Pilo when I was in Remedios at the beginning of my trip, and how I was trying to get enough phone cards to call him back and set up a meeting time. And now, there I was in the airport with no way to get word to him, to let him know what happened, to explain why I was no longer at the Hotel Vedado. I felt so bad knowing he would call the Hotel Vedado; it would be as if I had stood him up again.

The call came. It was time to board my flight. I handed the attendant my ticket and began the slow walk down the narrow passenger ramp and through the plane's door to find my assigned seat. Once I was seated and had my seat belt on, it took a while before the plane's door was finally closed. I felt the slow, subtle movement of the airplane's jerky motions starting before the plane moved out and taxied to the runway. After a long pause at the end of the runway, the engines revved; we sped across the runway and lifted off into the air.

I looked out my window and saw Havana one last time. I could see its beautiful grandeur, its centuries of history, and its air of faded glory below me. Sitting in a perpetual time warp, and with all its mysteries, the land of Cuba is both a paradox and an anomaly in today's Western world. I was leaving it behind as the plane flew off into the sky, filtering through the white tropical clouds. There was a sadness tugging at my heart, knowing that I was leaving a family of friends behind. But I also knew that I had another family at home that really needed me.

The flight took about an hour. As we were making our descent into Mexico, I noticed that a person sitting next to me was an American gal. She was a real estate agent from New York City who went to Cuba in defiance of the embargo. She said that she just wanted to go to Cuba and see it. After being in Cuba for two days, she was mugged. Fortunately, they didn't get her passport, and she was left with just enough money to get home. I was amazed that she went by herself. I thought, *She's one tough gal.*

We landed in Cancun without incident, but as we went through customs, it was discovered that I had forty rolls of film.

"You're only allowed to have twelve rolls of film, and I have to take these," one of the immigration inspectors said.

I turned to the New York gal who happened to be standing in line next to me.

"Here comes the shake-down." I said out loud to her.

I think the immigration officers heard me because, of course, I didn't do anything to hide it. By now, I was getting a little angry, as I remembered back to the time when I came through here with my suitcases filled with nothing but gifts for my Cuban family of friends, and these corrupt officials tried to steal everything I had. I made it out of one hot frying pan in Cuba, and into another one here in Mexico. The difference being that in Mexico, I was dealing with corruption as prevalent as rust building on a cast iron pan.

He took all my film. I could see my new dilemma was going to be trying to get all my film back. I would most likely have to pay bribe money.

In front of everyone, he pulled me aside and said for all to hear, "You're in my country!" he shouted loudly. "You have to abide by our laws!" he said, as he pointed his finger firmly in my face.

To which I thought, *We have laws in America, and you guys don't even give a crap! Mexico has no respect for the sovereignty of the United States!*

He pulled out a piece of paper.

"See here!" he said very piously and condescendingly. "You're only allowed twelve rolls of film, but I'm going to let you pass just this one time."

It became exceedingly obvious that I had to humiliate myself and play like I'm the stupid American gringo. "Oh, thank you. You are so kind. Thank you very much for having mercy on me." After the embarrassment of groveling, I was given all my film back.

I got out of there as fast as I could, in case any of those clowns decided to change their minds. I looked behind me and saw the lines backing up from the recently arrived flights. The people still standing in the lines were rolling their eyes, as they watched the nonsense of these Mexican officials and their blatant corrupt power charades going on.

I had to switch terminals, so I went outside and waited at the bus stop for the airport shuttle. I was hoping to have an airline ticket waiting for me there at the front counter.

I arrived at the new terminal and went to the ticket counter. I was happy to see that my wife had come through. A one-way ticket to Dallas-Fort Worth waited for me. All I could think of at that moment was, *Yee Haa! I'm going to make it home!* I had to wait several hours for my flight to Dallas, but I was happy knowing that I was going to make it back to American soil to be with my family.

It was a good flight to Dallas, although it did take a few hours. I managed to catch up on much-needed sleep. I had lost a lot of sleep the night before because of stressing about all the unknowns and all the very real things that could have happened while trying to make my way out of Cuba.

Once I landed in Dallas and entered the lines at customs, there was not much time to spare before my flight to Los Angeles. I was honest about the fact that Jesús gave me a child's baseball shirt and cap for my oldest son, Shane. On the immigration paperwork, I wrote down that I had been to Cuba, and that I could verify the legality of the trip with the paperwork I had on hand.

At one of the stations, I was stopped and kicked out of the line, and told that I had to go and follow a certain colored painted line on the floor that would take me to another area. I told the customs agent that I had the paperwork to show that my trip to Cuba was legitimate. Obviously, he didn't care. Of course, it was not like what happened to me in Cuba. Still, I got pulled because I claimed the Cuban items on my customs forms. Leaving the regular flow and the line of people, I made my way through the maze of painted lines on the floor to the next counter where I had been directed. Once at the counter, I saw the officer sitting there. I handed her all my paperwork and passport.

"Yes, I have been to Cuba, and it was legal." I told her. I informed her that I had some things from Cancun, and the two items from Cuba. I explained that the two items from Cuba were given to me, and that I had not spent money on them. I explained what the items were and why they were given to me. I told the story of how I brought a lot of humanitarian gifts for my friends and their families, and that at the end of my trip, Jesús, who has a child the same age as my son, surprised me with the baseball shirt and cap.

Regarding the humanitarian gifts, my attitude was that I was giving from my heart. I didn't need recognition like human nature sometimes dictates. Now and again, I've found that people have the need to validate themselves, or almost in a backward way, they want to name-drop, or they just want to toot their own horns at the things they have done. I personally just wanted to give with no strings attached. I realized that I couldn't take care of the world. There are so many people who want to save the world, but since the beginning of time, things have never been right on this Earth. We're still going to have the poverty. We're still going to have hunger. We're still going to have wars and rumors of wars. No matter how much we try, these things will always be with us in some form or fashion. Human nature dictates that. It's sad, yes! But what could I do? Well, I know these people who I'd come in contact with. I'd tried to do what I could, and that was the best I could do.

"You're not allowed to bring anything back from Cuba except CDs, artwork, or literature." the custom's agent told me.

"Yes, I understand" I said. I pointed to a copy of the Federal regulations that I had. There was some leeway in the wording of the regulations that could have allowed her to use discretion in deciding whether or not to seize an item. I also pointed to the paperwork where it said that no American money could be spent in Cuba. "I didn't pay for them. There was no American money spent. It was a gift. I'm not trying to be disrespectful of our laws."

The officer seemed to understand the point I was making, but felt that she should check with her supervisor. The supervisor was called over. Once the supervisor arrived, she looked at my paperwork and got really feisty with me. It was clear that with her, it was going to be, "No way in hell!"

I tried to explain to her, and I showed her the paperwork I got off the government website that clearly states under "What can be brought back from Cuba?" that "If US travelers return from Cuba with Cuban origin goods, such goods, with the exception of informational materials *may* be seized at Customs *discretion*."

But before I could finish, I was cut off.

"You're not getting anything," the supervisor said loudly. "Not on my watch, and not on my badge."

She abruptly walked away. With that, the other agent looked at me and said I would have to hand over the two items. As I placed the shirt and cap in front of her, I could see the look on her face. She shook her head as she realized the insignificance of these two items.

I felt so bad for my son. I knew that this was something that he would have liked. He would have known that he was thought about on this trip. I asked the customs agent what would happen to these two items. She paused for a second from the paperwork she was filling out, looked at me, and said they would have to be destroyed. All I could do was shake my head. To make matters worse, I only had twenty minutes left to catch my next plane to California.

There was a bunch of forms and paperwork that they wanted me to fill out. I said, "Look, I've got to catch a plane in twenty minutes. Do I really have to fill it out? Here are the items you're going to take from me. I've got to catch a plane. And you're going to destroy it anyway."

At that point, she called over another officer to see if I needed to be there to complete the rest of the paperwork, or if I could just leave to go catch my plane. They discussed the issue and agreed that I could go.

Just before I left, I turned to them.

"You know what?" I said to them. "This bothers me. I come here. I'm an American. I go to Cuba legally to document things, and I almost got obliterated over there through intimidating interrogations. I come to my own country, and I get hassled. There really should be no reason. I'm being honest with you guys."

The guy turned to me.

"Well, if it's any consolation, we do the same to them when they come over here." he said.

I thought to myself, *Wonderful! It's like a tit for tat. That really makes me feel great.*

As it turned out, I got out of there just in time to make it to my next flight. I did not even have an extra minute to spare to call home and tell my wife that I made it through the wall.

By the time I reached Los Angeles, it was very late at night. I still had to catch my prepaid shuttle for the hour and a half to two-hour drive home. I stood outside the baggage pickup area waiting for it to arrive. I had to be on the lookout for that certain shuttle-van that would be passing by amongst the hundreds of buses and taxis that were continually driving by.

I called my wife to let her know that I made it safely to Los Angeles. It was almost midnight, and I hoped to be home in a couple of hours. My wife told me that she didn't tell the kids that I was coming home early because she didn't know if I would encounter problems or delays. From my e-mails, she could sense that there might be trouble leaving Cuba. We caught up on the phone. I waited about forty minutes for the shuttle-van to arrive. I said good-bye to my wife, hung up the phone, and flagged down the driver.

After showing the driver my paperwork, I boarded and made the long drive home. It seemed to take forever. The shuttle arrived at my house around two thirty in the morning. It was great to see the familiar neighborhood and my house. Kids' toys were strewn about on the front lawn. Obviously performing a studendous job of forgetting to pick them up before going in for the night.

My wife had heard the shuttle-van in the driveway and came to the door to greet me. I was tired and exhausted from the day's travels. I only had enough energy to peek in my kids' rooms and look at them as they slept soundly. I thought to myself that it's amazing how their faces look like such angels when they're asleep, in contrast to when they're awake and sometimes can fight over the dumbest things with each other. It felt good to be home.

A few hours later, around six thirty that morning, I was awakened by the sound of my youngest son, Garrett, the one who thought I was dead. He jumped from his bed and came running from his room. Before I realized what was going on, he leaped on my bed and gave me the biggest hug!

"How did you know I was here?" I asked him.

"I heard your breathing," he said excitedly.

"What? Not me! That's mom, she's the one who snores," I said.

Without any delay, I received a swift kick from underneath the bed covers.

By now, my two other kids were happily filing into the room to see me. They gave me big hugs while I was still lying there in bed, still tired.

At that moment, my youngest son looked at me, as if he had just remembered something. He jumped off the bed and abruptly ran out of the room. I thought to myself, *I don't know what brought this on.*

After spending time talking to my two older children, out of nowhere came the words, "So, where are our presents?" I had to laugh a bit. After all I had done to try and get home to be with them, what they thought of now were their presents. Although I did feel badly for my oldest son, Shane, since his baseball shirt and cap were taken away at customs.

My youngest son, Garrett, came running back into the room with the biggest smile on his face and his hand held high. Inside his hand was the comb he had taken from my travel bag. Now, he wanted to give it back to me. All I could say about that was, "Why, you little stinker!"

I spent the next few days decompressing from this exhaustive and highly immeasurable visual adventure. I realized that today was supposed to have been my original departure date from Cuba. I wondered about El Comandante, what he was up to and thinking about. I would not be at all surprised if he was at the airport that day waiting for me, looking through the crowds with a renewed focus and intensity in his eyes, ready with a fresh, full round of new questions.

More days passed, as I continued to try and get back into the rhythm of my family's normal routines. I was surprised one day to receive an official letter in the mail from US Customs and Border Protection to officially notify me that they had seized my property at the Dallas-Fort Worth, Texas, airport. Upon reading their letter, I discovered that I was being asked a variety of questions and given procedures to follow if I wanted to pursue a claim for my property. I was quite surprised that they were giving me an opportunity to contest the seizure by submitting a petition for relief of the items they intended for destruction. For them to consider my request and possibly return my items, I had to complete the form they sent and attach it to a petition. The petition had to include all the facts that would support warranting relief from forfeiture. I thought that it was odd. Why are they asking me about this now, since they had previously told me that the shirt and cap were going to be destroyed? After thinking about it further, I realized that I did not sign off on anything at the airport because I had to catch my next flight. I thought, *That is probably why I received this letter. Well, what do I have to lose? I might as well check the box to contest, write a letter of explanation, and hope for the best.*

> Port Director of Customs and Border Protection
> Dallas/Fort Worth Airport, TX 75261

> Dear Customs & Border Protection officer,
> I respectfully request Customs & Border Protection to consider my petition to return the child's shirt and cap that were seized from me at the Dallas Fort Worth airport on March 20, 2009. I had a Travel Affidavit to travel legally to Cuba.
> I took humanitarian gifts for the Cuban travel guide. As it turned out, the travel guide has children the exact same age as mine. In appreciation for the gifts I brought him, he gave me a gift of a child's shirt and cap for my son. When I brought these two items into the United States, I did not want to do anything to disrespect or disobey our laws, and so I claimed these two items on my declarations. I did not hide anything. I declared everything I had. I did not purchase any Cuban merchandise. The only Cuban items I had were the child's shirt and cap and these were a gift to me for my son.
> With my Travel Affidavit, I received a copy of the US Department of the Treasury Office of Foreign Assets Control "What You Need to Know About the US Embargo—An overview of the Cuban Assets Control Regulations Title 31 Part 515 of the US Code of Federal Regulations." This document says the following about Cuban items being brought to the United States: "If US travelers return from Cuba with Cuban origin goods, such goods, with the exception of informational materials, *may* be seized at Custom's *discretion*." Since this document says that Customs is allowed discretion regarding property from Cuba, I respectfully request consideration of my petition to please return the child's shirt and cap that I did not purchase, but were gifted to me.
> Sincerely,
> Chris Messner

I was hoping that sanity would prevail with my letter and that I might still have a chance to get that special shirt and cap for my son returned to me. After more time had passed by, I received the response from US Customs.

US Customs and Border Protection

Dear Mr. Messner:

Reference is made to your petition for relief received on May 6, 2009 dated April 27, 2009, in the above-identified seizure case. Two (2) Cuban Products were seized and are subject to forfeiture under the authority of title (sic) 19, United States Code, section 1595a(c) for violation of title 31, Code of Federal Regulations, part 500 et seq, and title 50, United States Code, App. 5, because the merchandise was imported into the United States contrary to law, in that the items are embargoed products of Cuban Origin.

The above merchandise was seized in accordance with the Cuban Assets Control Regulations 31, Code of Federal Regulations, Part 515. In accordance with the above regulation, relief can only be granted if the petitioner received a license to import gifts received in Cuba from the Office of Foreign Assets Control. Your petition did not include such a license from the Office of Foreign Assets Control.

Therefore, after careful review of your petition and all of the circumstances of the case it has been decided to <u>deny</u> your petition and commerce forfeiture proceedings immediately.

If you have any questions regarding this decision, please contact Paralegal Specialist of the Fines, Penalties and Forfeitures Office.

Sincerely,

Fines, Penalties & Forfeitures Officer

I was feeling disappointed about the letter. Obviously, there was nothing more I could do about this matter, but shake my head again and move on. Because of the barrier caused by the political wall that's between us, Cuba's mosaic is more than just a distant and lifeless diorama frozen in time. The more I began to think about this whole mess between our two countries, the more I thought about how we got ourselves into this quagmire. That is when I realized that it began to solidify during the Spanish American War, and was fueled by William Randolph Hearst and all his tenacious yellow journalism. Historically, during its time, cotton was king in the United States and sugar was king in Cuba. Passing the Teller Amendment and giving Cuba back full control of their country was the prerequisite for entering in the Spanish American War in 1898. After the war, the Teller Amendment was simply never honored. It was ignored outright.

Judging by today's pork-laden bills and political romper-room games in Washington, some things never seem to change. Congress in 1901 attached a rider known as the Platt Amendment into an Army appropriations bill. The Platt Amendment overrode the Teller Amendment and denied Cuba its true independence. Why? There was so much money to be made from the sugar industry. By the 1920s, much of Cuba's farmlands were owned or operated by American conglomerates. Of course, over time, the commodity has changed, and now oil became king. Following the example set by his grandfather, President Theodore Roosevelt, Kermit "Kim" Roosevelt Jr., a political action officer in the Special Activities Division of the CIA, helped orchestrate a coup d'etat to help prop up the Shah of Iran in the early 1950s.

Regarding Castro and Ché, one could only wonder how their roles in history would have been if Theodore Roosevelt's and Franklin Delano Roosevelt's foreign policy had been different toward Cuba. If the Roosevelts had not meddled in Cuba and forced Cuba to cede full control of Guantanmo Bay, would Ché and Castro have risen to power? What kind of relationship would the United States have had with Cuba had there been no political deceptions to acquire control over Cuba? Without all this, one wonders what kind of relationship our nations would truly have: like the kind of relationship we have with Canada?

Now that I was solidly back into my daily patterns of life and the movement of my family's routine, I went to get my morning coffee, wishing that I had a Cuban espresso instead to light my morning up. I began to reminisce and wonder what my family of Cuban friends was doing. I wished that I could talk to them over a nice cigar and Havana Club 7 años rum. Of course, Jesús would have to pour the first few drops on the ground to ask permission to drink from that bottle, and by this, giving the first drink to the African deities, orishas, or gods. I missed them, as I wished that I could step back and cross over into that other world to be with my family of friends. With this wall that is between us, it is almost like a reality of two worlds.

From out of the blue, I could not believe it, I literally could not believe it, I received a letter from Pilo. I was so happy to receive his letter and could not believe the timing of it all!

Big Hello Dear Friend + fine art photographer, chris + The Messner Family

(Anne, Shane, Stephanie, Garrett.)

I hope you are all doing well + enjoying good health, Peace and harmony. At the end of your tour I called back at your hotel and I got a hold of Jesús on his mobile. He told me about your unexpected departure for family matters. I told him to give you my regards . . . I'm so sorry about what happened, I think it was just not fair what they did to you; anyhow they didn't give you the reasons at long last. It is good news to hear that you are well, safe and back there in the States with all your stuff. I wonder if will they allow you to revisit Cuba once again.?? Anyway, our friendship is ever lasting and I would like to keep in touch.... I'm cycling as usual, the bicycle + sunglasses are working well. The caps + T-shirts are in good shape. Painfully, my cycling shoes are now cycling sandals. I do a lot of cycling it is my only means of transport. We have been struck by the world Economic Recession. I see many difficulties along the way, and an uncertain future where everything has become fragile and unsustainable. Endlessly I very much appreciate your friendship ties, your hard work, your boldness and solidarity. I very much appreciate all what you are doing in order to keep in touch with each others + help us. We are waiting for the day when US Citizens will be allow to travel to Cuba + buy Cuba items. That would mean a boom for our economy. We would welcome them with out stretched arms. I wait patiently for the moment that we can meet again to talk and to enrich our cultural exchange. Till then, Our Best Wishes, Many Greetings, warm hug + happy and long lives to your family.

Sincerely yours with plenty of gratitude,

Yazmin, Elisana + Pilo.

ACKNOWLEDGMENTS

To those who from the very beginning appreciated my art and believed in my potential and those who supported and encouraged me during my Cuban endeavor. Richard and Karla Chernick, Corridan Gallery, Darin Sullivan, Don Parris, Dorothy Dearman, Gianna Sayre, Jane Litchfield, Jim Rowe, Keith Jones, Linda Gregory, Luminare Design, Marcel Mauceri, Rich Foster, Tom Schultz, Urban Optics Santa Barbara—Dr. Jerry Neel. I would like to express my sincere gratitude.

To my good friend, Jesús with the ponytail, I want to thank you for your sincere friendship and hospitality. I look forward to the day when you and your family will be able to come to my house. I will have a big barbecue in your honor and grill some of those big and fat T-bone steaks, the ones that you have always dreamed about but never had a chance to have. Of course, we will have to find a way to have Havana Club 7 años rum and that wonderful Cuban coffee. I will show you around my country like you showed me around yours. We will see the rolling hills of the wine country, the majestic giant redwood trees in the Sierra Nevada, which are the largest trees in the world, and even possibly see snow. I would love to take you and your family to Disneyland and make a run through the drive-through at In-N-Out for Double-Double cheeseburgers with fries, of course, But most of all, I would like to say, from my family to yours, from the bottom of my heart, "Thank You!"